EAVESDROPPING

We have only so much as to glance at another human being and we at once begin to read beneath the surface. We see there another conscious person, like ourselves. We see someone with human feelings, memories, desires. A mind potentially like ours.

NICHOLAS HUMPHREY

With the aid of a word I overhear in passing, I reconstruct an entire conversation, an entire existence. The inflection of a voice suffices for me to attach the name of a deadly sin to the man whom I have just jostled and whose profile I glimpsed.

VICTOR FOURNEL

Eavesdropping

AN INTIMATE HISTORY

JOHN L. LOCKE

OXFORD
UNIVERSITY PRESS

OXFORD
UNIVERSITY PRESS

Great Clarendon Street, Oxford OX2 6DP

Oxford University Press is a department of the University of Oxford.
It furthers the University's objective of excellence in research, scholarship,
and education by publishing worldwide in

Oxford New York

Auckland Cape Town Dar es Salaam Hong Kong Karachi
Kuala Lumpur Madrid Melbourne Mexico City Nairobi
New Delhi Shanghai Taipei Toronto

With offices in

Argentina Austria Brazil Chile Czech Republic France Greece
Guatemala Hungary Italy Japan Poland Portugal Singapore
South Korea Switzerland Thailand Turkey Ukraine Vietnam

Oxford is a registered trade mark of Oxford University Press
in the UK and in certain other countries

Published in the United States
by Oxford University Press Inc., New York

British Library Cataloguing in Publication Data

Data available

Library of Congress Cataloging in Publication Data

Data available

Typeset by SPI Publisher Services, Pondicherry, India
Printed in Great Britian on acid-free paper by
Clays Ltd., St Ives plc

ISBN: 978-0-19-923613-8

1 3 5 7 9 8 6 4 2

Contents

Contents

Acknowledgments

I DID the research for this book at the University of Cambridge, New York University, and the City University of New York, completing the manuscript while I was on sabbatical in the Department of Anthropology at Yale University. I have enjoyed the encouragement and advice of several scholars and writers, including Michael Studdert-Kennedy, Kathrin Perutz, Alison Wray, Anne van Kleeck, and Kim Oller, though none has seen the final version of the manuscript. I have also received assistance on specific matters from a number of scholars, including Adrian Treves and Marjorie McIntosh. My greatest debt is to my wife, Catherine Flanagan, who has offered personal encouragement, editorial advice, and countless hours of thoughtful conversation. This book is dedicated to her.

JOHN L. LOCKE

Cambridge, England
Old Lyme, Connecticut
July 2009

List of Illustrations

List of Illustrations

Prologue

O N a flight from Milan to London I was slumped down in my aisle seat, deep in thought as I reviewed an early draft of the manuscript that has become this book. Unbeknownst to me, I was being watched by a woman in the middle seat of the row immediately in front. After we had landed and the passengers were commencing the customary disembarking ritual, the woman startled me by looking over her headrest and pointedly asking if I was writing a book. I answered that I was. What's it about, she asked. I said my book concerned the intense desire of members of our species to know what is going on in the personal lives of others. At this, the woman burst into ironic laughter since first in watching, and then in asking, she had just expressed two different forms of that very desire.

Watching and asking produce a form of intimate experience, which can be enjoyable in its own right, as well as intimate images, which may be re-experienced when privately brought to mind or—as information—shared with others. Intimacies tend to circulate preferentially among people who know and trust each other, and they usually move swiftly. Since many of these "secrets" ultimately become public knowledge, a look at how intimate material travels enables us to understand the social foundations of scandal, rough justice, and the "news," even "history."

I smiled in response to the lady on the plane but I could just as well have laughed, too, for here I was, writing a book about a subject on which there was little in the way of directly relevant research. Indeed, until I began to study eavesdropping—one of the more important ways that ordinary people express the desire at issue—I had never, in many years of research, encountered a behavior whose actual significance was so greatly at variance with its recognized importance. Look for books on social behavior with the word "eavesdropping" in the index section and you are likely to be severely disappointed. Enter the same word in computerized literature searches and your screen will display a list of books on wiretapping and other forms of electronic surveillance. But the word was coined centuries before telephones and recording equipment were invented, and the practice of eavesdropping documented nearly a thousand years earlier, when people were happy to entrust to unaided senses the question of who was doing what to whom.

Just after I began my studies of eavesdropping, a colleague asked me why I had chosen to address this particular subject. It must have seemed a radical departure from my previous work on the psychology of language. I told him that I had come across Marjorie McIntosh's analysis of court records indicating that five and six centuries ago, English citizens had, in impressive numbers, been *arrested for eavesdropping*. I wondered what, in the medieval mind, would have caused this behavior to be criminalized, and what the "criminals" themselves were doing, or thought they were doing, when they went out at night and listened to their neighbors' conversations.

I had also begun to study ethology, a field that deals with behavior in a broad range of species, and had encountered the work of Peter McGregor. He pointed out that birds increase their chances of survival by monitoring the long-distance calls of *other* birds—signals that are not even intended for their ears. Such interceptions, McGregor noted, are ignored by all existing models of animal communication, which are uniformly dyadic, that is, focused exclusively upon two parties—"the sender" and "the receiver." These models contain no provision for any *other individuals* that might be partaking of the experience from obscure or distant positions.

Models of human communication are also dyadic. They empha-size the back-and-forth channeling of verbal information between two individuals. But in the lives of humans, not just birds, additional ears are often in operation—we know this because our own ears are among them. If real people also tune in to each other, and become usefully informed in the process, then theories of human communication must explain these things that real people do.

But they have not done so. Animal behaviorists have been able to document eavesdropping because they study birds, fish, lizards, and other species, either naturalistically or in structured experiments, and their research subjects do eavesdrop. The reason why social scientists have failed to document equivalent levels of eavesdrop-ping in humans, however, is not because they looked for it and discovered that there was nothing to be seen. They never looked in the first place.

Why they did not, I think, is linked to a long-standing tendency of philosophers and psychologists to put humans on a pedestal, to regard our species as more intelligent and rational than other animals. This view could not be sustained if humans were on a continuum with other primates and mammals, so they concen-trated on the behaviors accounting for, and related to, Man's best and highest accomplishments. Central to these was language, the symbolic code that enables speakers to consciously transmit thought to willing listeners. This kept other animals safely at bay but, paradoxically, also excluded important facts about *human* communication.

Eavesdropping is communication, and it has two features that make it unusually interesting. The first is that it feeds on activity that is inherently *intimate*, and is so because the actors are unaware of the receiver, therefore feel free to be "themselves." The second feature that makes eavesdropping so interesting relates to the way the information travels. It is not *donated* by the sender. It is *stolen* by the receiver.

My colleague nodded as I told him these things, but later I realized that he might have been wondering about *me*. Most of my friends do! When I describe my interest in eavesdropping, several have asked if I am, unbeknownst to them, an unusually serious practitioner. While admitting to a weakness for social eavesdropping—some of the methods described are my own—I'm afraid the answer is less exciting. I study humans for a living. Much of my graduate and post-doctoral training was in linguistics and psychology, fields that have a clear stake in human communication.

But this is only partially relevant because these disciplines take little interest in messages that are transmitted *unintentionally*, and they care even less about information that is received *surreptitiously*. What they usually investigate, instead, is the verbal behaviors that pairs of people willingly and consciously donate to each other. One of the two parties, usually designated Person A, is "the speaker." He or she tells Person B, "the listener," something that B will be interested to know. "When I communicate with another person," wrote esteemed mathematician and communication scientist Norbert Wiener, "I impart a message to him, and when he communicates back with me he returns a related message which contains information primarily accessible to him and not to me."[1] It is all very tidy and rational.

Just what human life is not.

The Person A–Person B models might make sense if the behavior to be explained is a telephone conversation between two colleagues who are attempting to consummate an important business deal under the pressure of time. But in more natural circumstances—like those in which our species evolved—the sender and receiver can see and hear each other, and they are frequently not alone.

In many species, individuals live close to each other, and to their predators and prey. The signals that they emit are designed to reach the sense organs of mates and competitors but they also come to the attention of others who have an "interest" in the existence and location—and business—of the signaler. Since humans live in close contact with each other, I began to wonder how social scientists could justify *not* dealing with eavesdropping.

My goal here is to address a number of questions pertaining to the voracious human appetite for intimate experience in the lives of others. How, I ask, did our evolutionary ancestors engineer this appetite, thus our modern craving for sensory images that will satisfy it? How has the appetite been expressed, from the earliest moments of recorded history? What were the benefits, and the risks?

I also deal with the things that people have done, and now do, with the perceptual "booty." Observation of intimate behavior, regardless of the reasons, leaves bits of information behind. What happens to it next, and how does this affect the personal lives of the perpetrators and the victims?

Premonitions of creeping "big-brotherism," once a source of nervous amusement, have been replaced by real and widespread alarm about hidden cameras and other forms of monitoring. Though currently acute, these fears are predictable from evolutionary and historical trends. Our distant ancestors were secure because they could see each other at all times. They were either trusted, or did not need to be. But on the way to modernity many things happened. A sequence of factors—from sedentism and population growth to the construction of durable housing—nudged our ancestors along a path that could only lead to long periods of personal opacity. The process took many millennia but only began to seriously impact supplies of social knowledge in the last several thousand years.

When residential walls were erected, it was the beginning of truer and deeper forms of intimacy. Walls also made it difficult—and ultimately unnecessary—to look around every few seconds to see what others were doing. A human vigil, one beginning with ancestors that we share with apes, was reduced to manageable proportions, freeing up many hours of undistracted time per day.

This would gradually increase opportunities to develop the kind of personal, marital, and familial relationships that we now hold dear.

At one time, the isolation-cum-privacy enabled by walls was about as welcome as incipient blindness. By blocking the eye, walls placed a premium on something that they knew very little about: trust. What was trust? Who could be trusted? With so few previous opportunities to *violate* trust, it was hard to tell. Predictably, suspiciousness and fear rose precipitously. If walls were to continue, more penetrant means of perception would be needed. Fortunately, a suitable cognitive mechanism was waiting in the wings.

It was eavesdropping, a term that I will use in its conventional sense to mean surreptitious observation as a technique for sampling the intimate experiences of others—whether the surveillant is peeking through a keyhole or just feigning inattention to ambient activity. But I also use the term metaphorically to represent the lifelong quest of all humans to know what is going on in the personal and private lives of others.

Much of what we call "information" begins as sensory images that acquire informational status with the recognition that others might appreciate the same material. When verbalized, these images are morphed into "intimate capital," which can be exchanged for needed resources. It is illuminating to see how power-hungry men and intimacy-seeking women, as traditionally characterized—if not caricatured—have spent the last thousand years accumulating and managing their funds of intimate capital. But the gender division is not always so tidy. For in blackmail and stalking we also see women trading their intimate knowledge for power and men exercising their dominance in pursuit of intimate experience.

A great deal of the most potent information is stolen, but all normal humans also donate privileged material about themselves to selected others. They do this in an attempt to relate intimately, and to be understood. Since intimacy is linked to selectivity, each of us also needs to limit this exposure. We must be skillful in how we act on these opposing impulses, but act on them we must. Doing so necessarily produces a spirited social dance, with alternate thrusts and withdrawals of our selves.

This dance reveals the interplay of biology and culture, for social monitoring is biologically mandated—we simply must absorb information about the behavior of others if we are to benefit from gregarious life. These objectives require acquisition of information that is valid, and much of this will necessarily come from "behind the scenes." Culturally, however, people have placed a premium on opacity; thus the scene is set for conflict, with the inherited drives of biology on one side and the acquired imperatives of culture on the other.

Taking the path of least resistance, watchers direct their gaze at electronic images of unfamiliar and invented beings. The media provide the images, and the beings. In some ways, our fascination with these figures is more, not less, interesting than real-life eavesdropping. For the functions, and the benefits, would seem to be entirely different, and yet it is possible that they are not.

At times I have worried about my own use of the term "intimacy," aware that it could raise expectations of a "pop psychology" book that tells women how they can get more of it, and men why they must quit avoiding it. Mine is an entirely different type of project, for I explore the deeper social and biological issues that provide the foundation for intimate experience. We will see some interesting gender differences, to be sure, but these are not at all like those addressed in the other kinds of books. They are less obvious, and they run deeper.

I have also worried that that an author who uses the word "eavesdropping" will be expected to deal with electronic surveillance of the type we associate with the FBI and criminal investigation. But where social eavesdropping is concerned, these sleuths are rank amateurs. They may know how to put a "bug" in a potted palm or hack into your personal computer but ordinary humans know how to tell when a friend is behaving unusually, an acquaintance is reluctant to share something, or a stranger is up to no good. These judgments require observational skills that were built up hundreds of thousands of years ago, and cannot be taught.

In doing the research for this book, I pursued threads of evidence from fields ranging diversely from social, sexual, and cultural history to biology, ethology, archaeology, anthropology, sociology, architecture, psychology, neurophysiology, urban studies, and the law. When woven into a coherent pattern, each has something to say about the theft of intimate experience in other lives—a central question of the book, a central issue in human life.

CHAPTER ONE

Passionate Spectators

For the passionate spectator, it is an immense joy... to see
the world, to be at the centre of the world, and yet to
remain hidden from the world...   Charles Baudelaire

IN May of 1598 an English housewife named Margaret Browne
was spending a quiet day at her home in Houndsditch, near
London. Records indicate that at one point she peered and
listened through a hole in a wall. It was a shared wall. By looking
out of her home, Margaret was gazing directly into the private
rooms of her neighbors, Mr. and Mrs. John Underhill.[1]

If the Underhills had been playing cards or taking a nap, nothing
would have come of Margaret's adventure, and nothing would be
known about it today. But on that spring day Mr. Underhill was
away, and the activities next door were anything but ordinary. What
Margaret saw was a series of rough-and-tumble sexual encounters
between Mrs. Underhill and a man named Michael Fludd, scenes
that Margaret was surprisingly able to follow even as the lovers
moved from place to place within the tiny home.

Once she saw what was going on, Margaret could have
turned away, but she remained at the hole like a sentry at his

post—watching and listening for an entire afternoon and some part of the evening. In an adultery trial, held just two weeks later, Margaret testified to everything, from the precise nature of each sexual maneuver to the couple's pre- and post-coital banter. From the transcript, we even learn the color of Mrs. Underhill's underwear ("seawater green").

Margaret could not have known it then, but four centuries later millions of married women would spend entire afternoons watching intimate activity from the comfort of their homes. These spectators would be glued to a different aperture, watching serial installments of *Days of Our Lives* on NBC where Margaret was forced to content herself with a single episode from her home in Houndsditch.

It is also possible that Margaret watched the hijinks next door because she felt a moral obligation to do so. Sixteen years before that fateful day in 1598, a highly placed official in the English Congregational church exhorted parishioners to "watch one another, and try out all wickedness," and it was wicked to covet somebody's spouse. What Margaret saw in the first few minutes was enough to make her pound on the wall, shout disapproval through the hole, or pay a visit to the local vicar—but there is no indication that she did any of these things.

Margaret may also have wanted to protect her own marriage. If Mrs. Underhill exercised no restraint when it came to Michael Fludd, what kept her from flashing her seawater green knickers at Mr. Browne? How, if women like Mrs. Underhill showed so little respect for the bonds of matrimony, would the married women of Houndsditch keep their marital and economic lives together? The court transcripts say nothing of Margaret's own marital relationship, of course. Did she pine for more tenderness; or crave more sexual satisfaction? It would be surprising if she failed to compare the sexual adventures next door to the activities in her own bedroom. Margaret could have marveled at the way Mrs. Underhill aggressively and repeatedly seduced Mr. Fludd, a fantasy that is now played out in romance novels.

Even if Margaret was satisfied in her marriage, the sexual scenery that day in June may have awakened feelings that had grown dormant. "I love my husband," a reader of true romance novels told an interviewer recently, "but it is a mellow, comfortable, long-married feeling. With each new romance I read," she said, "it brings back the excitement, the sparkle, tears and joy of falling in love."[2]

How did the tryst next door find its way to public trial? It's anyone's guess, but Margaret probably told someone what happened, perhaps her women friends. If so, word would have traveled quickly through Houndsditch. Out of sympathy, she may have told her cuckolded neighbor directly. What we do know is that Mr. Underhill immediately initiated an adultery suit—tantamount, in sixteenth-century England, to a divorce proceeding.

How separate was the telling of the tale from the acts that were told? Did Margaret eavesdrop *so that* she could send word of her observations up the civic chain of command, perhaps in revenge for some previous transgressions by Mrs. Underhill, or to give John Underhill the ammunition he needed to end a marriage that had so obviously gone awry? If her motive was not to recite the tale, why did Margaret spend so much time observing the activities next door?

She could have done so simply because the opportunity was "there." In Elizabethan England domestic walls lulled occupants into thinking they were alone when, in fact, neighbors and strollers were only a structural defect away. Margaret may have found the hole in the wall too tempting to pass up. But this would only account for the first few seconds. What about the next five or six hours?

One possibility is that Margaret enjoyed the view. Voyeurs, as we know, watch sexual activity purely for pleasure, and the pleasure can be very great indeed. Modern research indicates that sexually explicit films give hormonal levels a significant boost, a reason, perhaps, why some humans are able to subsist largely on visual images.[3] But the link between vision and sex is not particularly strong in women—laws against Peeping *Toms* were not written with women in mind—so it is probable that Margaret's true motivations lay elsewhere. Perhaps a better place to look for clues would be in the *frisson*—the feeling of doing something that is forbidden or illegal, as when peering through a keyhole, or reading a letter that was addressed to someone else.

As a late sixteenth-century housewife, Margaret was used to being told what she should enjoy and must endure. One of her principal tasks in patriarchal England was giving pleasure to Mr. Browne. But the day in question was different. For Margaret decided, without spousal assistance, what she wished to experience, and to do so, for once, without responsibility or commitment. Or disappointment. "The everyday practice of taking pleasure into one's own hands is a political act for women," wrote Mary Ellen Brown in *Soap Opera and Women's Talk*. "Women usually function in our society as givers, not takers, of pleasure."[4]

There is another possibility still, one that has less to do with images than speech. Adultery was illegal—for women. If Mr. Underhill took his wife to court, Margaret would be asked to testify. Her appearance in court would satisfy a civic obligation. Anticipating her testimony, Margaret may have taken unusually detailed mental notes as she watched, aware that doing so would improve her "performance" in the witness box. The color of Mrs. Underhill's underwear and other gratuitous details may have been offered up in an attempt to establish Margaret's legal credibility. Even if the neighborly romp was immoral, illegal, and exciting, Margaret could hardly have failed to anticipate a social benefit of having seen it—vocal empowerment. When she took the stand, for one brief juridical moment the most important men in the community—from the vice-mayor and alderman to the court scribe—would listen intently to what Margaret Browne, housewife, had to say about a matter of compelling local interest.

The jurists who thanked Margaret for her testimony did so in robes, but they wore breeches too, and some may have had mixed feelings about the role their star witness had played. To be sure, the aldermen, in their own domestic lives, were—or wished to be—free to leave home without worrying about spousal misbehavior. On that score, their sympathies would have lain with John Underhill. While he was away, his wife violated her husband's trust.

But there was a sense in which Mr. Underhill posed a problem too, for he had allowed himself to be cuckolded. The men of Margaret's era knew there was no way the husband of an adulterous woman could be certain that her children were blessed with his genes. Lacking such knowledge, he might feel justified in shirking the usual paternal responsibilities. In 1622 English writer William Gouge pointed out that female adultery, more than the male kind, presents confusions about paternity. The problem, wrote Gouge in his book about "domestical duties," was that the unsuspecting husband "may take base children to be his owne, and so cast the inheritance upon them; and suspect his owne to be basely borne, and so deprive them of their patrimony."[5]

The appetite

Margaret Browne lived in a tiny place in the distant past. It would be easy to think of her as "different" from ourselves. But there is a little of Margaret in each of us. We all have a desire to sample, even to experience, the private lives of others. This appetite has no name, but it is widely recognized, at least tacitly. It was at the core of *Le Diable Boiteux*, published by Alain-René Le Sage at the dawn of the eighteenth century. In this novel, a limping demon called Asmodeus magically removed the rooftops of Madrid's more elegant homes. Exposing the occupants, he told his young student, Don Cleofas, would reveal "the springs of their actions, and their most secret thoughts."[6]

In the decades to follow, revelation of thought and action continued to demonstrate broad appeal, as new generations of Asmodeus, dispatched by new authors, exposed pupils to the seamier sites of London and the more fashionable addresses in New York. Reincarnations of the original "devil on crutches" handled similar assignments in Germany and France. It seemed that whenever anyone wanted to witness private activity, they sent for Asmodeus.

But this expository demon was not just a plot device. Nathaniel Hawthorne confessed envy for Asmodeus, wishing that he, too, might hover invisibly around men and women, "witnessing their deeds, searching into their hearts, borrowing brightness from their felicity, and shade from their sorrow, and retaining no emotion peculiar to himself."[7] Charles Dickens also begged "for a good spirit who would take the house-tops off, with a more potent and benignant hand than the lame demon in the tale."[8]

Exhibit 1 *Le Diable Boiteux*

(Dessin de M. Karl Girardet.)

Exhibit 2 "Coupe de maison," image by Karl Girardet, *Magasin pittoresque*, 1847. The original caption read: "Asmodeus has borne you up above the big city. . . your eyes have come to rest on an elegant three-story house . . . Asmodeus has understood; he makes a gesture, and the walls that hid the interior from you have become transparent. Everything that happens there appears before you like so many moving pictures framed under glass."

The fact is that everyone wonders what other individuals do, feel, and think in private; they wonder what others are like when no one is around. The passionate spectator, Baudelaire wrote, "is an 'I' with an insatiable appetite for the 'non-I.' "[9]

The idea of unmasking our fellow humans also possesses a vaguely mysterious appeal. At one time, New Yorkers were purchasing up to a hundred telescopes a week. Most of these terrestrial astronomers, a shopkeeper told writer Bill Buford, "are not going home to count the moons around Uranus." What they are doing, he said, is taking advantage of the "comfort distance," the space between one's apartment and perceptually adjacent ones. It is a distance that, if sufficient, lulls occupants into thinking they are alone and, if the optically assisted viewer is lucky, acting accordingly. Buford saw this behavior as an expression of our "insatiable humanity, an appetite for more and more about the human species, the visual equivalent of gossip."[10] For that reason, he wrote, it is *bad manners* to close the drapes.

As we cast our own personal gaze on the things that eavesdroppers have witnessed through the ages, we discover some long-shrouded characteristics of our socially curious species that continue to this day. Eavesdropping is a deeply biological trait, with ancient roots. Few if any species do *not* eavesdrop—even plants do it—and the chimpanzees and other primates with whom we share so much of our DNA stop eavesdropping only when they go to sleep. Their societies require that members know who is who, and who is doing what to whom. Since they cannot gossip—there is no ape "grapevine"—others cannot do the looking for them.

When our own species was evolving, and the modern human brain was under construction, those who knew what their associates were doing, or might do in the future, were more likely to survive to reproductive age and to pass on their genes. In order to compete, they had to cooperate with a few selected allies, and this required social knowledge. These early humans, like modern apes, were good at looking and listening, and making the appropriate inferences. Twentieth-century studies of hunter-gatherers suggest that early members of the human lineage were no less interested in who does what to whom.

But something happened. Ten to fifteen thousand years ago—a grain of sand on the beach of human evolution and history—our ancestors began to live behind walls, and the pool of social information began to dry up. Where casual observation had been sufficient, new and more invasive intake strategies became necessary.

The drive to invade the private spaces of others is universal. The English term "eavesdropping" derives from the practice of standing under the eavesdrop—the place where rain water falls from the roof to the ground—in order to hear conversations occurring within the home. In French, to eavesdrop is *écouter aux portes*, to listen at doors, as is the Italian equivalent, *origliare alla porta*. In Spanish, *escuchar sin ser visto* means to listen without being seen. In Tzotzil, a language spoken in the Mexican Highlands, there is a verb that means "to observe in secret, from a hiding place."[11] In German, *horchen* means to listen at the door secretly. In Swedish, an eavesdropper is a *tjuvlyssnare*, basically a listen-thief; in Polish, *podsluchiwanie* implies a violation of privacy, by placing oneself "underneath the private conversation." In Russian, *pod slushivanye* refers not to "overhearing" but to "underlistening."

In all these cultures, people have chosen to name this particular temptation: that of listening secretively, especially to speech. But there is no reason why perceptual invasions should not include activity that is seen, smelled, or touched. A great deal of social monitoring is accomplished by eye. Several years ago, the managers of a private club near Washington, DC put silk screens, ficus trees, and potted plants in its spacious dining room to increase a feeling of intimacy. Club members objected. "Now I can't see who's on the other side of the dining room," one woman complained.

The deeper motive, of course, is not merely to see the outer surfaces of others. It is to enter and explore the interior, and to

Exhibit 3 *Overheard,* Jules Adolphe Goupil, 1839–83

inspect the more privileged material that is kept there; and that is
the motive that will concern us here.

As far as the "I" can see

There has never been a time when humans were free from evaluation. "Existence as a human being," wrote social philosopher

Exhibit 4 *Curiosity,*
Eugene de Blaas, from the
Pears Annual, Christmas
1892

Edward Shils, "entails being under scrutiny."[12] The urge to
eavesdrop is a natural disposition, one that evolved anciently,
develops early, is expressed universally, confers a number of important benefits, and has a long history, dating back to the Middle Ages.
But some people scrutinize more often, and differently, than others.
Men, more than women, have trained their senses on the periphery

of social space in order to vet strangers. Women, more than men, have monitored the social, sexual, and familial behavior of the members of their own social groups. Both men and women are unusually interested in sexual rivals.

As functional as it can be, eavesdropping is quirky. Information is received by someone to whom it was not intentionally or knowingly sent, and this occurs without the sender's cooperation or knowledge. Moreover, seeing is an act of reception, but looking—the thing we do in order to see—can also be a signal. Others notice that we are looking at something, and because it is easy to follow one's line of regard, they can usually tell what that thing is. Frequently, the object on the other end of our gaze is a face, one that is pointed in the direction of another face. We see people, who, like us, are watching people.

This tells us something that we need to know. In our species, as in the other primates, the individual who gets the most looks is usually the most important. The male ape that attracts the most attention usually holds the highest rank. He has powerful friends, and gets more of everything he wants. Much the same is true in our species.

Information has always been a precious resource—the psychologist George Miller once referred to humans as "informavores," individuals who cannot survive without a steady diet of information.[13] But "information" has an arid sound. We *are* informavores to be sure, but the information that is important here is not the coldly decontextualized sort that resides in libraries. It is the kind that radiates from our fellow humans, merely by their living. If we are to find out the answer to one of humankind's most important questions—who we are—it is necessary to know what others are like. This evaluation tells us to what degree, and in what ways, we are unique or ordinary, and whether we are justified in thinking of ourselves as being, among other things, intelligent, kind, or generous.

To evaluate others in this way, we must ascertain what it is like *for them to be them*. This requires that we enter their patch, the little piece of the world that is uniquely theirs. But we cannot really enter it. If we did, critical behaviors would change. Thus the only possibility, as Charles Baudelaire noted, is to see their world from a distance, or an obscure vantage point.

We investigators come equipped with powerful acquisitive mechanisms. This is particularly evident in the case of smell. True, we may be able to detect odors if they rush past the sensory receptors in the nose—under some circumstances, merely breathing is enough for this to happen. But if we wish to *investigate*, it may be necessary to *sniff*, and sniffing has its own brain mechanisms.[14] Recently, a test of olfactory ability was developed that is based purely on sniffing. When the test is administered, people are asked to identify an odorant that is pumped into the nose through plastic tubes. A transducer measures changes in air pressure. Predictably, research shows that when the odor is identified, the participants *quit sniffing*.[15]

If we humans are outfitted with specialized means of ingesting socially relevant information, one might expect us to have specialized ways of *blocking* the flow of this information too, and we do. Our ancestors evolved at least one signal that prevents interception—the whisper. By design, whispered words do not travel well over the kinds of spaces that normally separate humans, so it seems safe to assume that this way of speaking has entered our repertoire just so we can foil eavesdroppers.[16]

Eavesdroppers are interested in people, to be sure, but they are also perfectly willing to explore the places where people have been. Assignations leave clues. Anthropologist Thomas Gregor studied the Mehinacu, a small tribe of Arawakan-speaking Indians occupying a village in Central Brazil. In his report, Gregor noted that the paths are sandy, and that every tribesman was known by his footprints. But other parts of Mehinacu anatomy are also familiar. "The print of heels or buttocks on the ground," wrote Gregor, "may be enough to show that a couple stopped and had sexual relations alongside the path."[17]

Heel and butt prints are clues to intimate deeds, but intimacy is also to be found in the person who is alone with himself. When socializing, people are under the review of their friends. They are likely to be acting to some extent—performing or playing a role. But the solitary individual appears without any psychological make-up. He is alone with himself, trying to please or share the moment with no one but himself.

Oddly, there is something worth protecting here. Milan Kundera once wrote about a man who suddenly discovers that this hidden self is under the review of another. The man is alone in his room at night. "Head lowered, he paces back and forth; from time to time he runs his hand through this hair. Then, suddenly, he realizes that the lights are on and he can be seen. Abruptly, he pulls the curtain."[18]

What the man lost was the opportunity to spend an evening with his self, and all that self-companionship affords, from rest to reflection and creativity. He also lost the freedom to undress psychologically. Some years ago, this ritual was portrayed in an improvisational theater in San Francisco. Seemingly in preparation for bed, an actor took off his hat and placed it on a bureau, then removed his hair (a wig). The man took off his glasses and massaged the bridge of his nose where the glasses had rubbed. Then he took off his nose and removed his teeth. Finally he disconnected his smile and lay down to sleep, a man now finally restored to his natural state.[19]

Cough a little

In many societies there is an etiquette to personal observation, and has been for some time. In the thirteenth century Robert de Blois wrote that whenever people passed by a private residence, they should "be careful never to look in and never to stop. To stand agape or idle in front of a person's house is not wise or courteous behavior. There are things that one does often in private, in one's own home, that one would not want others to see should someone come to the door. And if you want to enter the house," he wrote, "cough a little upon entering to alert those within to your arrival, either by this cough or by a word."[20]

Cough to announce your presence? How about knocking? In the French Pyrenees the following century, Raymond Sicre was out checking his sheep one night when he passed the house of Jean-Pierre Amiel. There were lights burning, suggesting that Amiel had company. Sicre must either have felt intense curiosity or suspicion, for the next thing he did, remarkably, was *open the door*. Met by a rough curtain that blocked his vision, but not the sound, Sicre lingered for a while, taking in the conversation.

It was pretty tame stuff—they were talking about different recipes for bread—but Sicre was determined to find out who the talkers were. "I went to the corner of the house," he was later to tell the village bishop, "and with my head I lifted up a part of the roof," taking "good care not to damage the roof covering. I then saw two men sitting on a bench. They were facing the fire, with their backs to me. They had hoods over their heads and I could not see their faces." Sicre then proceeded to repeat in minute detail everything the men said to each other.

It's strange to read of a person who, fueled by curiosity, was so bold as to open the door to someone else's house, and when that supplied too little information, proceeded—and *was able*—to pry up the roof of the house with his head. But the people of early fourteenth-century France saw little shame in the odd act of de-privatization, and architecture was on their side.

The etiquette of Robert de Blois notwithstanding, there were no rules against eavesdropping in centuries past. People readily admitted that they did it. They knew that minding *one's own business* was the risky thing. If they needed to know about the nature of a relationship, or what a person was really like, or if someone who acted like a friend was really a foe, what was the alternative to eavesdropping? Polite observation picked up crumbs; consulting the subject or his associates was fraught with danger.

The information that is snatched, from unwilling—and unwitting—sources, is usually a higher grade than the material that is on offer. Eavesdroppers catch people with their guards down—sitting as they like to sit, dressed in a way that feels comfortable, behaving in ways that feel natural. Donations, by contrast, are contrived to please, or to meet a standard. Like "photo ops," they may be designed to impress.

At first glance there appears to be a mismatch between the effort and the yield. In ordinary life, little happens from moment to moment, but imagination and fantasy may be enough to keep eavesdroppers at their task. When closed-circuit cameras were installed in the lobbies of New York City apartment buildings, residents discovered new ways of watching their neighbors. Inability to hear them seemed to make the experience even more exciting, since the viewers were free to generate their own theories about what was going on. "This," said sociologist Peter Bearman, "may be one of the reasons that it is so much fun to watch essentially nothing."[21]

In an intensely social species such as ours, an unposed being, caught in an asocial moment, is something of an oddity. The image beckons. Who is this person; what is he thinking? From what life experiences has he derived his bearing? He may be alone in a crowd, wearing a mask that he chose for the occasion. Is he looking around, pleasantly, hoping to make contact with the others? Is he preoccupied with his own thoughts, or attempting to distance himself from someone in the group?

When people are observed while interacting with others, additional questions arise. What is the nature of the relationships between the individuals that we see? Are they breaking up, or reconciling? Is she pensive or sad or playing hard to get? Does he really care about his lady friend, or is he merely feigning interest?

Even before the emergence of public and private selves—a late development in cultural history—there were boundaries between a person's outer and inner lives. In order to earn a place in the tribe, individuals had to socialize, and occasionally to perform. In time of high interdependency, some minimal level of social presence was required. But thought is private, and our distant ancestors did not act on every impulse. Like us, they kept some things to themselves.

Domestic walls realigned and deepened these basic divisions between the human selves, leaving residents with two major "versions," one private, the other public. When they stepped out of their dwellings, they stepped into their public selves, assisted physically by clothes and other adornments, and psychologically by masks and social roles. When they came home, public personas were checked at the door.

The walls have ears

In the competitive environment in which our species evolved, individuals kept certain kinds of information to themselves—even took steps to conceal it. If others got the information they needed, it was frequently because they were able to *snatch* it. These early humans were hunters and gatherers, and they were eminently qualified to hunt and gather social information as well as food. When language emerged, our ancestors were able to tell others about things they had seen. Biological anthropologist Robin Dunbar has even suggested that it may have been the need to pool social information that pressured individuals to communicate in more complex ways, and at some point, to speak. This more recent evolution—manifested in the capacity to "tell tales"—would become one of the most subtle yet powerful of all social weapons. To this day the offspring of eavesdropping—gossip and its siblings, rumor and scandal—have the capacity to change fortunes, tarnish reputations, and ruin lives.

Information is power, but one may not have to go to unusual extremes to acquire it. The socially *embedded* eavesdropper is in the presence of others. He must be visible if they are to be audible. Merely by *tuning in*, the embedded eavesdropper can gain access to material that is unintended for his consumption. By adopting an "ultra-receptive posture," as a detective did in a story by the French writer André Breton, the embedded eavesdropper puts himself "in a state of grace with chance."[22]

Some embedded eavesdroppers are completely ignored. In Teopisca, Mexico, a place where a high value was placed on personal reputation, people sent their children to the town market and other public places with explicit instructions to spy. When the children came home, according to John Hotchkiss, the anthropologist who studied the Teopiscanecos in the 1960s, they were "extensively interrogated" by family members to find out what was going on in the village.[23]

Eavesdropping runs the gamut from casual to premeditated, from amusing to sinister, from personal and idle to historically eventful. But most eavesdropping is an adaptive solution to problems that are not of the individual's own making. It is, in that sense, entirely normal. "There is nothing intrinsically objectionable in observing the world, including its inhabitants," wrote philosopher Stanley Benn.[24] Investigating absolutely everything that others do, wrote German sociologist Georg Simmel, "does not overstep the boundary of external discretion; it is entirely the labor of one's own mind, and therefore apparently within the unquestionable rights of the agent."[25]

Assurances such as these may not be needed by ordinary people. In an investigation of England's neighborhood watch programs, many citizens said that they were *already watching their neighbors before the programs began*. One said that neighborhood watch "just sort of consolidated more or less what we already did but made it official." A second said he thought the program was a good idea but that he and his family had already "been doing it for years ... without thinking." The researchers concluded that "the surveillance habits of members and non-members are indistinguishable."[26]

Already doing it. This is an interesting confession. In 1889 a London woman described an average day in her apartment

Exhibit 5 *Spionnetje,* or "little spy". In some parts of Amsterdam, the monitoring of neighborly activities is facilitated by house mirrors that are mounted on the side of parlor windows. Little spies are relics of an earlier period when they enabled residents to preview visitors, but they are now used to see what is going on up and down the block. At one time, similar mirrors were used in America, including Society Hill in Philadelphia.

building. It is clear from her account that eavesdropping made apartment life intelligible. "At 5 o'clock in the morning," she wrote, "I hear the tenant overhead, Mr. A., getting up for his day's work." Her report continues:

Exhibit 6 "Spy hole" in Dinkelsbühl, an ancient village in Bavaria

His wife, who does a little dressmaking when she can get it from her neighbours, was up late last night (I heard her sewing-machine going till 1 o'clock), so he does not disturb her. He is a carman at the Goods Depôt of a Railway Company, and has to be there at 6 o'clock, so he is not long getting his breakfast of tea and bread and butter. But before he has done, I hear a child cry; then the sound of a sleepy voice, Mrs. A., recommending a sip of tea and a crust for the baby. The man, I suppose, carries out the order, for the crying ceases, and I hear his steps as he goes downstairs. At eight o'clock there is a good deal of scraping and raking on the other side of the wall. This means that my neighbour, Mrs. B., an old woman partly supported by her dead husband's savings, partly by the earnings of two grown-up daughters, is raking out and cleaning her stove. Then the door is opened, the dust is thrown down the dust-shoot [sic], and a conversation is very audibly carried on by two female voices. Among other topics, is the favourite one of Mrs. A.'s laziness in the morning—though Mrs. B. knows perfectly well that Mrs. A. has been up late at work, having indeed repeatedly complained of the noise of the sewing-machine at night, and though Mrs. C. openly avows that she will not say anything against Mrs. A., as she has always been very nice to her.

This continues in the same level of detail, through the morning and afternoon, only to end at bedtime. At various points other senses report in, for example, when the lady resident notices the aroma of food being prepared in other apartments. Toward the end of her description she offered an evaluation of life in apartment buildings. Loss of privacy was listed as a disadvantage, but chief among the benefits was its corollary, "the impossibility of being overlooked altogether, or flagrantly neglected by relatives in illness or old age."[27]

Similar reactions appeared a half-century later in sociologist Leo Kuper's account of day-to-day life in a residential housing unit in England. The homes were all semi-detached, and residents could easily hear radios and pianos, crying babies, coughing, shoes being dropped at bedtime, children running, laughter, and loud talk. Though some residents complained that they could "hear everything," one said, "I don't feel so lonely when I know there's somebody about." Another said she enjoyed the "company."[28]

In 2004 an article in the *New York Times* carried a similar description by a Brooklyn man who liked to sit in his backyard on a summer night, where he experienced a "soundtrack-only version of 'Rear Window.'" "Over the last four years of night-sitting behind my house," he wrote, "I've become good at figuring out what my neighbors are doing just by listening. I hear dinners being cooked (clinking pans), dinners being enjoyed (light clink of silverware on plate) and dinners being cleared (loud clinking of plates and pans). I hear vacuum cleaning and blow-drying and screaming fights and bad guitar solos and birthday parties, all echoing around in the real sound stage created by a small block of interlocked brownstones."[29]

If there had been an angry altercation, the Brooklyn man would have heard that, too, and he might have been able to call the police in time to prevent it becoming dangerous. To understand the quest for intimate experience as a proximal motive, consider the real *Rear Window*, the 1950s Hitchcock film starring Jimmy Stewart and Grace Kelly. Stewart played the part of L. B. Jefferies, a photojournalist who, as the result of a leg injury, was confined to his apartment during a sweltering summer in New York City. Jefferies is bored until he discovers that he can see other apartment-dwellers across the courtyard, forced by the heat to open their windows and curtains, move out onto their balconies, and sunbathe on the roof. And then Jefferies instantly becomes un-bored.

The set of *Rear Window* was ready-made for people watching, a virtual smorgasbord for the visually curious. Merely by playing his naked eyes over the apartment complex, Jefferies is able to see a woman brushing her hair, a man lathering his face for a shave, and a couple sleeping on their balcony. In the kitchen of one apartment, Jefferies discovers a scantily clad woman doing dance routines; in the living room of another, a songwriter playing his piano and entertaining friends. Through other windows Jefferies observes a pair of amorous newly weds who foil his gaze by pulling the shade, and a lonely widow preparing dinner for two.

It's central to the film, and no less interesting here, that in one of the units across the courtyard there is also an overtly angry husband and an ailing wife. Something is rather different, even sinister, about this apartment, for it is here that Jefferies begins to sense the possibility of a serious crime. At this point, he begins to augment his normal senses—first with a pair of binoculars, then by looking through a camera fitted with one of the tools of his trade, a massive telephoto lens—and his reasons for looking change too.

Eventually, *because Jefferies is already looking*, he sees something amiss, and new reasons for watching develop. It is then that he becomes "concerned citizen, looking for evidence of a crime." And when he reports what he has seen, the police are persuaded to act, eventually arresting the murdering husband who behaved so suspiciously.

My point is that eavesdropping is usually done in order to satisfy an evolved appetite for intimate experience in other lives, not, in the first instance, to solve some environmental problem. Of course, there are frequently some tangible *benefits* of eavesdropping, such as personal power and social control, but these may occur because the eavesdropper is already tuned in, on a purely psychological motivation, in the first place.

The drive to monitor the behaviors of others is built into the human psyche, but its strength varies with local conditions. Features of human societies determine who sees, hears, and eavesdrops upon whom, how often they do so, what they get out of it, and what happens to the victims. As we saw earlier, Mrs. Browne's housing arrangement provided her with a treasure trove of data. But there are other factors, from religion and morality to government, politics, the law, internal competition, and external threat. All these things affect the degree to which people exercise their desire to invade the private space of others. After 9/11 many Americans began to look at strangers more suspiciously.

Fig leaf on her face

One of the more influential factors in social monitoring is interpersonal spacing. In urban centers, people are just close enough to eavesdrop, and just separated enough that they can do so without detection. But everyone with a stake in knowing about a particular individual can only be in sensory range part of the time. We would surely benefit if we could pool our images with others, and this is one of the more important benefits of language.

When there is no spacing, people have a way of creating their own psychological distance. In close quarters, one may be spared unwanted attention by erecting psychological boundaries. The philosopher John Silber once noted that strip teasers, by virtue of their

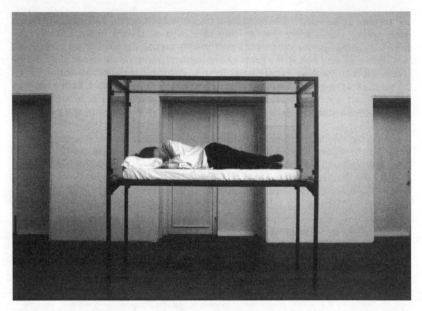

Exhibit 7 *The Maybe*: woman sleeping in a glass case

calling, seem to relinquish to others the right to examine their body. "But in the blank, dead expression on the face of the dancer," Silber wrote, "one sees the closed door, the wall, behind which she hides an intense, if limited, privacy. She wears her fig leaf on her face."[30]

Some amount of perceptual freedom may also be conferred by others. Erving Goffman called this "civil inattention."[31] Years ago, social psychologists discovered that people tend to look into the eyes of others less when in very close proximity than they do at greater distances. Most of us assiduously avoid looking into the eyes of our fellow passengers in a crowded elevator, and we usually grant each other more space when in cramped quarters, such as an ATM area.[32]

There is a fascination with the boundaries between public and private. In 1995, an English actress spent a week sleeping in a glass case in an art gallery in London. "It was very unsettling looking at her," wrote art historian Lisa Tickner after she had viewed the actress, Tilda Swinton. "You couldn't look at her as an exhibit: she was a human being. But you couldn't look at her as a human being without feeling guilty. This was an art gallery. We were licensed to look. But she couldn't look back and sleeping is private: the simplest involuntary movements cast us as uneasy voyeurs."[33] Five years later another actress, Daniela Tobar, spent two weeks in a small glass house. Like Tilda, Daniela was an exhibit at a museum in Santiago, Chile. The purpose was to stimulate debate about public and private space in Chilean life. The crowd could not get enough of Daniela—a human specimen under glass—even though she simply read, slept, cooked, and engaged in other ordinary household activities.

We modern humans take our privacy very seriously, but once, when the ability to domicile oneself was still new, eavesdropping was amusing, and not as wrong as it seems today. In the Roman comedies of Plautus and Terence, there were at least ten bouts of eavesdropping per play. They added little or nothing to the dramaturgical action, suggesting that eavesdropping was inherently entertaining.[34]

These comedies make it clear that eavesdropping was "in" over two thousand years ago, and it has surely stayed in. In a French novel by Marivaux, published in about 1714, a young man eavesdrops on a conversation between his lover and a rival on four different occasions. In some of his plays, the eavesdropping is so pervasive that a literary scholar, William Trapnell, referred to it as "spontaneous compound eavesdropping."[35] In one play, a piece of information acquired though eavesdropping caused a poisoning, and another piece of information, similarly obtained, enabled administration of the appropriate antidote.

Trapnell expressed surprise that in Marivaux's plays there is no hint of regret that the characters were "secretly intruding upon the intimacy of their victims. Does this intrusion," he asked, "not amount to the theft of information belonging to others, a reprehensible act according to most systems and traditions of morality?" But of course, as Trapnell immediately conceded, in early eighteenth-century France "close and frequent contact between individuals and classes precluded a high degree of privacy and imposed much tolerance of eavesdropping and hearsay."

Today most eavesdropping is done artfully. In places where we find ourselves embedded with others, as in a restaurant or waiting room, we tend to take in visual information with a series of nonchalant glances. If the object of our curiosity suddenly looks up, we may attempt to disguise the invasion with a gracious transition to an adjacent area, as though a continuous sweep of the room was in progress when the "interruption" occurred; or by glancing just behind the prey, as though something there was the real object of attention. When it comes to listening, we can only be glad that human ears do not visibly swivel into position, as they do in dogs and some other animals. But we still must avoid inclining the head or eyes toward interesting conversations.

Embedded eavesdropping brings to mind anthropology's "participant-observer" method of gathering information about individuals in groups. Participant-observers walk a fine line. If they remain aloof, they cannot see and hear what they must, but are able to retain their objectivity. Familiarity, on the other hand, gets them close to the subject matter, but threatens scientific impartiality. Sociologist Susan Murray has written about the dangers of emotional involvement faced by researchers working in the field. In her case, she became so involved with her subjects (labor union members) that she felt guilty when taking notes over the telephone. She was playing two roles but only one was fully understood by her subjects, who had become her colleagues.[36]

There is another problem with embedded eavesdropping. It produces information, but since the subject knows he is not alone, this information may not meet the highest standards. Merely by "being there" the observer alters the flow of behaviors from the actor. Something may be concealed. Best feet may be put forward. To the eavesdropper, embedded observation also may not produce the most interesting psychological experience. Lost will be the rush

Exhibit 8 Trojan horse eavesdropping. Woman taking a bath while her maid secretly conceals a voyeur. Early nineteenth-century French painting

that comes from doing something naughty, but, more importantly, the thrill of seeing a psychologically naked human being in his pure, unadulterated, socially unprepared form—a person, possibly, with his worst foot forward. Perhaps the purest case of this rush may come from what might be called *Trojan horse eavesdropping*, in which the viewer is not *personally* visible, at least as the person that he is. One variant of this is depicted in an early nineteenth-century painting of a woman taking a bath, while her maid conceals a voyeur under her smock.

On one occasion, Benjamin Franklin committed a different kind of Trojan horse eavesdropping.[37] Franklin had left his family home in Boston as a child. When he had a chance to visit his mother many years later, Benjamin—always the scientist—decided that he would withhold personal identification in order to see if some sort of maternal intuition would enable his mother to recognize him. He

Exhibit 9 *L'Armoire*, etching by Jean-Honoré Fragonard, 1778

spent one night sleeping in her boarding house, and spent an evening observing her as a person who was presumptively not her son. It was in this sense that Benjamin Franklin watched his mother without her knowledge. She had no idea that the lad observing her was *Benjamin*.

At some point in their life, most people also engage in *concealed eavesdropping*, observing from an obscure position. In childhood the tiny eavesdropper is able to peek at others from a hiding place— often under a staircase or piece of furniture—without being seen or suspected. In adulthood, the appetite is no less intense, and the means may be only slightly more sophisticated. The classic case is looking through a keyhole or listening through a wall. But one can also safely eavesdrop merely by turning out the lights and gazing out at an adjacent apartment building.

The irresistible allure of the other

"I'll bet you," the film director Alfred Hitchcock said in an interview, that "nine out of ten people, if they see a woman cross the courtyard undressing for bed, or even a man puttering around in his room, will stay and look; no one turns away and says, 'It's none of my business.' They could pull down their blinds," said Hitchcock, "but they never do; they stand there and look out."[38]

Even if a person *never* eavesdrops, he cannot claim to have played *no part in the process*. He would frequently have participated as *a victim*, and he may have attempted to prevent interception by whispering or pulling the shades. Kafka complained that a man named Harras, in the next apartment, "has pushed his sofa against the wall and listens; while I on the other hand must run to the telephone when it rings, take note of my customers' requirements, reach decisions of great consequence, carry out grand exercises in persuasion, and above all, during the whole operation, give an involuntary report to Harras through the wall."

Harras was engaged in what might be thought of as "recreational eavesdropping," a way to while away the hours. This was especially popular before the spread of mass media, and it is a role that the media have come to play in modern life. Thanks to reality TV shows, we can eavesdrop on people we will never encounter in real life, people whose lives will never intertwine with our own. With function out of the picture, what can explain such "couch potato" eavesdropping? Is it purely the evolved appetite at work?

Perhaps the explanation lies in what the experience does to the spectator. After sampling the intimate experience of another, the eavesdropper may be unable simply to withdraw as though nothing had happened. "Once we eavesdrop," wrote Ann Gaylin, "we are implicated in the story we have acquired. Once it becomes part of our repertory of stories, it also becomes part of ourselves."[39] Everything else the eavesdropper knows and feels relocates itself in internal space. Should she do something with the new experience? Should she talk about what she knows? What if she encounters the people she has observed socially? They don't know what she knows, and would be shocked if they knew how she found it out. Can life go on much as it was before?

It couldn't for a New York journalist when she found herself on the telephone with a woman who, much to her surprise, happened to live on the same floor in the adjacent apartment building. Mischievously, the two neighbors waved to each other. "From the moment of that wave, life was different," the journalist wrote. Over the previous decade, neither had been particularly concerned about privacy—they were two anonymous beings—but after the meeting, the other woman began to keep her shades down, and when her shades were up, the journalist wrote, "I felt awkward about looking out the window, an act that used to be innocent but now felt uncomfortably like peeping. If I did catch a glimpse of her, I'd look away quickly, wondering if she'd seen me."[40]

When Alain-René Le Sage led his readers across the rooftops of Madrid three centuries ago he was on to something. We humans do have a strong and continuing desire to expose and experience private moments in the lives of others. When perceptual access to other people became more difficult to achieve, our ancestors became more strategic, and more stealthy, but they did not give up. For, if anything, walls only whetted the Asmodean appetite, intensified the allure of the closed door, the enigmatic smile, the inaudible whisper. How did other people's business become our own?

CHAPTER TWO

Under the Leaves

No man in the tribe can keep his social place unless the
other members are able to foresee how he will act under any
given set of circumstances. This is the necessary basis of all
gregarious existence, even that of animals.   E. L. Godkin

I N the previous chapter we saw that a number of diverse
cultures have a word for "eavesdropping." By itself, this
could mean that the disposition to invade other lives evolved
once, and subsequently was maintained wherever people distributed themselves around the globe; or that this tendency emerged
independently in a wide range of human societies. Either way, the
hand of biology would seem to be at work, directing the perceptual
invasions of our socially curious species. But the naturalness of
eavesdropping is also implied by another fact—it cuts across species. Long before men and women began standing "under the
eaves" in order to hear domestic conversations, lizards, blackbirds,
and chipmunks—not to mention quail, iguanas, dik-diks, and
baboons—were already tuned in to their neighbors "under the
leaves." When we see what this does for animals, and what it
does to them, we develop some fresh insights about how eavesdropping might work in our own species.

We begin with the fact that all animals have to *do things* if they are to acquire food, build nests, and fulfill their other biological commitments, and this puts them in the public eye. They also have to send signals if they are to maintain contact with group members and warn them of imminent threats. Calls are naturally audible to conspecifics, members of their own species, for it is these individuals that signaling systems evolved to reach. But they also inevitably come to the attention of other species, including predators and prey. According to cybernetics expert Lawrence Frank, "everything that exists and happens in the world, every object and event, every plant and animal organism, almost continuously emits its characteristic identifying signal." This world of signals, he wrote, resembles "a myriad of To Whom It May Concern messages."[1]

This universe of signals was dramatized in 1934, when a physiologist at the University of Hamburg, Jacob von Uexküll, published "A stroll through the worlds of animals and men." In this quaintly titled essay, readers were invited on an imaginary stroll through a meadow that is strewn with flowers and alive with the sounds of insects and butterflies. Left to their own devices, readers would naturally enjoy their own impressions of these things, but von Uexküll suggested an alternative. The strollers, he said, could bask in the same sights, sounds, and smells as the meadow dwellers themselves if they would "blow, in fancy, a soap bubble around each creature to represent its own world, filled with the perceptions which it alone knows." If we then magically stepped into these bubbles, as von Uexküll urged his readers to do, a whole new world would appear. "Through the bubble we see the world of the burrowing worm, of the butterfly, or of the field mouse," he wrote, "the world as it appears to the animals themselves, not as it appears to us." Von Uexküll referred to the unique perceptual world of individual animals as an *Umwelt*.[2]

Note the reference to the animals *themselves*. The emphasis is not on the perceptual world of the *typical* worm or butterfly, but on the experience of *this* worm and *that* butterfly. For each animal has its own personal *Umwelt*, a unique sensory collage that reflects the material—and only the material—that it alone has chosen to ingest. Outsiders may be able to infer the content of this collage by noting the orientation of the animal's head and body, and especially its eyes, ears, and other sensory receptors. They can then look in the same direction or breathe the same air, and this is exactly what they do.[3]

Each of us humans has a personal *Umwelt* too, a perceptual world that includes all the individuals we encounter *in situ*. "When we see other people walking around us," von Uexküll wrote, putting aside his bubble metaphor for the moment, "they are walking on our stage while we do so on theirs. These stages are never identical, and in most cases are even entirely different."[4]

There is an allure to these separate spheres. Something about them intrigues and beckons us, draws us in. We must take to the stage—their stage—but we cannot do so physically. That would burst the bubble. Our only choice is to travel as far as our eyes and ears will carry us, completing the journey with inference and imagination.

For von Uexküll, appreciation of another animal meant entering its "self-world" without becoming a part of it. What does it mean—really mean—to enter the "space" of another; and what kind of space is this? A mental space? An emotional or spiritual space? What are the risks and benefits of "entering"? These will be our questions—our questions about *human beings*—but we will get a huge headstart if we first look at eavesdropping in other forms of life.

In the early 1990s, zoologist Peter McGregor pointed out something that now seems simple and obvious. In the wild, everyone's sensory equipment is permanently turned to the "on" position. Thus, when Bird A *calls to* or *squawks at* Bird B, these sounds are also *heard by* Birds C, D, E, and F as well as heterospecifics—the members of other species. McGregor referred to this arrangement of signalers and receivers as a *communications network*, to capture the idea that the signals of isolated individuals usually reach all those who inhabit the same perceptual arena. These other animals, however lowly or primitive they might seem, are exquisitely adapted to their evolutionary environments; and they tend not to do things that would serve no useful purpose. So if they spend a great deal of time observing others, they must be getting something in return. What?

One thing they get is food. If an animal forages on his own, he must personally inspect every promising nook and cranny, a hit-and-miss endeavor that can be tiring. But it is possible to scan a fairly large area visually without roaming around, and when other animals are discovered with something appetizing in their clutches, the observer—merely by sidling up to them—stands to gain far more calories than scanning and sidling consume.

The relative ease of this process is perhaps why "free loaders" and "scroungers" have been given such unappealing names, just as "snoops" and "eavesdroppers" have. But as degenerate as they may seem from a puritanical perspective, there is much to admire about such individuals from a cognitive perspective. Species that are devious enough to steal something as coveted as food, and to do so on a regular basis, may be smarter than those that meet their nutritional needs "honestly." In fact, studies indicate that they have significantly larger brains.[5]

Another benefit of vigilance relates to safety. By sampling their environment, animals get information about predators, enabling them to take evasive action before it's too late. The Galápagos islands are home to diverse species, including mockingbirds and marine iguanas. As different as they are, these species have something in common. They are both prey to a third resident—the Galápagos hawk. When mockingbirds see a hawk, they issue an alarm call, as their species evolved to do, presumably for the sake of other mockingbirds. But iguanas can hear the alarm calls of mockingbirds, and they too run for cover.[6] Much the same is true of the African dik-dik, a miniature antelope that goes into alert mode when it hears the alarm call of the white-bellied go-away bird.[7]

To survive, iguanas and dik-diks must pay attention to hetero-specifics, whether they be predators or fellow prey, but there is one thing, preeminently, that requires animals to attend exclusively to their own species. It's sex. If males are to procreate, they must be able to locate willing females. In primates, male senses should also be tuned to the signs of ovulation. When females become sexually receptive, there are visible changes in the genital area. Males must notice these right away, for there will be, at most, a tiny window of opportunity before other males move in.[8] In our own species, the female speaking voice becomes more attractive to male listeners when women are able to conceive.[9]

Females must be vigilant, too. In most species, females are "choosier" than males, and this is adaptive. They have more to lose from a poor choice of mates since they have fewer off-spring, and make a larger contribution to infant care. To get a good father for their offspring, and a suitable companion for themselves, females must review the available material very carefully. But how will a superficial scan tell them who the best mate is? In many bird species, brains—especially female brains—may be *pre-tuned* to melodious voices and bodily orna-mentation, and helpfully so: vocal ability is linked to testoster-one, and thus to sex and territorial defense; and brightly colored feathers are supported by melanin and chromatin, which imply some level of fitness.[10]

Color and music would seem to take us into the aesthetic domain, but in the animal world these properties are strictly functional. By holding out for attractive males, females increase their chances of bagging a good-quality mate, and the benefits may continue past their own lifetime. For any sons that are born are likely to be *more* colorful or melodic than the sons of less attractive fathers. They will easily find a mate and reproduce, passing on their mother's genes along with their own.[11]

In animal communication, there are two arrangements in which the information flows mainly in one direction. In one arrangement, the recipient takes in information merely because he is alert, though he may be unusually sensitive to the threat of predators or out-group challengers, or to the existence of prey. I will use the term "vigilance" for this tendency to look *for something* outside the group. In the other arrangement, attention is selectively focused on members of one's own group. This inclination to look *at someone* is eavesdropping, and I will refer to it as such, in keeping with the scientific literature on mammals, primates, birds, fish, insects, lizards, and plants.[12]

Plants? Yes, plants. When attacked by herbivores, some plants send an SOS signal—a bouquet of volatile chemicals. These chemicals attract the natural predators or parasitoids of the herbivores, who eavesdrop on the plants. In some cases, neighboring plants—no more exotic than lima beans—have also been caught eavesdropping.[13] These "bodyguards" then release their own concoction, sympathetically, in what one biologist has called "a botanical cry for help."[14]

Whether eavesdropping is practiced under the leaves, or by the leaves themselves, there are indications that it played a role in the evolution of communication systems. In fact, there are suggestions that the ability to send and receive signals may have co-evolved. Biologist John Endler has proposed that in evolution, signals were designed so as to increase the fitness of the *senders*. But there was a delicate balance that had to be achieved, for it would have been necessary to maximize the reception of conspecifics—the evolutionarily "intended" *receivers*—while minimizing interception by potential predators.[15]

Endler's hypothesis is appealing, for it combines with other evidence to suggest that eavesdropping—far from being a trivial thing or, in our species, a "naughty" thing—played a significant role in evolution, shaping the neural control and processing systems that are now used for communication. Ancient eavesdropping, it would appear, contributed to the design of modern brains.

Information about all of these things that animals care about, from food and predators to sex and fitness, is in the public domain, available to individuals who are generally alert to the possibility of certain events. It is critical to survival and reproduction and, as public information, it can be intercepted with little risk or effort. Are animals that acquire material which benefits them in the moment, or their offspring in the future, supposed to pretend that they didn't see it?

That would be tantamount to genocide. Signals and displays are in a species' repertoire for a reason. They met millions of years of ancestral needs, and continue to do so today. The ornamental and behavioral displays of males provide information to observers, who use it to make adaptive choices. The probability that this information will be ignored approaches zero. In fact, some biologists believe that it was the perceptual appetites of females that caused the appearance of male traits in the first place.[16]

All of these cases of eavesdropping are *one-on-one*. One eavesdropper is focused on one *individual*. It is true, of course, that the eavesdropping may have been inspired by a third animal. The eavesdropper may also be able implicitly to relate what he sees to some feature of his own life—certainly, as we will see, this is possible in our own species. But as we saw with Margaret Browne, *one-on two* eavesdropping is also common, and in these arrangements the spotlight is on an interaction, or a *relationship*, between two (or more) individuals. What kinds of relationships do animal eavesdroppers favor?

Most involve sex or dominance. These desiderata go by different names, but they are as entangled in the wild as they are in Harlequin novels. In many species, females base their choice of mates partly on fighting ability, and in primates, aggressive and dominant males typically produce more offspring than subordinate ones.[17] Sex and dominance also converge in some songbird species, where dominant males use their voices to shout down male competitors. Other males, who eavesdrop on these slanging matches, avoid the winner later on, but female eavesdroppers do just the opposite. They approach this warrior, and more: they sexually display to him.[18] This makes good biological sense, for a winner is exactly what they need. He will defend his territory and fight, successfully, for everything else that his family requires.[19]

But what if a female has set her sights on a male that *looks* like a suitable mate but has never fought in her presence? Should she take the plunge, trusting her own evaluation, or wait until a fight breaks out, with the risk that some other female will enter the scene in the meanwhile? In many species, the females experience no such conundrum. They select a convenient male and proceed to mate with him. Then, at some point during the act, they emit a loud copulation cry. Most or all of the unmated males in the group hear this, and treat it as a challenge. They hurry to the spot, descend on the male, and begin fighting with him—and each other. The best fighter is the last one standing, and he is the one that is "chosen" by the female.[20]

There are connections between sex and aggression in our species, too. In men, a single hormone, testosterone, promotes both, and women favor males with physical and behavioral characteristics that are correlated with high levels of testosterone. Men with low-pitched voices have more testosterone than others, sound more dominant and attractive, have sex more often—and with more different partners—and father significantly more children.[21] Men with large shoulders and hips, and a large shoulder-to-hip ratio, have more testosterone than other men, and women like these physical features too.[22]

Sex and dominance are also linked in human cultures. Romantic bestsellers rarely if ever feature gentle heroes.[23] According to romance novelist Doreen Malek, women prefer to read and fantasize about "a strong, dominant aggressive male brought to the point of surrender by a woman." There is no sense of triumph, she wrote, in "winning against a wimp."[24]

HETERO - NORMATIVE!

46

Under the leaves, the criteria used in mate selection are the "standards" that evolved. They may appear somewhat fixed, but there is room for environmental influence. In a surprising range of species, from guppies to quail, females put aside innate preferences for certain male features when they see other females consorting with males that lack these qualities, or have different attributes.[25] This is especially true when the female "model" is older than the eavesdropper.[26]

Males also base their courtship tactics on what is going on around them. In song sparrows, eavesdropping males will literally "change their tune" if they pick up the telltale signs of sexual competition. In an experiment carried out in Denmark, audio recordings of male courtship calls were played to see how mated males would respond. Predictably, they increased their own courtship behavior. They did so, it was assumed, in an effort to outshine their imagined rival, and to avoid being cuckolded.[27]

If eavesdropping can help an animal get a mate, or dodge an unwinnable fight, it may also produce a perceptual experience in and of itself. Rui Oliveira and his colleagues in Portugal put two male cichlid fish in chambers that were separated by a partition. For three days these solitary "actors" were viewed, without their knowledge, by other male cichlids on the other side of a one way window. Then the partition was removed. Predictably, the actors instantly began a fight for dominance. What they experienced is unknown, but it must have been exciting to the audience, for their testosterone levels were elevated by the fight, and they remained high for some time afterwards.[28] Sporting events do much the same thing to men.[29]

Stealth and strategy

I have discussed two perceptual targets, a sole individual and a dyad, or pair of individuals. The flow of information in these cases can either be *passive*, inasmuch as personal facts are "given off" because the actor is unaware (or does not care) that he is being observed; or *active*, where information is "given" or donated by the actor to particular recipients, as in a dominance or courtship display.

This active–passive distinction refers to the sender. Where the receiver is concerned, personal information can be acquired *openly* or with *stealth*. Under the leaves, animals take steps to minimize or conceal certain activities, or to render them difficult to interpret. This makes it necessary for others to observe them *strategically*, or to interpret what they have seen and heard in a way that is socially shrewd. It is here that *theft* enters the picture.

The fact is that in the wild, animals constantly attempt to *outsmart* each other. One animal acts, hoping—if animals can hope—that no one will see him; another watches, in an effort to discover what it is that the actor wishes to conceal; then the eavesdropper reacts, hoping his reaction will pass unnoticed.

In studies conducted off the coast of Canada and Alaska, cetologists have discovered something interesting. Killer whales that feed on seals make fewer pulsed calls than whales that feed on fish. The reason, it is thought, is that the whales are vaguely aware that seals have better hearing than fish—which they do—and that any seals that are eavesdropping will be alerted by the calls and immediately swim for cover.[30]

In at least six avian species there is evidence for a *quiet song*, one that functions like human whispering. In one of the species, blackbirds, it's called "twitter" song. This song has a number of acoustic features that limit its transmission, being higher-pitched, quieter, and more directional than ordinary song. Twitter song is sung by highly aroused males that are approaching or interacting with a conspecific at close range. In one of the classic conflations of sex and dominance, females are courted with twitter song and males are threatened with it. Female blackbirds also have a quiet song of their own. Known as the "copulation trill," this song is acoustically different from the male twitter and is obviously used under different circumstances. Both twitters and copulation trills, according to Torben Dabelsteen and his colleagues, are used when blackbirds have "a distinct need for privacy."³¹ These adjustments have the effect of preventing eavesdropping in others, but in some respects their use seems to be more furtive, perhaps "sneakier," than eavesdropping itself. Why should efforts to prevent the theft of personal information involve *more* stealth than attempts to steal it?

For one thing, animal eavesdroppers rarely need to maneuver into position. Under the leaves, signals tend to carry. Animals often find themselves positioned to receive without any special maneuvering. But they still need to know what eavesdropping can tell them *about others*—this requires interpretive skill, a strategic mind. They also must deduce what their eavesdropping tells other animals *about them*. This means anticipating how some number of individuals will react if they have seen them—or not seen them—doing certain things. In fighting fish there is evidence that males who lose a fight are less likely, later, to court a female that was around at the time—and therefore was in a position to have witnessed their defeat—than one that was elsewhere.³²

What about the females? Were the male losers right to assume that any females in the audience would actually have rejected them? I'm not sure the relevant experiment has been carried out with fighting fish, but in chickadees there is evidence that females who have seen their mate lose a song contest subsequently "divorce" him—researchers actually use that word—and cast about for some other male.³³

It is adaptive, of course, for animals to conceal their interest in anything they would rather not share with others. When females become interested in a male, they may avoid detection by others of their sex, whose pulses may be similarly quickened at the sight. It also may not benefit a male to be seen approaching a female, for this may arouse the interest of other male suitors. This can be troublesome even if competitors find out what is happening later on. Marc Hauser noted that primates sometimes suppress a copulation cry when others might hear them—like suppressing an orgasmic scream when visiting the in-laws.[34]

Perhaps one of the better ways to conceal possession of a valuable resource is to make off with it. In chimpanzees a male will occasionally form a consortship with a female and remove her from the group for a period of time. Jane Goodall wrote about one chimp, "Leakey," who tried to abduct two females simultaneously (he ended up with neither). In extreme cases, consortships continue for several months. But the motive usually has more to do with the avoidance of hassle by sexual rivals than it does with romance—frequently, the females are browbeaten into compliance.[35]

By leaving the scene, chimps avoid interference and achieve successful sex, with no doubt about paternity. Since they also avoid detection when approaching food, and seek seclusion in their nocturnal nesting patterns, it will be tempting to ask, at some point, if what we are seeing in our closest evolutionary relatives is simply isolation or something that approaches what we call *privacy*. We will devote a great deal of thought to this later because fully fledged privacy, when it emerged in human societies, posed a whole new set of challenges and opportunities.

In the meantime, we have an "internal" issue that is nearly as important as privacy, and just as relevant to the acquisition of personal information by theft. This is deception, a cognitive aptitude that supports the ability of various species to play some form of hide and seek.

Consider the western scrub-jay, a species that stores food in hidden caches. These birds know when they are being watched. They continually relocate food that they have hidden previously if another jay is watching, relaxing these efforts if a barrier is placed between the cacher and the observer. They also hide food in faraway places if they can see that they are being monitored by another jay.[36] Jays who customarily steal food themselves go to unusual lengths to hide their food, doing more to conceal it than an honest jay.[37]

The jays' reaction to barriers raises questions about the role of secrecy and privacy in the animal kingdom, and the ability of animals to infer knowledge in other animals from acts of selective attention. This issue comes to the fore in the higher primates. Chimpanzees routinely follow each other's gaze, and know what other animals can and cannot see. Implicitly, they appear to recognize that if another animal sees something, he has some awareness of that thing.

They use this information in devising strategies for acquiring food.[38] When foraging, chimps prefer to approach food that is hidden from view, even if that means approaching it circuitously,[39] and they also prefer invisible or silent approaches over ones that are transparent or audible.[40] In an experiment by Juliane Bräuer and her colleagues, subordinate chimpanzees approached a banana that a dominant chimp was not in a position to see, in preference to one that was in the dominant animal's line of vision.[41] These kinds of findings make chimps seem "sneaky" but of course they are merely behaving intelligently in competitive circumstances, and their goal, if they could be said to have a goal, is merely to get the food they need without being attacked.

Do any of these animals know what others are *thinking*? Under the right circumstances, chimps may be able to generate a crude inference or two, but it would be daring to assume that jays and fish can do this. Yet all these species seem to be aware, on some level, of the information that *would* be received by an eavesdropper *if* they were behaving in certain ways at the time that the eavesdropping occurred. We may underestimate the intelligence of animals if we ignore their ability to steal and conceal personal information.[42] But the link between intelligence and deception is even more compelling, and more tangible. I mentioned earlier that in birds, scrounging species—kleptoparasites—have large brains for their body size. Chimpanzees may be more deceptive than any of the other higher mammals, and they also have very large brains for their body size. We humans are clearly the best liars in the animal kingdom—even such laudable things as diplomacy and civility require "white lies"—and when adjustments are made for body size, we have the largest brains of all, especially in the cortical regions where acts of deception originate. We will discuss this further in a while, but there is another issue to consider before we take up the evolution of eavesdropping. It's the size of animal groups.

Sentient webs

To defend themselves against predators, solitary animals have to be vigilant. They must constantly swivel their heads like periscopes. This makes it hard to look for food, build nests, have sex, rear infants, and do anything at all in an undistracted manner. Clearly, something has to suffer under such an arrangement. Dik-diks and iguanas deal with this by outsourcing a portion of their vigilance to heterospecifics, as we have seen, and this surely makes good sense if one lives in a place where there happen to be airborne sentinels with a shared predator and a built-in disposition to issue audible warnings. But if no such species exists, and there are conspecifics nearby, would it not be wise to keep eyes and ears focused on *them*?

A century and a half ago the English geneticist Francis Galton spent some time observing wild oxen in the deserts of South Africa. These beasts, he noticed, tended to huddle together very tightly. They never gave any indication that they *liked* each other, but when something happened to separate them, the oxen became agitated. Galton surmised that herding reduces the probability of surprise attack. "To live gregariously," he wrote, "is to be a fibre in a vast sentient web." Merely by living in close proximity to others, Galton wrote, one becomes "the possessor of faculties always awake, of eyes that see in all directions, of ears and nostrils that explore a broad belt of air."[43]

Galton's idea has occasioned a great deal of research. A century later enough evidence had accumulated to justify a conclusion, and it was that individual vigilance and probability of attack do indeed decline as group size increases.[44] But there is a hitch, a serious hitch.

In apes and monkeys, groups have a typical size, ranging from as few as four to as many as twenty-five, and size matters. Groups—like dinner parties—can become too big, at least for certain purposes. If groups enlarge past the point of optimal monitoring efficiency, the new members can do little to provide additional protection, and just by existing they ramp up the competition for available resources.

Animals in larger groups interact more often than they do in smaller groups,[45] and this increases the chance of friction. There is also more competition in larger groups. In primates, there is a constant struggle for power, and battles are fought over everything, especially food.[46] Where groups have enlarged, the threat of predation was replaced, to some extent, by new fears of attack by conspecifics and, more ominously, members of one's own social group. There is plenty of evidence that large-group apes are physically aggressive, even homicidal, particularly in the context of competition.[47] The competition within primate groups "is so intense and potentially costly to reproductive success," according to Brian Hare, who led much of the research on chimpanzee deception, "that it has been a challenge for behavioral ecologists to develop theories of why primates might live in groups at all."[48]

With so much danger posed by one's associates, it would not be surprising if group expansion caused a shift of attention from the periphery of an occupied space—the area *around* a group, the outer line of defense against predators—to the *center* of that space, literally the inner circle, and it appears that this is exactly what happened. Where *vigilance* had been the ancient and primary means of investigation, there was an evolutionary tilt toward *eavesdropping*.

There is no shortage of evidence that competition engenders eavesdropping. In one of the more elegant demonstrations, squirrel monkeys—who live in large groups that are characterized by cliques, subgroups, and dominance hierarchies—were compared to cotton-top tamarins, which live in more egalitarian family groups known for cooperation, sharing, and relative peacefulness. The investigators found that the more competitive squirrel monkeys, as anticipated, devoted significantly more attention to other group members than the tamarins did.[49]

Within-group competition can create a tension between eaves-dropping and vigilance. The time that animals devote to eavesdropping upon "their own kind" takes away from the time spent looking out for predators. There are some human issues here. Police departments that once were dedicated to crime fighting now must deal with terrorism as well.

Sex differences

When I have told friends that I was writing a book about eaves-dropping, the men nodded, often without comment, but a number of women spontaneously declared—sometimes blushing—*"You must be writing about me!"* There are intriguing "gender" distinctions in our species, and we will take a good look at them in the chapters that follow. But it makes sense to look first at sex differences in the eavesdropping of other species. These will alert us to possible trends in the history of human eavesdropping, trends that go back nearly a thousand years.

Although we may be tempted to ask which sex "eavesdrops more," and may even feel that we can guess, the question, as framed, is too simple. Males and females attempt to protect their interests. Some of their interests are the same, others are different, and the areas of overlap and difference shift with various external factors. One has to do with space—the way that males and females distribute themselves and make use of physical space. There are strong and consistent trends here. In various primate species, males display and court, challenge and threaten each other, and advertise themselves—their existence, emotional state, and motives—publicly and loudly.[50] They also travel more widely and, in that sense, make more extensive use of public space.[51]

Many female interactions, by contrast, are carried out quietly, in close proximity to other females. They produce a large number of social vocalizations, a category that includes soft coos and grunts, and somewhat speechlike sounds called girneys. Social vocalizations are not and cannot be yelled out across the forest canopy. They are murmured by clustered females during bouts of manual grooming.

In many primate species grooming is done predominantly by females, and in macaques, females—far more often than males—participate in *grooming chains* in which as many as three or four animals groom each other simultaneously.[52]

In a study of Japanese macaques, 90 percent of all the girneys were produced by females.[53] In research on rhesus macaques, females issued more than ten times the number of social vocalizations as males, and vocalized socially to other adult females more than thirty times more often than they vocalized to adult males.[54]

Space is also gendered in our own species. Starting in childhood, females naturally form smaller groups—which are less competitive than large ones—and situate themselves closer to each other than males do.[55] Some time ago, students of proxemics (the social use of space) found that short distances between people indicate intimate relationships.[56] Females, more than males, prefer these smaller interpersonal distances.[57]

In apes and monkeys, females enjoy closer same-sex relationships than males. Primatologist Joan Silk has pointed out that female baboons spend far more time socializing than males, and continue to do so even when food is scarce and they must spend more time foraging than usual. When a close companion dies, females also appear to be more strongly affected than males. Gluco-corticoid levels may rise following the death of a relative, indicating increased stress. Females also spend more time grooming after a loss, subsequently increasing the size of their grooming networks.[58]

Now that we have seen some of the more important differences in the social ecology of primate males and females, we are ready to look at the vigilance and eavesdropping of the two sexes.

Of course, we have already discussed a few sex differences in animal surveillance. We saw that female birds prefer to mate with males that they were *in a position to hear* when the males won a song contest; and we have noted that male fish avoid tangling with other males that they *would have been able to see* when the males won a fight. But in these species it has been difficult to actually see eavesdroppers taking in the information—to catch them in the act.

Fortunately, it is often possible to detect primates (and some other animals) *looking up* from their foraging and *scanning* in particular directions. This has helped investigators to ascertain the sex and, in some cases, the social status of the target animal. Moreover, by following their line of regard, researchers have also been able to make inferences about whether the animals were looking *for* predators or *at* members of their own group; and it has also been possible to evaluate the effect of ongoing issues, such as breeding or infant rearing, which would naturally affect the two sexes differently. That said, it has been witnessed in various primate groups that males exhibit a vigilance bias for individuals located outside the immediate area—presumably they are looking for competitors or predators—and that females tend, more than males, to direct their attention to individuals that are physically close, even within an arm's reach, and these would be familiar members of the group.[59]

But males also devote some vigilance to subsections of their own groups. Low-ranking males look at more dominant males, who look for, and at, other males, especially potential challengers and interlopers from outside groups.[60] There is little that excites competition among males so much as the sight of a female in estrus, and there are indications that male watchfulness increases as the breeding season approaches.[61]

In monkeys, mating periods, births, and infant excursions all boost maternal looking time. Maxeen Biben and her colleagues at the National Institutes of Health found that when they played tape recordings of infant vocalizations, the time adult females spent looking for predators increased fivefold. Studies of black howler monkeys indicate that female vigilance rates increased after the birth of infants,[62] and that females were more vigilant when their offspring were young—neonates or infants—than when they were older, and they were more watchful when their young vocalized, played, or moved about in a conspicuous manner.[63] In a study of rhesus monkeys on La Cueva island in Puerto Rico, it was found that mothers looked up more often when they were separated from their young by more than an arm's length.[64]

In these findings on nonhuman primates we are beginning to see a fairly general sex pattern that will re-emerge in our own species later. The motivation for male monitoring—mainly in the form of vigilance—is frequently tied to a self-oriented control function. Looking is directed outside the group, from whence predators and strangers emerge, and inside the group, where holders of power, and challengers, reside. By contrast, much of the visual monitoring of primate females is directed to genetically and socially related individuals within the group or to outsiders that threaten those individuals.

The brain of an eavesdropper

"As you go through life," wrote author Norman Mailer, "you ... observe everyone, wittingly and unwittingly. Out of the corner of your eye, you glimpse someone in a restaurant who represents a particular menace or possibility, potentially a friend or a foe." In this remark Mailer allied himself with Georg Simmel and others who have commented on the naturalness of human eavesdropping. But he went on to say something more interesting—that once the diner has observed what is going on around him, "the unconscious goes to work on that. It needs very little evidence to put together a comprehensive portrait, because, presumably, *it has already done most of that labor."*[65]

Up to a point, the to-be-human brain evolved under social conditions similar to those in which the apes now live. But our groups became larger than theirs, and the competition keener, and it was largely in response to these changes that we humans acquired proportionately more social brain than the apes have.[66] So it makes sense to ask how our enhanced intellectual capacity would have affected the ability to observe and make sense of subtle and intimate human behaviors, especially ones that are not intended for public consumption.

Arthur Conan Doyle's detective, Sherlock Holmes, occasionally admonished his investigative assistant, Watson, for overlooking important details. You look, Holmes would chide Watson, but you fail to see. To eavesdrop, one must be able to *intercept* the physical images—the light and sound waves—that flow from others, but these would be of little value if one didn't know how to *interpret* them. These processes are almost certainly related, of course; how can one know whether to eavesdrop in the first place, or which features to observe, without having some sense of what it means? To make these decisions, one needs a mind that is endowed with some very particular properties.

The ability to interpret complex social behaviors. Primate societies have an intricate structure. It has been pointed out that dominance hierarchies require that every animal be able to recognize and remember things about group members and kin, and that exchange systems require primates to know which individuals owe and are owed favors. Additionally, according to a recent summary by Joan Silk, primates must be able "to compute the value of resources and services; keep track of past interactions with group members; make transitive inferences; discriminate between cooperators and defectors; and assess the qualities of prospective rivals, mates, and allies."

They must also know something about the relationships between all the other group members.[67]

To service social relationships one needs a socially serviceable brain. In the early 1990s Robin Dunbar initiated a series of demonstrations that speak to this point. The first and most significant was a correlation between the size of primate groups and the size of the cognitively critical neocortical areas of the brain, ultimately leading to what Dunbar called the "social brain hypothesis." This hypothesis holds that the challenges of living in social groups produced expansion and reorganization of the primate brain. This made it possible to solve ecological problems socially, through the operation of brain mechanisms that enhance social cohesion.[68]

What Dunbar failed to realize, but Swedish neuroscientist Patrik Lindenfors did, is that increasing group size only explains changes *in female brains*. Lindenfors argued that females were "the driving sex in primate social evolution, with female group size changing first and male group size subsequently adjusting to female number."[69]

The ability to understand personal (especially intimate) relationships. In general, the primates are fairly well adapted to the challenges of group living but social animals also spend a great amount of time and effort on *relationships*. In fact, Dunbar has suggested that it was the capacity for relationships that *enabled group living*. As we will see, the ability of primates to form and maintain relationships may itself derive from something more basic—the capacity for males and females to bond, to live monogamously. Recently, Dunbar and a colleague, Susanne Shultz, observed that in a diverse range of animals and birds there is an association between brain size and monogamy.[70] In primates, ungulates, carnivores, four orders of mammals, and well over a hundred species of birds, large brain size is associated with social monogamy.[71] Dunbar and Shultz suggested that at some early point in their evolution, primates began to redeploy the kinds of cognitive skills that had evolved for pair-bondings to create and service *other kinds of relationships*. This meant that two individuals of the same sex could form

relationships that were nearly as intense as those enjoyed by reproductive mates in other species.[72]

The ability to understand deception. Nicholas Humphrey has observed that if social success enhances biological fitness, then any
heritable trait that increases an individual's competitive ability will
soon spread through the gene pool.[73] In these circumstances, animals will continually attempt to outfox each other, with predictable
increases in the ability to deceive and to spot acts of deception, until
these abilities peak in the species—if they ever do. To eavesdrop,
and to avoid being eavesdropped upon, one must be able to deceive
tactically. Tactical deception refers to attempts to mislead another,
to the misleader's own advantage. This ability has been found in all
major groups of anthropoid primates, but is particularly common
in chimpanzees and baboons.[74] It has been shown, using field data,
that the frequency of tactical deception across primate species is
highly predicted by neocortical volume.[75]

The ability to imagine possible worlds. Dunbar suggested that
group living is *inherently virtual* since it requires members to imagine the future behavior of other individuals, which, in turn,
encourages them to imagine other individuals' mental states.
"These aspects of the world," he wrote, "cannot be observed or
engaged with directly, but have to be constructed in the mind."[76]
There is no problem here, of course. We come equipped for virtual
experience. Imaging research carried out by Perrine Ruby and Jean
Decety in France indicates that a region of the human brain, the
right inferior parietal cortex, was activated when their subjects
mentally simulated actions as they would appear *to others*, but not
as the same actions would appear to the subjects themselves. This
region of the brain was also activated when participants were asked
to imagine how others would feel in situations that would normally
elicit an emotional response.[77]

These findings lead us to an interesting conclusion: every normal
human has the brain of an eavesdropper—a brain that is wired up

to do the things that eavesdropping requires. Possessed of this facility to a unique degree in the animal kingdom, we naturally enough seek regular opportunities to use it. With brains like ours, it would be surprising if our ancestors had adopted anything but the most open plan of living.

CHAPTER THREE

Open-plan Living

There are no recognised and respected ways in which the
public gaze can be cut off, no ways of separating oneself
out from others present. Any conversation between two
may be freely invaded... Privacy can only be achieved by
hiding from others. Frederik Barth

E VERY night, just as it starts to grow dark, all the chimpanzees, gorillas, and orangutans in the jungle get ready
to retire. They begin by making their beds, but they do
this not by fluffing up the leaves and branches that were used the
night before. Rather, they build an entirely new place to sleep,
first by settling in, then by pulling branches over and around
them.[1]

Lots of wild animals appropriate physical areas for their personal
use. In doing so they convert spaces to places, and these places
became the property of the animal. Swiss zoologist Heini Hediger
called them "fix points," zones of maximum security to which
animals withdraw when threatened, or when they need to rest,
sleep, give birth, or care for the young.[2]

Wild humans

Wild humans also make places out of spaces, and use them for their own specifically human needs. I refer here to human beings who *live in the wild*, naturally, as our distant ancestors did, without significant contact with individuals who live in any other way. There is nothing wild about the *behavior* of these individuals—many of them live in relative peace, and do an excellent job of rearing their children—but they live without walls. They share space with wild animals.

Wild humans are interesting because they tell us something about the adaptive value of various behaviors, including ones that shaped habitual residential and communicative arrangements long before the influence of contemporary cultures.[3] I believe there are messages in their behavior for what it means to live a completely domesticated life, as we now do; and for what we and others must know, and should not be permitted to learn, about each other.

Today small-scale societies are dwindling, but in the previous century a number of anthropologists studied the tiny, relatively unadulterated hunting and gathering bands that inhabited Africa, Australia, India, South America, and other places. Their detailed accounts tell us a great deal about the value placed on openness and privacy by wild-living humans.

One thing we will look at is their huts, for the form, spacing, and orientation of these structures tell us things about the perceptual requirements of the builders. We will see what wild humans valued, and find that this was revealed less by what they created than what they kept the same. It is something that we care about very deeply today.

In using the term "open plan" I am recalling a trend, beginning in the 1960s, toward open-plan offices. In these physical arrangements, office workers were distributed across large, open spaces—with few if any walls or partitions—in preference to small, enclosed, private offices. Predictably, when workers made the transition into these new spaces, they said that they missed something to which they were accustomed: privacy.[4] Is this a basic human need?

The Kung

If we look at the Kung, the answer would seem to be no. These hunter-gatherers inhabit the Kalahari Desert of Botswana and Southwest Africa. In the mid to late twentieth century, when they were studied fairly intensively, most of the Kung lived in bands of fifty or sixty, but they periodically dispersed into smaller groups or concentrated into larger ones, as suited their needs.[5]

The typical Kung camp was laid out in concentric circles. In the center was a public gathering place. Rimming this plaza were the huts of the band members.

Huts built for the rainy season were the most elaborate. They were circular, about five feet in height and diameter, made of branches that were set in the ground around the circumference and bent inward, then lashed together to form the peak of the roof. The frame was covered with grass. Facing inwards, towards the plaza, was the front of the hut—a small opening. This opening could easily have been confused with *an* entrance, or *the* entrance, but in reality it was not really *any* kind of entrance, at least in the normal meaning of that word.

For the fact is that the Kung *went* in far less often than they *reached* in. The huts were places to store belongings or, less often, to seek momentary relief from the sun or rain. They were not really habitable, but this was no design flaw—the builders never expected to be occupiers. What the huts gave each family was a territorial claim—squatters' rights in their most literal meaning—and in a more socially constructed sense, an address. This place was considered "private property" in the sense of its being one's own.[6]

Just how a tiny piece of ground can become an address was discovered by anthropologist Jean Briggs' who, while conducting her doctoral research in the early 1960s, shared an igloo with an

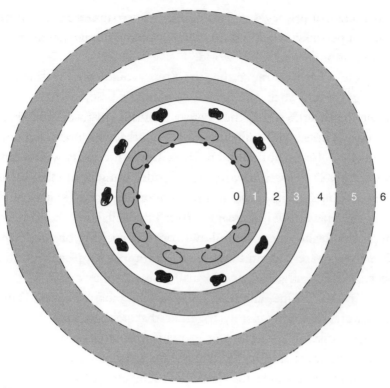

Key

!*gau* {
0 Central plaza, chu/o
1 Circle of huts and fireplaces, da tsi
2 Ash dumps
3 Cooking pits
}
4 Empty area
5 Zone of defecation, z/o
6 The bush, t'si

Exhibit 10 Plan of a typical Kung village showing the central plaza (o), circle of huts and fireplaces (1), and other functional zones

Eskimo family. Briggs chose, or was given, a tiny place to sleep that was between one of the family members and the wall. "That spot, just the length and breadth of my sleeping bag, very quickly became my home, in a real sense," she would later write. "I possessed my spot, and from it I always looked out on the same view. The sameness of it gave me a sense of stability in a world of shifting dwellings, a feeling of belonging in a family; it even gave me a sense of privacy, since no one ever encroached on my space without permission, and sitting there I could withdraw quietly from conversation into an inner world."[7]

It is in no sense strange that the Kung would come to think of their grass and stick enclosures as a home base, perhaps even homes, even if they were not houses.[8] This is particularly clear in the case of huts built for the non-rainy months, which amounted to about three-fourths of the year. These huts were made with a few sticks and a little grass. It would be ridiculous to suppose that these were *dwellings* in any sense of the word, or even visual shields, and they were never used to escape scrutiny. Indeed, it was considered improper for anyone to withdraw from the sociality of camp life. The Kung "rarely spend time alone," wrote Richard Lee, "and to seek solitude is regarded as a bizarre form of behavior."[9]

Partly to escape anything approaching solitude, the Kung huts were spaced so closely together that people sitting at their hearths—essentially "dine out" kitchens in front of the huts— could hand utensils to each other without getting up. This arrangement made it possible for next-door neighbors to converse at a normal level of loudness. It also enabled them to eavesdrop on the latest camp gossip. Indeed, I would suggest that the huts and layout of Kung villages were designed—consciously or unconsciously— with eavesdropping in mind. To block the flow of personal information would have been unthinkable, and extremely risky.

Western Desert aborigines

On a different continent, an Indian Ocean away, a tiny band of aborigines lives in similar huts, or at least they did in the late 1960s. That's when archeologist Richard Gould excavated an area in the Central Australian Desert and, while there, photographed the huts of the indigenous Pitjantjatjara people.[10] At that time there were just over thirty aborigines living a fully nomadic existence in the area where Gould was doing his archeological work. He found that in

the winter, when temperatures dropped to freezing, the Pitjantjatjara built "cold camps" by erecting windbreaks to shield them from
ground winds. Like the Kung's, the Pitjantjatjara camps were
generally circular, with the huts on the periphery and the entrances
of the huts facing towards the center.[11] In the summer, when there
was sweltering heat, the aborigines built small, dome-shaped shelters from boughs. These "shade camps" provided relief during the
hottest part of the day.

Photographs indicate that the shelters of the Pitjantjatjara and
the Kung were almost identical. Although Gould said nothing
about any resistance to privacy the Pitjantjatjara might have felt,
there is little indication from the design of their huts that they
wanted to spend any time in them, or to be alone.

The Semai

In the early 1960s Robert Dentan studied the Senoi Semai, another
aboriginal group that lived in the mountains of central Malaya. The
Semai people characteristically banded together in time of danger,
and therefore needed to know who was under threat. Their houses
were built to foster this awareness. "Because the outside walls are
usually thin and the whole house open to the breeze," Dentan
wrote, "people near a house can hear what is going on inside . . . In
the evening after the lights were out we would often chat through
the walls for a quarter of an hour or so with any of our next door
neighbors who were awake."[12]

It would not be wrong to refer to the Semai huts as shelter, for
they were designed to protect people against wild animals and the
elements. But they were not supposed to shield people from each
other. "To refuse someone admission to one's house," Dentan
wrote, "would be an act of extreme hostility."[13] Recognizing this,
and secure in the knowledge that the friendly anthropologist would
not want to hurt their feelings, the Semai sometimes entered
Dentan's house, even if he and his wife were sound asleep at five

o'clock in the morning. In his book he described a typical entry. "They would cough a few times to see if we were awake or ask in clear, pleasant voices, 'You sleeping?' If we pretended to be asleep and they had nothing urgent to do," Dentan wrote, "they would settle down to chat with each other. A person who dropped in by himself might just sit for a while, humming a little tune, or he might rummage through our belongings in hopes of turning up something interesting." In response to these invasions, the Dentans tried tying the door shut, but this made little difference. "Serene in their knowledge that we liked them and were therefore always glad to have them visit," he wrote, "they would reach over the top of the door and untie the fastening."[14]

The Nayaka

The Nayaka, a forest-dwelling group in south India, were studied about thirty years ago by Nurit Bird-David. She reported that the "walls" of Nayakan domiciles were made of interwoven strips of bamboo, offering little or no privacy. The people moved into these huts before construction was complete, and lived there for many weeks, in full view, before they began to build walls.[15]

Even when the huts were finished, the Nayaka continued to spend much of their time outside. "They remain seated by their respective fire-places, and talk across space from fire to fire," wrote Bird-David; "[and] they rarely try to conceal their domestic activities." Almost all interactions are overheard by others, she went on. "Normally, they do not even try to keep their conversations private."[16]

The Samoans

The Samoans also lived in a fishbowl. In the 1980s the typical house (called a *fale*) had no walls. Except in bad weather, when they lowered blinds, the occupants were completely exposed to public view. This, according to anthropologist Bradd Shore, helped keep everyone in line. One woman told Shore, "People want to know what happens inside a house. Many Samoans feel that if your house is all closed up, then you'll do secret things inside that others cannot see."[17] Another said that in a walled house (called a *pālagi*), a structure that aroused suspicion, "you cannot see the kind of behaviors that go on inside. If people do bad things you cannot see them."[18]

Here one begins to see tensions between two quests, one for the nutritional and other resources that are needed to sustain individuals, the other for interpersonal feelings that are necessary for group solidarity. Aroused by these tensions, eavesdropping flourishes at the boundary between individuals and their societies.

The Mehinacu

The Mehinacu Indians of central Brazil, who were mentioned in the first chapter, are the most interesting for our purposes, for they offer insights into a tribal group's extraordinary need for transparency and a rare glimpse of its equally unusual need for periods of relief.

In 1967 Thomas Gregor studied a small Mehinacu tribe living along the headwaters of the Xingú River. It is clear from his report that Mehinacu life was built to accommodate the senses. Each of the five huts in the village housed a family of about ten or twelve. The dwellings were oval in shape, with hammocks in the ends and an open area in the center. There were no internal walls. These thatched domiciles were situated around an open circular plaza. Anyone crossing the plaza was seen by one or more villagers. Some of the watchers merely sat in the doorway of a hut; others peered out of openings in order to keep an eye on local activities.

When the Mehinacu were not immediately visible, which was rare, their activities could be inferred from various clues, which were eagerly sought by their curious fellow villagers. We saw earlier that they were quick to notice the telltale prints of butts and heels on the sandy paths around the village, but the Mehinacu also recognized each other from their footprints. When asked by Gregor, several tribesmen drew each other's footprints from memory, doing so with sufficient accuracy that other villagers could use them to make a positive identification.[19] Such clues enabled the Mehinacu to reconstruct not only the activities of others, but also their intentions—what they were "up to."

Many of the Mehinacu activities that could not be seen were audible. The thatch walls of the huts did little to keep conversations inside. When a person speaks, wrote Gregor, "there is a chance that a third person is listening, and that in a short time everyone else will know what he said. Even the most intimate details of his sex life often become a matter of public knowledge." Incidentally, this feature of Mehinacu dwellings—the ability to overhear sensitive conversations—is the single most important complaint about open-plan offices,[20] but the Mehinacu considered it a benefit.

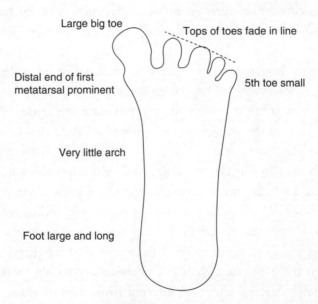

Exhibit 11 The chief's foot, as drawn by one of the villagers

Benefits of open-plan living

A naive visitor might think that the collage of personal sights and sounds in these tiny villages was the result of shoddy construction materials or primitive building techniques—the best that wild humans could come up with, having little or nothing to rely on but bamboo and grass. But it was not what these tribes *didn't know* that accounted for their transparency. It is what they *did know.* The under-building of huts and the openness of encampments were *intended*, and the benefits they offered were of critical significance.

What does it mean to be fully exposed? What does the choice to live a transparent life give those who choose it? From a psychological standpoint, we may suppose that complete access to the lives of others is expansive. It gives people a sense of the possible. "As one's ability to monitor surrounding activities increases," wrote architecture professor John Archea, "so does one's awareness of emerging behavioral opportunities." Paradoxically, full exposure can also be restrictive in ways that are also beneficial, especially from a social perspective. When "the likelihood of being monitored by others increases," Archea continued, "so does the person's accountability for his or her own behavior."[21]

But exposure was also protective. In small, open societies, people were able to achieve some level of personal security without surveillance cameras, police, or an aggressive press—mechanisms that are required in larger societies. But there was a price to pay: openly living beings could not quit monitoring, and when they observed wrong-doing they had to take action personally or spread the word.

In small-scale communities, even subtle events are likely to reach public notice. Since each person is known to everyone, his conduct will automatically be of interest, and since the material featured in gossip usually involves some sort of indiscretion, the person's "news" will travel rapidly. In Semai communities there are few ways that Semai can be forced to conform to community standards, according to Robert Dentan, but "each person knows that his neighbors are watching him." If a man does something that offends a neighbor, "the news will be all over the settlement by bedtime."[22]

Small-scale societies are usually egalitarian. Everyone is happy, more or less, as long as no one is trying to get ahead, because in such arrangements personal advancement can only occur at the expense of others. To avoid being victimized, villagers keep a close eye on the activities of everyone else.[23] "Egalitarian societies," wrote Anthony Forge, "can only be maintained at the cost of continuous vigilance by their members."[24]

A specific thing that members maintain with vigilance is their systems for sharing food, which might, at first glance, appear to be supported by trust. But trust is not a well-formed concept in societies in which there is little possibility of violations, and round-the-clock surveillance makes those unlikely. Individuals who have food—that is, are *seen with food*—are expected to share it, and if they hoard it—that is, are *seen not sharing it*—they are chastised. One Samoan told Bradd Shore that if a family wished to eat a pig in an open *fale* house, the pig would have to be shared with other families because the family would be seen eating it. If, on the other hand, they were among the few that had a closed *pālagi* house, they would not be forced to give food away, because then no one would know what the family was eating.

Eavesdropping offers psychological benefits as well. In order to preserve some level of peace and harmony, people in interdependent groups need to be aware of mood changes, and if they live in close proximity to each other, they are. They see facial expressions, a tightening or loosening of the body, and subtle movements of the hands. When people are close to each other, they can see eye gaze, and by following lines of regard they can tell what others are looking at, or refuse to acknowledge. They can detect emotions in the voice, and may be able to make out whispered messages, including ones that are not intended for them.

Collectively, these subtle behaviors tell the observant individual what others are doing and intend to do. To fully benefit from group living, people must have this information, but they will not have it if everyone is widely dispersed. To benefit from group living, people need to huddle.

Psychological escape

From the perspective of the unwitting "sender," however, there may be psychological problems with proximity. The English psychologist Nicholas Humphrey has written that people require at least the *possibility* that they will be able to keep the existence of their thoughts and feelings to themselves. "The capacity for mind-reading and for being mind-read is all very well," he wrote. "But human individuals even in the closest knit cooperative groups are still usually to some degree in competition. So there must certainly be times when individuals do not want to be a completely open book to others."[25]

A great deal of the shielding needed for personal activities is achieved by psychological escape, that is, with behavioral signals rather than structural barriers. Earlier we looked at Nurit-Bird's account of psychological shelter offered by the Naiken people of India. In a later paper she described the way that they "sit scattered, staring in different directions," displaying a reticence that protects them from direct encounters with others. Since they live openly, reticence provides relief against what Nurit-Bird called "involuntary intimacy."

The averted gaze has always been an effective way of isolating oneself from others, and it continues to be today, especially when people are crowded into small places such as elevators and ATM kiosks. We may suppose this signal worked overtime in the case of anthropologist Jean Briggs, who, as we saw, lived with an Eskimo family in an open-space igloo or tent. Briggs quickly discovered that all her normally private (physiological) activities would have to be carried out in front of these potential observers. Yet this scrupulously polite family of six never really looked at Briggs, nor did she watch them when they engaged in intimate personal and family activities.

Similar observations were made by Paul Fejos, an anthropologist who studied the Yagua people of northeastern Peru in the early 1940s. All the families of a clan, which ranged from twenty-five to fifty members, lived communally in one large house. Fejos noted that although there were no partitions, members could achieve privacy at any time simply by turning away. "No one in the house," Fejos wrote, "will look upon, or observe, one who is in private facing the wall, no matter how urgently he may wish to talk to him."[26]

This sort of civil inattention is rather different from structural privacy. For one thing, one's associates cooperate. Their ability to attend is not, as with physical enclosure, removed from them unilaterally. The privacy achieved by these individuals is *requested*—directly or, more often, indirectly—and freely *conferred*. In open living arrangements, others retain the ability to detect an abuse of privacy, and to restore scrutiny at any time. *They know what it is they are not watching*.

These benign concessions by a group carry rather different implications than unilateral withdrawal by an individual. This is especially true where the individual cannot be trusted, and in face to face societies there are few ways that one can earn trust. If we are eating a pig, one Samoan woman said, we give it to other families because they can see into our house and they know that we are eating it. It may be impossible for a man to know who can be trusted and who cannot, wrote the jurist Charles Fried, "unless he has a right to act without constant surveillance so that he knows he can betray the trust."[27]

We thus find eavesdropping and trust in odd juxtaposition. In today's closed societies, eavesdropping is precipitated by distrust, but in the open societies of the past, eavesdropping—then an easy thing to do—rendered trust unnecessary.

Growing pains

Eavesdropping works well with tiny groups, which may be responsible for the fact that small-scale societies may be able to get by without police or courts.[28] But as groups enlarge, it becomes more and more difficult to "keep tabs on . . . the alliances and maneuverings of others," as Berkeley anthropologist George Foster put it, and under the circumstances it is easy to imagine that these activities "may be prejudicial to oneself."[29] But why is it difficult to keep track? Are we concerned, here, with limits on the information processing capabilities of the human brain? "*Homo sapiens*," wrote a British anthropologist, Anthony Forge, "can only handle a certain maximum number of intense face to face relationships, successfully distinguishing between each."[30]

Of course we are not speaking here of limits on the capacity to store and recognize faces. This capacity goes into the thousands, far outstripping the size of small villages. But there is almost certainly a problem with personal familiarity, of knowing what others have done, are doing, and may be planning to do next. How many of these ambiguous beings can one stand to live with?

In his own field work in New Guinea, Forge noted that there were usually about 150 people in the average settlement. Groups of this size normally included about thirty-five men. This number, he reasoned, should certainly be able to cooperate without too much rivalry. If the group swelled to double this size, however, or climbed even higher, the fighting over resources would surely escalate. Little would be known about other people's reliability and intentions, so it would be difficult to predict their future actions under various circumstances or the likelihood that they would offer help in time of need.

Now this is interesting. If people become suspicious of each other when there are too many faces to keep track of, and fractious when they don't know who they can depend on, how would we expect them to act if key members of their group periodically disappeared from view and, for fairly long periods, remained out of sight?

CHAPTER FOUR

Reluctant Domestication

For working and talking, people sit on mats under spreading trees . . . To stay alone in the house is considered a sure sign of evil intent.   Gillian Feeley-Harnik

GERMAN biologist Paul Leyhausen once recited a parable about some porcupines that on a winter night decided to huddle together for warmth. They quickly discovered that their spines made proximity uncomfortable, so they moved apart again and got cold. After a bit of shuffling in and out, the porcupines eventually found a distance at which they could be warm without getting pricked.[1]

Our human ancestors also experienced environmental threats of one sort or another, and discovered that they had collective action on their side if they maintained close contact with other members of their group. But if their associates drew too close, and remained so for too long, they began to rub each other the wrong way. The challenge for them, no less than for the porcupines, lay in finding the right distance.

Authorities from various disciplines have commented on the need for a proper distance. Most species, according to ethologists

Peter Klopfer and Daniel Rubenstein, have "an equilibrium level" where even a small increase in privacy or exposure threatens rather than enhances reproductive success. Sociologist Barry Schwartz suggested that for humans there is "a threshold beyond which social contact becomes irritating for all parties." Thomas Gregor, the anthropologist who studied the Mehinacu, referred to "a narrow optimum range between what constitutes too little and too much interaction and exposure." Philosopher Thomas Nagel has written that "social life would be impossible if we expressed all our lustful, aggressive, greedy, anxious, or self-obsessed feelings in ordinary public encounters," but "so would inner life be impossible if we tried to become wholly persons whose thoughts, feelings, and private behaviour could be safely exposed to public view."[2]

In this chapter we take a look at the initial reactions of humans to their own domestication, and especially their search for an optimal social distance—one that would enable the benefits of a proximal life without danger of over-exposure or friction, and periods of solitude without loss of social connection and support. We will see clear evidence that many individuals spent their lives attempting to establish this boundary, without ever succeeding.

The first humans to build and occupy walled domiciles were strongly conflicted about their use. Walls were a new technology, one that paradoxically threatened the security of human groups while offering tempting opportunities for relief from mounting external pressures. It would be difficult to overstate the effect of walls on social monitoring, for they snatched from eyes and ears material that was essential to the management of peaceful and morally tidy villages. But, as we will see, domestication never gave our ancestors complete control over how much of their private life would be truly private.

If we could take a tour of the world as it existed fifteen thousand years ago, we would be able to see a great many of the human beings then alive. The missing ones would be the foragers and lovers who happened to be off in some leafy glade or desert dunes when we went by, doing something that could only be done there. The rest would be *at or near their home base*, but they would not be *in their homes*. They had no homes.

Contrast this with a different tour, one that could be conducted almost anywhere in the world today. If we were to drive through any number of cities, we would see only a fraction of the citizens who live there and were actually there at the time. But the invisible people would not be *away* some place. They would be *there*, at home, *inside*. Herein lies the appeal of our demon, Asmodeus, who offered readers the fantastic possibility of peering under the roof-tops of Madrid's finest residences. Why did our more recent ancestors build and occupy homes and the earlier ones not do so? Was it just to tantalize and tease all the outsiders?

The road to domestication

The answer cannot be that *Homo sapiens* had no tools; even their own distant ancestor, *Homo ergaster*, could make these; nor can it be that they lacked building materials, because mud, wood, and stone were everywhere; or that they could not figure out how to build dwellings, because they had more than enough intelligence to do this.[3]

But ecological factors were operating. At the transition from the Pleistocene to the Holocene, some ten thousand years ago, most people were still nomadic. They lived on wild food of one kind or another, from plants to large animals, and wild food had a habit of moving whenever it saw someone chasing it; or its own source of nutrition went elsewhere; or there was a change of seasons or the weather.[4] To spend much time building anything, or to make it larger or more secure than necessary, would have made no sense.

It would be easy to rest our explanation here, content that we had provided a respectable account of human domestication. The openly living nomads, according to our story, had no real reasons for living transparently, it was just easier than constructing something that would *coincidentally* have blocked the senses. But we already know that this is not correct. In the previous chapter we saw that our wild living ancestors craved sensory access to each other. Indeed, as egalitarians they would have had great difficulty living without it.

The need for constant relocation had to subside before it became labor-efficient to build permanent dwellings. Even when it did subside, however, dwellings were not built, and this suggests some degree of resistance to sensory interruption all along. We will discuss the source of this resistance shortly, but in the meantime we need to ask, what eroded our ancestors' peripatetic ways?

Anthropologists differ as to the precise sequence of events, but certain factors can be identified.[5] One is the dissipation of large animal herds. Increasingly, hunters were returning with insufficient food to supply their small camps. A second factor—possibly related to the first—was an increase in the rate of population growth, increasing the competition for whatever large animals that remained. Fortunately, an alternative developed. It was *global warming*, a significant increase in temperature and rainfall, occurring between eleven and fifteen thousand years ago. This climate change stimulated the proliferation of annual cereals and legumes, giving our ancestors new nutritional possibilities on a more local scale. Where dwindling herds had necessitated a change in the human diet, these new plants enabled it. The new cuisine, small animals, vegetables, and wild cereals,[6] were less palatable than horse and reindeer, but they could be reliably found in one place.[7]

These changes enabled people to get by, but the population continued to rise, and this increased competition for the new diet. Fortunately, solutions lay in the large and inventive human brain. Having enough intelligence to modify the natural environment, and more time to themselves than ever, our Holocene ancestors discovered that seeds and shoots, with proper handling, could become an important new source of nutrition. They also found ways to domesticate pigs, goats, and other animals. About twelve thousand years ago, people began to herd, farm, and fish, and it was around this time that people began to settle down.[8]

Settling down

The new ways of acquiring food required little or no roaming. So for the first time in history, it made sense for most humans to develop fixed areas of residence. It was also discovered that farming was ideally pursued on a cooperative basis, with the possibility of formal systems of storage and exchange, and this led to the establishment of farming communities. Population centers arose in Egypt and Mesopotamia as well as China, the Americas, Africa, and other places.[9]

In time, agriculture and sedentism made their own contribution to population growth. When migration stopped, infants no longer needed to be carried from one place to another, reducing the rate of infanticide. With grain in their diets, it also became possible to wean infants earlier. This shortened the period of lactation, enabling women to bear more infants in their reproductive lifetime. Adults were also living longer. These additions to the populace encouraged even more sedentism and farming.

The transition into sedentism increased the frequency and stealth of eavesdropping. For one thing, sedentary societies were larger, more complex and competitive, and more stressful than nomadic ones. In the event of a heated conflict—something that was increasing—it was harder for disputants to vote with their feet. Wars of words—which might once have remained at the verbal level—became violent. Moreover, many of these transitional groups were still attempting to live in a structurally flat, egalitarian way, and with no tribal leaders to resolve their conflicts, sedentist villages became more militant than nomadic ones had ever been.[10] These social changes encouraged the construction of more substantial dwellings. The walls were weight-bearing structures that supported the roof, protecting occupants from the sun and rain, but they would also serve as shields, protecting residents from the perceptual invasion of others.

Having social as well as climatic functions, the new domestic walls could only have been regarded as a wonderful new invention. But it was not so simple. There was still a hidden factor, one that is missing in most anthropological and archaeological accounts of human domestication.

Resistance

In some places, people *resisted the construction of dwellings*. In his book *House Form and Culture* anthropological architect Amos Rapoport described the housing that existed, or had existed, in a wide variety of places around the world. After surveying countless dwellings, he concluded that "house building *is not a natural act* and is not universal."[11] He based this on housing patterns in various places, from southeast Asia to South America and Australia, where tribes continued to live without houses.

One of the places was Tierra del Fuego, an archipelago off the southern tip of South America. The climate is almost arctic there, but the natives contented themselves with windbreaks made of seal or animal skins, sewn together and attached to a circular arrangement of poles that were stuck into the ground.[12] Very similar shields were built on the Pampas, in southern Buenos Aires Province, and by the aborigines in Tasmania. In many places where it was hot, however, people built elaborate houses. Witnessing these paradoxes, Rapoport concluded that from a climatic perspective, the housing pattern of primitive and peasant builders is "*irrational*."[13] A similar conclusion was reached by Edmund Carpenter after he inspected Eskimo igloos that feature large open areas rather than the series of small internal enclosures that one expects in frigid climates. The Eskimos, wrote Carpenter, display "a magnificent disregard for environmental determinism."[14]

In places where people did build houses, many *resisted the temptation to live in them*. Sedentism had encouraged the construction of houses in some places, but it was not enough, by itself, to produce homes. Why? By modern standards, it seems strange that a person would go to the effort to build a house, store all of his possessions in it, spend the bulk of his free time around it, develop a sense of territoriality about the place and the structure, but continue living on the outside.

What was being resisted was the cessation of social transparency. Peter Wilson pointed out that this meaning of privacy, a by-product of domestication, was "not natural to human existence."[15] Private living, in any form, drew curiosity and suspicion.

Evidence of this was acquired in the early 1970s, when anthropologists John Roberts and Thomas Gregor investigated the relationship between certain aspects of small-scale societies and the amount of privacy afforded members by their houses. Roberts and Gregor constructed a privacy index based on the permeability of dwellings to sight and sound, and the presence or absence of closable windows, doors, and internal partitions. It also took into account the number of persons that lived together under one roof, and the openness of the villages. By these criteria, *in fully three-quarters of the societies people were considered highly visible.*[16]

The residents of tiny villages were reluctant to live privately, but it is not as though their homes were luxurious. By modern standards they were cramped and dark, and in many parts of the world they were cold and damp. The early homes were also malodorous— domesticated animals slept inside with their owners—and none had tables, chairs, or beds. The new "insiders" slept on the ground. It was like camping "in."

One might suppose that the new homeowners set about rectifying these problems as soon as they got the hang of indoor living. But there are no indications that they did. In fact, homes—what they were, physically, and what they afforded, psychologically—remained unchanged, essentially, for *thousands of years*. In seventeenth-century

England most lower middle-class families still had little or no furniture—they continued to sit and sleep on the floor—and in semi-rural areas the situation was little better a hundred years later.[17]

With so little comfort in their homes, and so little interest in home improvement, one gathers that our ancestors were ambivalent about walled life. Were they, like porcupines, struggling to find the right place to draw the line between safety and warmth? Clues are available in two societies, the Sakalava and the Zinacantecos.

The Sakalava

Some sort of domestic ambivalence was evident among the Sakalava people of Madagascar—a perfect society for us to examine since, by coincidence, they were in transition when anthropologist Gillian Feeley-Harnik studied them in the 1970s. At that time, Sakalava villages numbered between twenty and eighty people.[18] The interesting thing is that the Sakalava still subsisted on hunting and gathering, but had also begun to farm.

The primary dwelling place of the Sakalava was a one- or two-room structure with a doorway and no windows. Feeley-Harnik described it as "a portable set of walls, lashed to a timber frame and covered with thatch."[19] The reference to "doorways" is because there was a taboo on the use of doors—or even, in most places, door curtains. The Sakalava also disapproved of fences around their houses. A house with curtains on the outside doors, or with fences and walls, was seen as a threat to normal sociality.

The Sakalava were generally to be found—and were supposed to be found—outside their houses, in the company of others. "To stay alone in the house," wrote Feeley-Harnik, "is considered a sure sign of evil intent."[20] Even the house itself could pose problems, Feeley-Harnik wrote, since it is meant to remove the occupants from the larger social order. "Secrecy and separation," she continued, "indicate at best a lack of generosity, a suspiciously anti-social striving for distinction."[21]

The language of the Sakalava also contained an interesting clue to some perceived linkage between domestication and personal dishonesty. The word *mody* meant "at home" or "heading home," but it also meant "to pretend to be what one is not."[22] Later we will have opportunities to return to this intriguing connection when we examine a new being that was nurtured behind domestic walls—the public self.

The Zinacantecos

A few years after Feeley-Harnik presented her study of the Sakalava, Leslie and John Haviland described the village of Nabenchauk, Mexico. Nabenchauk was one of a cluster of Indian villages known collectively as the township of Zinacantan, nestled in the high valleys of the mountains in southern Mexico.[23]

Like the Sakalava, the Zinacantecos had ambivalent feelings about privacy. "There are," wrote the Havilands, "strict canons of privacy which pertain to the physical intrusion by others into private space."[24] These canons were implemented, in part, with fences. All the houses were fenced in, and villagers were forbidden from passing through the fence without permission. They also had no windows—if the Zinacantecos wanted more light they had to open the door. This was not a matter of neglect; it was due to active resistance. A few years earlier the government had given them houses with large, unshuttered windows. When the Indians moved in, they papered the windows over or bricked them in.

But as private as the Zinacanteco homes were built to be, staying indoors, or even closing the house door, was considered "a gross and open admission of being up to no good." "Prying," wrote the Havilands, "with the eyes and ears tuned to all goings on around one, is an ordinary behaviour in Nabenchauk. One expects that all one's business that is carried on where it *could* be seen or overheard is, in fact, seen and overheard. Similarly, one presumes that ignoring any aspect of others that can be perceived is simply foolish."[25]

To escape this microscopic existence, the Zinacantecos avoided using the area outside the house—even seemed, in some sense, to be afraid of it. Entering truly public places like the waterhole, the village paths, and the shops was tantamount to going on stage, for "the eyes of any of fifty houses may be watching."[26] Even conversations were a contest in information control, with one party "trying his best to pump information from his interlocutor, while the interlocutor uses every ploy he can to evade and deflect the other's purpose."[27]

Clearly, the Zinacantecos and the Sakalava—two of many small-scale societies in which there was nervousness about personal information—were ambivalent about domestic walls. They were also hypocritical, for they were desperate to know what was going on behind the walls of others, but just as desperately fought to keep secret what was taking place behind their own. What was going on here? What were the *perceptual* consequences of living behind walls?

It helps to consider the structure of sedentary societies. Where tiny hunter-gatherer bands had been mostly egalitarian, the larger agriculture-based settlements were structured in a more hierarchical fashion.[28] In such arrangements there is heightened competition to acquire resources. Those who succeed may be seen as selfish, their success occurring at the expense of others. It is likely that many of the early settlers were tempted to conceal obvious signs of success, including any unusual possessions, like scrub-jays that bury their food more strategically when other jays can see them, or Samoans who eat in closed houses.

This hierarchical structure was functional. As hunter-gatherers, they had used their eyes and ears to prevent squabbles from arising, frequently by nipping things in the bud. When disputes were irresolvable, they occasionally appealed to outside sources for mediation, or as Richard Lee said, "voted with their feet."

But relocation was no longer an easy option when people began to see themselves as residential, with fixed addresses. In agricultural villages, leaders were needed to deal with the more complex issues arising within these larger communities, and to resolve the increased number of disputes.[29]

The new sedentists needed to keep an eye on each other, and they were acquiring new reasons for doing so.[30] Less and less did they look *horizontally* at individuals who had to be reminded of the need to share, collaborate, and play by a common set of rules. Increasingly, they looked *vertically* at people who had achieved higher status, or at competitors who were aspiring to greater power.

Over-exposure

Rapoport was not sure why people built houses in places where the weather was pleasant, but he speculated that the reasons may have had something to do with religion, status, or some "other" factor. In his book on *The Domestication of the Human Species*, New Zealand anthropologist Peter Wilson speculated on what this "other" factor might be. It was surveillance. When groups enlarged, he suggested, openly living people couldn't stand the perceptual pressure.

It is widely known that human settlements, like primate colonies, have an optimum size. When they exceed this size, as the Kung camps occasionally did, they tend to fragment. Some of the members take off, a serious threat if the evacuees are skilled hunters. But Wilson had a different idea. "One immediate cause of such fission," he suggested, is "the strain between neighbors unable to trust one another's privacy or countenance one another's surveillance . . . too diligent a scrutiny of the comings, goings, and doings of neighbors can quickly build to resentment, evasion, and the eruption of hostility."[31]

What Wilson's idea boils down to is this. Life in transparent or even semi-transparent societies can become hard to handle. If it does, continuous self-exposure is likely to be withdrawn when the objects of this attention—the other tribe members—cannot take it anymore. But it may not be enough to feign a preoccupation with objects, or face silently away from the group.

The most dramatic exercises in withdrawal occur in precisely those societies that display the greatest exposure. The Mehinacu pushed the two extremes about as far as they could. On a personal level, they had a number of ways to achieve social isolation. They could plunge into the forest that surrounded the village, taking any of the paths that led through the thick foliage to small clearings. There, the villagers were free to carry on clandestine activities with little fear of detection.

When they were at home, villagers were protected by a code of etiquette that forbade spontaneous invasion.[32] But the more signifi-cant feature of Mchinacu life was the existence of *formal seclusion rituals* when, by custom, villagers were expected to remove them-selves from village life for extended periods of time. These intervals coincided with important stages in human life history, including infancy and adolescence, as well as important life events, such as parenthood and the loss of a spouse. These absences, according to Gregor, gave the Mehinacu "relief from socially abrasive interaction and surveillance."[33]

Peter Wilson's claim related to surveillance as suffered by the "victim." But consider a reverse issue: the schedule of the observer. If small groups of openly living humans spent much of their time looking, then as their groups swelled, the lookers would eventually reach some outer limit on their capacity to observe, and something would have to give. The choice would not be an easy one, however. If individuals cut back on their looking time, in a short while the rising tide of humanity, and the machinations of an increasingly complex society, would leave them frightfully unaware, vulnerable, and out of step. If, on the other hand, they continued to crank up their vigilance in pace with population growth, they would soon be unable to do *anything else*.

Vigilance fatigue

With more and more strangers to keep track of, individuals living with free and easy sensory awareness were driven to distraction in the literal sense of the phrase. They needed a way of reducing the time they had been spending, like monkeys in small groups, looking up and over their shoulders every few seconds. Work—pounding grain, making clothes and tools, raising infants—was suffering, and the human nervous system can only take so much.

Before the construction of substantial walls, our historical ancestors had to keep an eye on the area around their encampment. Like the other primates, they needed to glance up every few seconds in order to survey the immediate area. Lacking perceptual shelter, they were susceptible to the scrutiny of others at any given time, and they had to continually look out for potentially meddlesome people. After their occupation of secure dwellings, the inhabitants were able, to an unprecedented degree, to relieve their senses of external responsibilities. But now there was no easy way to keep track of whatever was going on outside.

Withdrawal let all the watchers off the hook. "The value of isolation as an exposure-reducing device becomes much clearer," wrote Gregor, "when we examine not only the relief afforded the individual in isolation, but also *the reduction in surveillance and exposure that his seclusion provides for the rest of the tribe*."[34] When an over-exposed member of the tribe sought perceptual refuge, it freed everyone else from the possibility of being observed and engaged by him. But walls, being bidirectional, also offered perceptual benefits to the insiders. At the same time, walls made it harder for outsiders to eavesdrop in, and for insiders to eavesdrop out. Walls enabled residents to quit looking up and around every few seconds, the way wild humans, and wild animals, do. Privacy in its first installment—social privation—gave everyone a break.

An important benefit that was enjoyed by the newly privatized was solitude—the freedom to rest, reflect, and enjoy one's own company, the feeling of peace that comes, in the words of Janna Malamud Smith, from "not having to take account of others."[35]

Years later Sasha Weitman would write that privacy, though "ordinarily thought of as the right of a person against the encroachment of society," is "also *society's right*, that is to say, *the right of others* not to have to be subjected to the sights and sounds of desirable experiences that they have not been invited to share. In short, walls, fences, curtains, venetian blinds, doors, and generally, all the partitions erected to ensure privacy are just as necessary for those *outside* as they are for those *inside*."[36]

In many of the new dwellings, the walls were made of mud or wattle-and-daub, a network of sticks and twigs that were woven together and covered with mud or clay. Others were made of stone.[37] These new barriers could be trusted to block a great deal of visual information and suppress some of the sounds of speech. If eavesdroppers were to keep abreast of socially relevant events, they would have to look for structural faults, and to work harder than ever to extract what they needed.

Everyone was building. Walls were in. For the first time in their history, humans were on the road to domesticity. People, everywhere, were beginning to settle down. They pulled off this amazing feat in less than ten thousand years, from start to finish. But something was not quite right.

An unsettled feeling

Our ancestors were discovering interior life, finding ways to reside within it, but the transition to domesticity was proving difficult. When the first settlers began to build walls, they were, unbeknownst to them, experimenting with social technology. To be sure, when the weather turned nasty they could go inside and momentarily escape discomfort. This satisfied what our elementary school teachers described as the basic human need for shelter. But when they *stayed* inside, these more committed domesticates were interrupting a visual conversation that had been going on for the entirety of human history.

In this sense, the retreat to enclosures was an adventurous use of space, one that put into play whole new sets of physical and social meanings. When space is inhabited, as social geographers remind us, it is changed into a place that is bounded and controlled by rules. Going indoors was one thing, but living there could be inadvertently asocial. It was one thing to seek relief from bad weather. In the new cultures that were forming, this would only be seen as an exercise in good judgment. But what were outsiders to think when a person *remained inside* when it was not all that inclement or, indeed, was even pleasant? This lent itself to sinister interpretations, as when a neutral article of clothing like a balaclava is worn on a hot summer day or in the boarding area of an airline terminal.

When people occupied their homes *unnecessarily*, it aroused suspicions, as the Sakalava experience reveals. Privacy was inseparable from secrecy. What were people doing *in there*, people wondered, that they cannot do *out here*? The partially domesticated mind could imagine almost anything, from sexual misconduct to child abuse—things that in the past were discouraged by community gaze. But this was not purely a matter of morality and personal safety. Civil beings had always granted each other "space," had voluntarily extended necessary amounts of psychological freedom. When groups were small these concessions, along with the occasional furlough, were enough for people to keep things on an even keel. But walls were not a civil accommodation, granted by others.

As it turned out, the personal cost was surprisingly low for most of the visually deprived, at least in the short term, for the newly sequestered had an ability that the other primates lacked: they could talk, and privacy was extending the utility of this uniquely human talent. Speech enabled perceptual bystanders to pool their individual observations and piece together a complete story for each of their associates.

Like physical distance, walls gave neighbors new reasons to talk *about* each other, while providing new reasons to talk *with* each other. Walls thus altered the relationship between visual and linguistic communication—the only one our species had ever experienced—while changing the nature of human discourse and the street value of personal facts. They also promoted the feelings of conspiracy and closeness that accompany the sharing of secrets.

Clearly, everyone was seeking a blend of public and private activity, a balance between independence and autonomy on the one hand, and reciprocal sharing and assistance on the other. There was, by reference to Leyhausen's parable, a "chill factor" that drove our ancestors from solitude to socialization, and a "quill factor" that prevented others from getting too close. What they sought was a "quill-to-chill ratio" that worked best for them. For all their concerns with things that were happening on the outside, they were discovering some precious new resources on the inside—ones that we, their distant progeny, would be willing to fight for.

CHAPTER FIVE

Privacy, Intimacy, and The Selves

Most people are afraid *not* of being what they seem to be, but of seeming to be what they are ...

Arthur Gardner, criminologist

WHEN people went behind walls, eavesdropping was needed to reestablish sensory contact. But it did far more than that, for the person *encountered* on the other side of walls was not the same person that had *disappeared* behind them. In his place was a different soul, one more revealed and vulnerable. When eavesdroppers breached the outer skin, they were rewarded with perceptual riches that exceeded, and in the future would embellish, their wildest dreams.

Whether the first homebuilders knew it or not, walls were a form of social technology; and when it came to definitional issues, walls behaved much like other technologies. The telephone was created with one function in mind—Alexander Graham Bell would have been happy if receptionists had simply used it to announce visitors—but took on other uses as time passed. Even if walls were originally thought of as barriers against the outside world, they also kept domestic activities safely on the inside. In this sense, structural privacy could be seen as "a technical by-product of domestication," wrote Peter Wilson. It was a resource that one could not reasonably consider *"natural* to human existence."[1]

From the beginning of domestic life to the present, this *unnatural* condition of privacy has been responsible for a steady stream of social conflict. We saw evidence of this in the tensions of the Sakalava people of Madagascar and the Zinacantecos of Mexico, but these were not isolated cases. In the 1960s, Oxford anthropologist J. K. Campbell studied the Sarakatsani sheepherders of Greece. He found them "insatiably curious about the details of domestic life and relations in other families." But the Sarakatsani hut was considered "inviolable." "No stranger may invade it without an invitation," wrote Campbell. "It is a sin, and a source of the greatest shame, if a man is caught with his ear to the wall of his neighbour's house or hut."[2]

For a peasant hut to be *inviolable*, and for listening at its walls to be a *sin* and a source of *shame*, raises serious questions. What was happening on the outside of the Sarakatsani hut that was so awful that the occupants fought *to keep it out*? Or was something happening on the inside that was so special that steps had to be taken *to keep it in*? Were the insiders seeking the architectural and social equivalent of Gore-Tex, content for things to flow one way as long as they didn't flow the other?

When openly living individuals had wanted to be alone, they went elsewhere. But wherever they went, they were still outside. Any aloneness they achieved was tenuous. Someone could burst on to the scene at any moment, possibly without warning, especially if the solitude-seekers had been seen leaving camp earlier. If they wished to take advantage of their isolation; if they planned to do something that could not be done in the company of others; they would have to remain perpetually wary. Under the circumstances, it would be hard to do much with, or to discover much about, solitary experience—leaving it to qualify, at most, as privacy in the third degree.

Privacy in the second degree

It is obvious that the construction of walls offered something new. But what was it? How can we know, a good ten thousand years later, what the first domestic privacy was like? Was it mainly a form of social shelter; an interruption in what had been, until then, a species-long conversation?

It is safe to assume, I think, that the first walls were valued mainly as shields against the eyes and ears of outsiders. Even in modernity, this sensory connotation has been captured in definitions of privacy. Law professor Anita Allen recommended that privacy be treated as "a condition of *inaccessibility of the person*, his or her mental states, or information about the person to the senses. To say that a person possesses or enjoys privacy is to say that, in some respect and to some extent, the person . . . is beyond the range of others' five senses."[3]

That the first domestic privacy was experienced as a form of *privation* is implied by the Latin *privatus* and *privare*. "To live an entirely private life," wrote Hannah Arendt in *The Human Condition*, "means above all to be deprived of things essential to a truly human life: to be deprived of the reality that comes from being seen and heard by others, to be deprived of an 'objective' relationship with them that comes from being related to and separated from them through the intermediary of a common world of things, to be deprived of the possibility of achieving something more permanent than life itself. The privation of privacy," Arendt concluded, "lies in the absence of others."[4]

On one level, this seems uncontroversial. When people went behind walls, they lost touch with human activity that was occurring on the outside. But which "others" did Arendt have in mind? Perhaps she meant the neighbors, or the other residents of the village or town. Walls offered unprecedented separation from *these* outsiders, to be sure, and this raised moral and civic concerns.

There was, as we discussed earlier, a special and rapidly growing class of individuals whose senses the insiders wished to be safely beyond: strangers. Between 1500 and 1700 the continent of Europe was populating and urbanizing. In London, for example, the population at the end of that period was *nine times larger* than it was at the beginning. Such a period of rapid social change, wrote Paul Delany, "arouses anxieties about status even among people whose own position is fairly secure."[5] The stranger, according to a second historian, Robert Muchembled, was "always dangerous, always feared." He was "that *other* who resembled him like a brother but whom he trembled to encounter."[6]

Behind walls, people were safely beyond the senses of strangers—and everyone else. They would no longer have to ask questions such as Who is out there? Who is approaching me, and with what intentions? Who is looking at me, and in what way? Are they merely glancing in my direction or are they watching me? Where are my friends, and what are they doing? Released from the usual concerns, the new privacy—call it privacy in the second degree—would naturally have increased opportunities for several things that are now highly valued.

One is relating. In the past, the individuals to whom one was physically closest and might know the most about were neighbors. Now one had his own reception room. One could have guests. They would enter and leave at the behest of the owner, and it would be these invitees who enjoyed privileged access to the dweller in his most congenial and unguarded moments. When everyone lived on the outside, how close people stood or sat, whether they touched or whispered, and how they looked at each other gave observers the information they wanted and, in egalitarian societies, needed. Structural privacy changed this. Behind walls, interactions with familiar others would be carried out without fear of public scrutiny and the possibility of negative reaction.

In a population boom our ancestors had found a way to achieve a measure of peace and security. Without the stares and glares of their fellow villagers, insiders would find new opportunities to reflect, and perhaps the first good chance to ask where they wanted the world—the outside world—to stop and their own interior lives to begin. But when these refugees stepped over the threshold, they got more than a goal of flight, something that nested animals had. They got a "zone of immunity," something that French historian Georges Duby defined as "a place to which we may fall back or retreat, a place where we may set aside arms and armor needed in the public place, relax, take our ease, and lie about unshielded by the ostentatious carapace worn for protection in the outside world."[7] This zone is what newspaper columnist Pete Hamill called a *Great Good Place*, a place "where the harshness of the real world is fended off."[8]

But the new dwellings were not actually as secure as one might suppose—or the inhabitants might have liked. In thirteenth-century France, Raymonde Testanière told the village bishop in Montaillou that her neighbors had built a *solier*—a room above the kitchen— and that she suspected some heretics of sleeping there. One day, hearing some men speaking quietly in the *solier*, Raymonde decided to investigate. She went out into the courtyard and climbed a dungheap from the top of which it was possible to see into the *solier* through a chink in the wall. From there, Raymonde said, she was able to observe the heretics "speaking to each other in low voices."[9]

The heretics were acting *secretively, while in private*. Not a bad idea considering the chink, the dung, and the very real threat of being burned at the stake. But this raises a question: how do privacy and secrecy differ, and what do they share? Secrecy guards against others "coming too near, learning too much, observing too closely," wrote philosopher and ethicist Sissela Bok. "It serves as an additional shield in case the protection of privacy should fail or be broken down."[10] Long before our ancestors adopted a structural approach to privacy, they had regularly sought secrecy, and it was adaptive that they did. Secrecy enabled them to exercise their Machiavellian human minds—to discuss ways to deal with their rivals and forge alliances with their allies—things that the heretics may have been doing.

Walls immunized residents from outside forces, and homes provided them with a new ecological niche, a crucible that would shape the development of minds, personalities, selves, and personal relationships. "The skins of houses are shallow things that people are willing to change," wrote folklorist Henry Glassie, "but people are most conservative about the spaces they must utilize, and in which they must exist. Build the walls of anything, deck them out with anything, but do not change the arrangement of the rooms or their proportions. In those volumes—bounded by surfaces from which a person's senses rebound to him—his psyche develops; disrupt *them*," Glassie warned, "and you can disrupt *him*."[11]

How did the insiders regard their new niches? Surely they would have felt less transparent than the openly living generations that had preceded them: they were surrounded by opaque barriers. Just as surely, they would have assumed that privacy gave them much of what secrecy had offered in the past, and that few things that happened "behind closed doors" could be used against them. Freed from these concerns, it became possible to contemplate life as it was being lived on the outside. Secure in their homes, they could reflect on their work and the people in their lives without fear of review. They could ponder and ruminate without interruption. Through more thoughtful comparisons of themselves with others, they would discover their own unique properties. Walls also gave inhabitants more intimate contact with *other* humans—their cohabitants—than had been experienced by any previous generation in history. For none of the new dwellings was subdivided by *internal* walls. Everyone lived in the same small room.

Individuals and families would be the first beneficiaries of this new life. Before homes were built and occupied, looking around had always produced a range of person-images—from family and friends to acquaintances, rivals, and strangers. By contrast, people in homes could focus on the members of their families; they could relate to each other without interruption or the scrutiny of others. Still, the family, according to Robert Muchembled, was mainly "a shield against pressing danger . . . a unit of production and of consumption" that "made it possible for its members to pool their efforts in order to survive." It was not, he said, "the principal focus of affective relations."[12]

With uncertainties about survival, it would take time for insiders to develop a rich or complete concept of privacy and the things that privacy facilitates—including intimacy and conditions that foster deeper forms of intimacy. But nascent, second-degree forms of these things were literally on the doorstep.

Intimacy in the second degree

Among those who lived openly, privacy was fleeting and fragile. Walls offered a richer and more intense form of privacy, taking over the role that had previously been played by reticence. With a new outer skin in place, people were free to spend more time in their minds, as implied by the Latin *intimus*, or "inmost." But they were also free, at the same time, to express that experience in a way that was less calculated and more honest than in the past.

We know the first houses were small, and remained so for thousands of years. Would this, by itself, have fostered intimacy? When we refer to an "intimate" space we usually have in mind an area that is small and bounded. Is there a relationship between small spaces and "inmost" experiences? Do people who share a niche *necessarily* enjoy intimate feelings?

Not if you look at the historical uses of beds. For thousands of years there were no "bed-rooms." As recently as the late eighteenth and early nineteenth centuries, people were still sleeping all over the house.[13] But it was not just that there were no special *rooms* for beds and the things that people did in them. On a tour of France in

1878, Robert Louis Stevenson found himself in a sleeping room that was furnished with two beds. "I had one," he wrote in his journal, "and I will own I was a little abashed to find a young man and his wife and child in the act of mounting into the other."[14]

There were quite commonly too few beds for each person to have one to himself. In some peasant homes, entire families slept together, partly in response to serious heating problems.[15] In late eighteenth-century Paris the lower classes still "did not consider sleeping to be an entirely private activity," according to historian Rafaella Sarti. "Overall," she wrote, beds "were a more crowded and promiscuous affair than they are today, and much of the population did not have one entirely to themselves."[16] Among rural peasants in Europe, sleeping alone was still fairly rare a century later.

Family members were not the only ones who slept two or more to a bed. In a court case in Boston, Ann James testified that Mrs. McCarthy, a fellow lodger, had shared a bed with a gentleman named William Stone. This meaning of "sleeping together" is one that we readily understand, but Miss James testified that while Mr. Stone "lay with Mrs. McCarthy in one Bead," she herself "lay with her two Sisters Abigail and Elizabeth Floyd in another bed in the Same Roome." In another case of bed sharing, a lodger testified—in clear contrast with most adultery trial testimony— that an unmarried couple had *not* had the sexual intercourse of which they were accused. The woman knew, she said, because she *had slept with the couple*. The bed itself was "very Narrow," she testified, and it was therefore most unlikely "if not wholly impossible that they should be guilty of that Crime without her knowledge and She observed no such thing."[17]

These cases merely indicate that intimate spaces were not necessarily interpreted as opportunities for intimacy in the *emotional* or *sexual* sense. In fact, joint occupation of intimate space *guarantees* little in the way of emotional intimacy. Psychologist Howard Gadlin has written that even where physical intimacy was imposed by living conditions, "the closest of relationships was formal to a degree we would find not only awkward but contradictory to intimacy." In male–female relationships, this formality reflected, among other things, "a fundamentalist Christian distrust of uncontrolled earthly pleasures and human passion."[18]

Still, domestic privacy encouraged the removal of protective armor and this, more than physical intimacy, encouraged honest personal expression. Free of external constraints, occupants were able to open themselves up to new ways of thinking and behaving. The old checks and balances were no longer needed. Broader and deeper forms of emotional access were literally on the doorstep.

Of course, dropping one's guard makes one vulnerable. In privacy, lovers "lay bare their innermost feeling to each other," wrote philosopher and legal scholar Edward Bloustein; "they are lewd and foolish with each other, they stand naked before each other... nothing is held back." But, he went on, all this is shared on the premise that it will be shared with no one else.[19]

The "no one else" clause is of course what makes eavesdropping so irresistible, for the practitioners of this interceptive art are not party to any understandings between the intimate principals, nor are they bound by the agreements of others regarding the disposition of any verbal or visual images that may surreptitiously come their way. Free of any such constraints, eavesdroppers are all too glad to share in the intimate experiences of others, and to share the images, as best they can represent them, with others.

As new resources, second-degree privacy and intimacy posed challenging adjustment problems. In their ecological niches, humans would have to learn how to manage intimate experience, the role of reciprocity, the need for trust, and the necessity of keeping close to the vest any acts that had occurred in private, and especially those that took place in secret.

Any progress that has been made on these issues has been decidedly nonlinear. Many behaviors that were previously shielded are now displayed openly, and historically public behaviors are now kept under wraps. Anita Allen has pointed out that battles over what should or should not be private, and what should or should not be public, are intensifying, with almost daily shifts in the boundaries.[20]

From the first days of domestication, there were undoubtedly significant differences between the sexes on both sides of the walls. On the inside, allowing oneself to be witnessed in a moment of "weakness" is something that might well have been avoided by anyone—especially men—who cherished their independence and autonomy. In social milieux, to regard with indifference the intimacies of others might have seemed unnatural to individuals—especially women—with a need for deeper levels of connectivity in their own lives.[21]

In time, insiders would have to learn how to deal with privacy and other new resources. One lesson is that the images flowing from intimate activity can be less important than their mode of transmission. If donated, personal material may or may not be interesting. But if it is stolen, the same material—insofar as it can be considered the same—can be exciting, breathtaking, even erotic. In the late nineteenth century, English sexologist Havelock Ellis related a story about a Parisian model who had posed in the nude at the Ecole des Beaux Arts, surrounded by aspiring young artists. Suddenly, without notice, the model screamed in terror and ran off to retrieve her clothes. What sent her running was the sight of a workman on the roof, peering through a skylight.

The reason for the model's reaction reveals an interesting generalization about intimacy. When she went to the Ecole that day, the model had expected to be seen in the nude by strangers. But she had only agreed to her body being viewed by artists. She had not consented to any other process—certainly not theft—nor to any other consumers.[22] The same goes for the woman in a scenario offered by legal scholar Richard Parker. He asked his readers to consider the case of a man who, after leaving the bed of his lover, peers back through the window in order to see her once more in the nude. The man knows that his lover's body has not changed, and that she has not had time to put on her clothes. His look threatens the woman's control, but control over what? "It is," Parker said, "a loss of control over who, at that moment, can see her body."[23]

Trust

There is one case in which information may be worth a great deal more if donated in confidence than if learned by accident. It concerns an important component of intimacy—trust. People tend to divulge little in the way of personal information unless, as Bloustein suggested, they feel that it cannot circle back to hurt them. How do they develop the confidence that it will not? One way is to reveal one's feelings, and to expose one's inner self, in degrees, waiting for reciprocal acts before continuing, or before any increases in intensity. Mutual disclosure of this kind tends to build trust while, paradoxically, making trust less necessary, since each party possesses the tools to hurt the other.

In their privacy, the insiders were more intimately exposed than ever before—to their fellow insiders. In the case of family members, this was undoubtedly beneficial, but not everyone living under one roof was genetically related. One morning in 1680, Nicholas Manning of Salem, Massachusetts got in a great deal of trouble. It began when three female servants walked through his bedroom en route to the kitchen. They did this not because they were rude or poorly trained or disoriented. It was because they had no other way to get there.

Manning's house had no corridors, but this was hardly a distinguishing feature. When houses were first built, the residents were clearly concerned about privacy, but the privacy they sought was against outsiders. As a consequence, little thought was given to the idea of building *interior walls* that would separate parents from children, or one lodger from another. The corridor, Raffaella Sarti has written, was a fairly late invention.[24]

When the servants walked through Mr. Manning's bedroom, he was in bed with his sister. This, by itself, was less strange than it might seem, given the tendency of family members to bed down together. But, peeking back through the bedroom door, which remained slightly ajar, the servants noted that the rapidly disembedding Mannings were stark naked. This came out in a public trial—a trial for incest.

People spent many centuries living in homes before they got the idea or motivation to create private areas *within* homes. In the sixteenth century, according to Philippe Ariès, the wealthier home-owners in France began to build private halls, stairways, and vesti-bules.[25] Privacy was becoming a value, but there was something else. People were beginning to think of themselves as individuals, as people who differed in important ways from all others, and they sought spaces that would reinforce these differences.[26]

Individualism

Earlier, I suggested that privacy fostered truer, deeper, and more emotional forms of intimacy, not just whatever feelings may have been produced by shared occupancy. It also contributed to an aspect of personality that would favor intimacy. This was individu-alism, a sense of one's own personal boundaries and distance from all others. Having one's own space would help to mold this separate being, enabling individuals to make a unique, and uniquely intim-ate, contribution to personal relationships.

In the nineteenth century, according to historian Alain Corbin, there was a strong and steady current toward individualism in France, and it expressed itself in a number of ways. For one thing, there was an increase in the acquisition and use of Christian names. People also began to acquire domestic mirrors and have their portraits taken by commercial photographers, and they continued a practice, dating from the late sixteenth century, of keeping a diary in which they wrote about *themselves*, including their own thoughts and feelings.[27] In the same period, Alexis de Tocqueville wrote that individualism was becoming a goal in America.[28]

People were obviously spending more time thinking about themselves. "For the individual," wrote Howard Gadlin, a "separation of the public from the private leads to a great expansion of personal consciousness," and in ways that would have enriched interpersonal methods of relating. "Individualism and intimacy," Gadlin concluded, "are the Siamese twins of modernization."[29]

The private self

Individualism implies a division of one's self from the selves of others, but privacy also caused deeper fissures *within* each person. The external life of an individual, the life led in the company of others, is his public self. "Behind every man's external life, which he leads in company, there is another which he leads alone, and which he carries with him apart," wrote English sage Walter Bagehot over a century and a half ago. "We see but one aspect of our neighbour, as we see but one side of the moon; in either case there is also a dark half which is unknown to us. We all come down to dinner, but each has a room to himself."[30]

In the past, people had lived *out*—in nearly continuous sensory contact with practically everyone they knew. When they achieved an interior space, they had two spaces—one that was public, the other private. Each day, individuals ventured into public space and returned home. In time, it was predictable that these broadly different niches would cultivate two broadly different ways of being.

The insider believes that he—unlike those on the outside of his walls—is the only one who knows what he is doing, or habitually does; that no one will see or judge him for any acts that he carries out. He believes that if he does something—anything—he alone will know about it. It is possible to locate antecedents of conscience and morality here, things that were virtually impossible when the public eye prevented individuals from making their own choices. At home, there were opportunities to live a more self-guided life.

On the inside, a person lived within a few feet of everything he owned. These things would bring back memories of the day he made or found them, or received them as gifts, and this would affect the way the insider thought about himself. Private possessions may be counted among our secrets, since they silently remind us of what makes us different from everyone else. They not only "concern nobody else," wrote Georges Duby, they "may not be divulged or shown because they are so at odds with those appearances that honor demands be kept up in public."[31] Studies of domestic burglary suggest that the inviolate nature of personal possessions contributes to the inviolacy of their owner's unique "personality."

Having their own niche, filled with their own things; having no possibility of scrutiny by, or negative reactions from, external others, the insiders would come to discover—or to invent—a deeper and more contemplative form of themselves, and this form would almost certainly contrast, in specific details, with their public persona. They would have a private self. Today, according to psychologist Roy Baumeister, people think of this self as "the way the person *really* is." This created an object of endless fascination and, for those who would eavesdrop, new temptations. For behind the walls there were new and more intimately behaving beings.[32]

A new public self

But this was not just a matter of titillation and prurience. Everyone needs to know how others behave in their *public* lives. It must be possible to see how they dress and what they do.

This process, which psychologists call "social comparison," enables individuals to conform to or deviate from the behavioral patterns established by others. People began to feed this appetite. Private quarters became dressing rooms where residents prepared themselves to "go out" and be seen. Now it was possible to *manage* one's images, thus to define oneself in the eyes of others, and there are indications that people began to devote more attention to grooming and bathing.

In eighteenth-century France, wrote director and dramatist Nikolai Evreinov, "the competition between life in actuality and life on the stage had reached the point where no one could say which was more theatrical. In both there were pompous, over-studied phrases, a mannered refinement of bows, smiles and gestures; in both, showy costumes...powder, rouge, beauty spots, monocles, and very little of one's 'natural' face."

People have been intrigued, and perhaps somewhat dismayed, by the deception that is involved in the maintenance of two selves. In *Le Diable Boiteux*, Asmodeus exposes Cleofas to a "superannuated coquette" who, in readying herself for bed, removes her hair, eyebrows, and teeth; and an "amorous dotard of sixty," who, having finished making love, has removed his eye, false whiskers, and wig, "and waits for his man to take off his wooden arm and leg to go to bed." In an adjacent house, Cleofas is excited by the sight of a beautiful and charming young woman. Asmodeus responds that she is, in actuality, "a machine, in the adjusting of which all the art of the ablest mechanics has been exhausted: her breasts and her hips are artificial, and not long since she dropped her rump at church, in the midst of the sermon."[33]

Everyone now had questions: what was the *real*, behind-the-scenes version of each public self like? How did others act when no one could see them? Answers would be needed if these others were to be understood, but there was an additional issue. How could one design a private life for himself without knowing how others lived? How was social comparison to be carried out in this new sphere that lacked visible models? If one's own private self—increasingly a major constituent of one's complete self—was to conform to contemporary models of private behavior, one would have to inspect this. But the inspection would have to be carried out from the outside.

Eavesdropping's new allure

There is always a great deal of interest, wrote Victor Hugo, in "a wall behind which something is happening." Fortunately for those on the outside, the walls were cracked. When insiders began to speak and act without the usual inhibitions, new levels of intimacy became available not just to them, but to those who peered and listened through the available orifices. There is something of the cinema here, the exposé or peepshow, the real reality TV show. The things that people did in privacy were valuable new resources, and they held a special allure for everyone, especially those on the outside.

In the so-called "back stage" areas of their lives, individuals were free to display personal vulnerabilities on a scale that would have shocked their transparent ancestors. When eavesdroppers went on their usual rounds, attempting to restore the basal knowledge required for orderly village life, they stumbled upon these new behaviors. These were far more intimate than anything they had witnessed in the past, and this added functions, and dimensions, to eavesdropping. It had become a flexible, multi-purpose strategy, serving the old civic and moral purposes while offering a new psychological experience. To be sure, that experience was compelling, but it also offered benefits to those who were merely seeking greater understandings of their own interior selves.

Court records make one thing very clear: for much of the time when there were walls and people could peek through cracks, they did peek. But the personal motivation to eavesdrop and the recognized value of doing so were fundamentally different. One day in early seventeenth-century Virginia, John Tully and Susanna Kennett heard the sound of snoring from an adjacent residence. Their curiosity aroused, John and Susanna got up on a hogshead of tobacco and peeped in. They saw Richard Jones in bed with Mary West. Enthralled, they watched as Mary placed her hand in the "codpiece" of the snoring Richard and "shaked him by the member," an act that caused Susanna to laugh so uncontrollably that she and her friend had to leave. Moments later, Susanna and John heard the adulterers enter a different room and start "Laughing and playing upon the bedd." Susanna displaced a loose board, allowing her to see Mary again, this time "with her cloathes up to her eares" and Richard "betwixt her leggs."[34]

Like Margaret Browne, Susanna amused herself for an afternoon. When the next-door lovers moved, Susanna moved too, keeping them in sight at all times. That she did so is due, in the first instance, to an appetite for intimate experience in the lives of others. But her foraging produced images that had a larger value. Because the lovers wrongly thought they were (mis)behaving in private, and Susanna was naturally drawn to the experience, she was able to augment her own personal power and exert a measure of social control.

CHAPTER SIX

Personal Power and Social Control

Monsieur Chatard . . . suspected that his wife was having an affair with a young man named Péchet, and so he, along with a friend and two gendarmes, hid in a closet in his house until the two "had attained the highest degree of criminality possible in such a situation."

Patricia Mainardi

WHAT might a moral man do if nobody could know that he was doing it? One classical philosopher's answer is to be found in *The Republic*, where Plato recites a fable about Gyges. A poor shepherd, Gyges experiences a sudden change in fortune when an earthquake opens up a giant fissure in the earth. In his curiosity, Gyges enters the chasm and discovers a naked corpse wearing a gold ring, which he removes and puts on his own finger. Later, while together with his fellow shepherds, Gyges discovers that if he turns the ring one way, he becomes completely invisible—the other shepherds speak about him as though he were gone—and if he turns the ring another way, he is instantly visible again. Deciding to put his new power to advantage, Gyges gets himself appointed a court messenger and in rapid succession seduces the queen, kills the king, and takes over the kingdom.

At the end of the fable, Plato asks his readers to imagine that there were *two* magic rings, one worn by a "just" man, the other by a man who is "unjust." Without fear of detection, Plato reasoned, the two men would be indistinguishable. For no man "would keep his hands off what was not his own when he could safely take what he liked . . . or go into houses and lie with any one at his pleasure." Indeed, it was Plato's opinion that a man who *could* get away with wrong doing but failed to take advantage of the opportunity would be widely ridiculed as "a most wretched idiot."

Plato's fable reinforces some basic facts about human life. First, visibility—exposure of oneself to the eyes of others—tends to suppress misbehavior. Second, when in their homes and able to do whatever they want without fear of detection, people do things that they wouldn't do in public, and these things may not be good, either for them or for anyone else. Acutely conscious of these facts, our medieval ancestors began to fear that villages would become disorderly, even dangerous, without optical control. In response, pressures mounted on ordinary citizens to monitor events occurring on the inside of walls. This required them to learn what they could from the outside.

To outsiders, lack of visibility was a regulatory concern, but insiders had a libertarian worry—that their own walls might be breeched by individuals who expected first to extract intimate experience, then to exchange the sensory information (whether auditory or visual) for personal power and social control. In fact, for several thousand years, this trio—experience, power, and control—moved through villages, homes, and lives as a unitary mass.

Around the time that Plato was writing about Gyges, vision was playing a conspicuous role in the public and private lives of real

Athenians. Ancient Athens was said to be a "face-to-face society" owing to a population that was small, residences that were concentrated, and a Mediterranean climate that enabled people to spend a great deal of time outside. It was also considered a "shame culture" inasmuch as there was a great deal of concern about "what people would say."

That Athens had no police was scarcely noticed. Most of the tasks that are normally carried out by law enforcement personnel—investigation, arrest, and prosecution—were carried out by the citizens themselves.[1] But the people never had to *seize* the powers of government. "Athenians were *encouraged* to pry and to probe," wrote Virginia Hunter in her book *Policing Athens*, "to know what their neighbors were doing and had done."[2]

But it didn't stop there. When a case came to court, the litigant, ideally an adult male Athenian citizen, also *presented it to the jury.*[3] Where did this ideal citizen get his evidence?

In Athens, there was an intimate connection between vision and knowledge, and the most trusted testimony was informed by the visual sense. Eye witnesses were needed. Frequently they were slaves, who were found everywhere in the Athenian home, from the courtyard and kitchen to the workrooms and *gynaikonitis*, an upstairs area that was reserved for women. Some slaves slept in the same room as their master and mistress. "As they moved about their tasks by day and into the night," wrote Hunter, "they shared in their masters' secrets. The latter were, in a sense, under constant surveillance."[4]

But their masters tended to forget about all this. Many acted, according to Elizabeth Fox-Genovese, "as if their house servants had neither eyes nor ears—as if they hardly existed at all." As a consequence, slaves were privy to practically everything that their masters said, did, and heard. If something was proved or disproved in a court of law, it was frequently because a slave had sworn to it.

Ordinary invisibility

Even ordinary people try to avoid exposure and control. Fortunately, it has long been possible, without magic rings, to achieve invisibility merely by going behind walls. In the privacy of their own homes there was nothing for the *occupants* to fear, of course. They knew that *their behavior* posed no threat to themselves or to anyone else. Moreover, domestic freedom enabled them to act as they wished. But *other people* were also free from observation, and this was worrying. Who knew what their standards were? How could *they* be allowed to act on impulse?

Other eyes would have helped. A few years ago the controlling effect of eyes—*artificial eyes*—was documented by Melissa Bateson and her colleagues at the University of Newcastle. They placed an image of a pair of eyes in a university coffee room to see what effect this would have, if any, on contributions to an "honesty box" used to collect money for coffee, tea, and milk. It was found that people put nearly three times as much money in the collection box when the eyes were displayed than they did when a control image was used. This suggests that even a black-on-white line drawing of eyes may naturally deter dishonest behavior.[5]

The power of optical monitoring is implied by the ways we talk about vision. We "have" someone in our sights, according to linguistic custom; we "hold" them in our gaze, possibly even "capture" them, much as a wildlife photographer might be said to have "captured" a moose drinking from a pond. The visual sense is implicitly linked to domination and control. In some places, especially the Near East, the Mediterranean, and South Asia, it is believed that certain people can harm others merely by looking at them or their property. In this "evil eye" belief, there is a conviction that "power emanates from the eye," according to anthropologist Clarence Maloney, and thus can strike whatever the eyes fix upon, whether a person or a valuable object.[6]

Visibility is also associated with threat. In hierarchical societies little attention is devoted to individuals on lower rungs of the social ladder. If these lower-downs want to get ahead, they can put their invisibility to good use by acquiring information about the vulnerabilities of their political superiors, and then reveal it—or threaten to do so. If they do, the higher-ups may take a great fall, and many have reasons to fear that they will. Economic and other forms of success require a good reputation, something that takes years of hard work to build. But a good reputation can be whispered away in seconds, especially if there is something to whisper about.

In this chapter we will see in vivid detail why it has been necessary to keep intimate experience behind closed doors. There is, as discussed, an evolved appetite for precisely this kind of experience. Like the main character in *Rear Window*, the eavesdropper may sample this experience purely because it is enjoyable to do so. But once he has absorbed intimate images and ascertained their meaning, the eavesdropper may discover *uses* for this material, uses that may be injurious to one of the intimate parties but beneficial to himself. One benefit is personal dominance over one of the intimate parties. Another benefit, related to the first, is social control.

Blackmail

Fear of personal injury is the reason why there are laws against blackmail. Blackmail is an ancient crime. As of 1567 it was already illegal, according to Scottish law, to *pay* blackmail. The first English statute, in 1601, made it a crime to pay or receive money, or any other form of compensation, in order to protect one's person or property.[7] Laws against blackmail are also quirky, since they criminalize the conjunction of two things that are individually legal: talking about what one knows to be true and asking a person for money.[8] But our own interest in blackmail is due to a different conjunction. Like eavesdropping, blackmail sits squarely on the intersection of intimate experience, personal power, and social control.

Harriette Wilson, an early nineteenth-century courtesan, used the first of these to achieve the second, and in doing so exerted an influence on the third. Harriette managed to sleep with several hundred of the most important members of the British aristocracy, and blackmailed almost all of them, including the Prince of Wales, the Lord Chancellor, and four future prime ministers. She had the perfect vehicle—her diary, published in 1825. Any of Harriette's numerous lovers who failed to pay an exclusion fee found himself in *Memoirs*, and if that wasn't enough, the book also sold well, especially to the lower and middle classes.[9]

In the early 1990s blackmail was the subject of a detailed analysis by legal scholar Richard Posner. He examined 124 cases with a known motive that had occurred in the previous century. Of these, fifty-four involved a threat to divulge a criminal act that had not been previously prosecuted. In thirty-eight percent of the remaining cases, the act in question had been, by Posner's classification system, "disreputable, immoral, or otherwise censurable," a category that, in the mode of Harriette Wilson's clients, included fornication and adultery.[10]

Posner's statistics indicate that nearly half of the cases involved a threat to publicize a crime. It is obvious why these were so numerous. No one wants to be exposed or punished if he can avoid it, and these people had been avoiding it. Why, then, did they spill their own beans by contacting the police? One possibility is that the blackmailer's demand exceeded the severity of the punishment likely to be meted out by the courts. Another possibility, however, is that payment would not have ended the matter. By demanding "just a little more" the blackmailer could continue his relationship with the victim, to no certain conclusion. Law professor George Fletcher pointed out that the most objectionable feature of blackmail is often not financial at all, but relational. The question, according to Fletcher, "is whether the transaction with the suspected blackmailer generates a relationship of dominance and subordination."[11]

I assume that this feeling of subordination was unusually difficult to tolerate in cases where the victim was a person of some wealth, breeding, or stature, as he would have been, and the blackmailer was a sleazy character, as most certainly were.

Since cases of *successful* blackmail do not usually come to light, one wonders how many maids, repairmen, and others have happened upon, or positioned themselves to see, a single act that under threat of revelation set them up for life. When one considers the loss of social standing, marriage, employment, self-respect, and everything else that stands to fall when a wrongful act is publicized, the blackmailer might actually be offering his victim *a good deal.*

There might not have been much risk of the blackmailer's being exposed, either, especially if he or she operated anonymously. When literacy reached the masses, poison pen letters enabled the middling classes to intimidate the rich and famous without fear of reprisal; handwriting experts did not appear for a century or more. Letters with a personal target were numerous, if the novels of Balzac are to be believed, though such letters were likely to be crumpled up and burned.

Public letters were another matter. British historian E. P. Thompson looked at the anonymous threatening letters that were sent to the *London Gazette* over a seventy-year period beginning in 1750. There were nearly three hundred letters in all. The majority were aimed at gentry and nobility, others at manufacturers or merchants. Clearly, some of these writers were attempting to get revenge, but others were seeking to redress various wrongs.[12]

In a pre-existing relationship, the mere *possibility of disclosure* can alter the distribution of power between the present "possessor" of personal images and the individual from which they came. This process resembles blackmail, but is far less dark. I call it "graymail." In a typical case of graymail, a person surprises a friend or associate in an embarrassing act, or is found to have learned something that he is not supposed to know. Nothing directly is said about this, and the parties being proper, nothing would be said. But the knowledge is now in the mind of another, and this produces an automatic tilt in the balance of power, and possibly the offer of some sort of favor or unearned privilege—also unlikely to be discussed. Everyone has experienced graymail.

One of the oddest things about eavesdropping is the degree to which it is able to straddle both ends of the moral continuum. Historically, a violation of personal privacy was prosecuted if it produced community tensions, and was welcomed—even rewarded—if it served religious, political, or judicial interests. But there was a fine line, if there was any line at all, between looking *for* immoral or illegal behavior and looking *at* it.

Holy watchfulness

The church wanted people to look for it. As we saw in Chapter I, the Congregational church had said in 1582 that each parishioner could better serve the church "by overseeing and trying out wickedness. Also by private or open rebuke, of private or open offenders."[13] They called this "Holy Watchfulness."[14]

In all societies, everyone—neighbors, tradesmen, servants, and lodgers—kept an eye out for sexual misdeeds, and they could claim that they were doing the Lord's business. In eighteenth-century Paris, a neighborhood was "a place where everyone was watched by everyone else," according to Arlette Farge.[15] Two hundred years later, it still was. In Gévaudan an unusually informative social pageant took place in the village churches. "People noted," wrote Michelle Perrot, "who attended mass, how frequently they received communion . . . and how long young girls remained in the confessional. Tongues began to wag," she wrote, "when faces swelled and waists thickened only to thin down suddenly."[16] Villagers also kept their eyes on another class of women—widows—counting how many months from their husband's death they continued to wear their veil. "Woe unto the widow who, one torrid summer day, lifts her veil in order to breathe," wrote Françoise Mauriac in 1926.

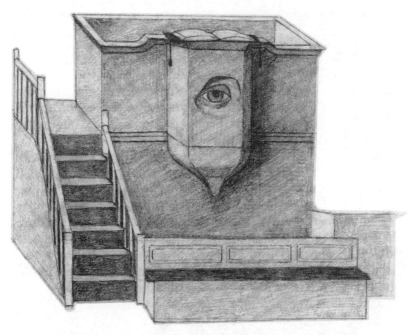

Exhibit 12 Holy watchfulness

"Those who see her will say: 'There's another one who quickly got over her grief.' "[17] Several decades later the writer Annie Ernaux would write of her village in Normandy that "the neighbours inspected the washing on the line to see how white and worn it was, and they knew exactly whose night bucket had been emptied. Although the houses were separated by hedges and embankments, nothing escaped people's attention, not even at what time the men rolled in from the café, or which woman's sanitary towels were conspicuous by their absence."[18]

These testaments are interesting, but they do not tell us who eavesdropped upon whom, what they saw and heard, how and why they did it, and what was done with the experience afterwards. Under the circumstances, it is hard to discover the deeper things that we need to know. What can we learn about the eavesdropping that occurred in previous centuries, when many people could not read and write?

Exhibit 13 *L'épouse
indiscrète* (The indiscreet
wife), engraved by
Delaunay, 1771

Adultery

A great deal, thanks to the English, who were good at keeping track
of such matters. For one thing, adultery was illegal, and the enforcement of adultery laws was being taken very seriously. But in
English courts, accusations had to be supported by eye-witness
testimony. This caused individuals—usually at least two—to
come forth and describe what they knew and how they knew it.
Court reporters took down their statements in detail, even, in some
cases, preserving subtle differences in the witnesses' manner of
speaking.

Frequently these citizens were investigating suspected misbehaviors. In other cases, they were already eavesdropping when they

Exhibit 14 *L'amour à l'épreuve* (Love on trial), Pierre-Antoine Baudouin, c. 1777

saw or heard something newsworthy or scandalous, which then snaked its way through the village until it reached the ears of the authorities. Given the sequence of events, one might be excused for thinking that a bout of domestic surveillance had somehow *caused* the criminal behaviors that, in fact, simply got caught in the eavesdropper's net.

In July of 1666 Mary Babb was at home in York, England with Mr. Babb. But she was too much at home with him, given that he was her brother-in-law Richard, not her husband Ottiwell. These in-laws were clearly enjoying their moments of presumptive privacy, without realizing that a neighbor, Elizabeth Tullett, stood silently watching them through a hole in an outer wall. Her eavesdropping was possible, Elizabeth would later tell a court, because there was *"only a wall* betwixt them.''[19]

In fact, Elizabeth had been watching Mary and Richard for some time, and had seen the two cavorting around York with less than a wall "betwixt" her and them. On at least one occasion she had seen the lovers "together both on foot and horseback," Elizabeth said, and had watched them "commit incontinency together and to carry themselves too lightly and wantonly" in a way that was "not becoming civil persons."

The domestic incidence of the Babbs' misbehaviors started in May. Elizabeth saw Mary Babb pass by the hole in the wall, "having her clothes and smock pulled up to her breast none being in the house with her but . . . Richard Babb." Two months passed before the next incident. Then, in early July, Elizabeth saw the couple alone together in Ottiwell Babb's house, where "they two did frequently kiss each other with as much eagerness and familiarity as man and wife could do." Richard "put his hand under her clothes in an uncivil manner which," Elizabeth added, his sister-in-law "allowed without resistance."

That was on a Tuesday. On Wednesday, Elizabeth—at her post once again—saw Richard Babb return to his brother's house several times. On one visit, Elizabeth saw him take his brother's wife "on his knee and there kiss each other very freely and too familiarly and he put his hand under her clothes in very uncivil manner several times." If that scene was not sufficient reward for her patience, the next one was, for Elizabeth then saw the siblings-in-law "in the very act of adultery or incest in a very beastly manner she the said Mary holding up her hinder parts and having her clothes and smock pulled up above her loins and he thrusting . . . "

I'll spare you the rest, except to say how the scene ended. Two other eye witnesses, Mr. and Mrs. Richard Vintin, happened along and joined Elizabeth at the hole in the wall. Enraged by what they saw, the Vintins *charged into the house*, hoping to catch the incestuous adulterers in the act. Unfortunately for them, the lovers quickly composed themselves. By the time the door swung open, Mary was sitting on the hearth with her brother-in-law on a bench beside her. "Lord Bless me," Mary was heard to exclaim at the sudden entry, to which Mrs. Vintin replied, "The Lord hath nothing to do with thee." Supportively, her husband Richard accused Babb of "playing nought" with his brother's wife. The truth out, the adulterous couple slunk away.

Elizabeth was a next-door neighbor. Did she eavesdrop because she wished to preserve the moral purity of her neighborhood? She was married. Was she attempting to shore up the institution of marriage? Elizabeth was a young woman, in her mid-twenties. Was she interested in the intimate experience she witnessed purely for its own sake; or was she bored in her marriage and seeking a voyeuristic frisson from observing her next-door neighbor's tryst?

It is possible, of course, that until the Vintons appeared on the scene, Elizabeth had *no plans* to convey her perceptual images to the authorities. After all, she had seen Mary and Richard doing "wanton" things in the past and had said nothing; had seen them behaving "incontinently" and had kept it to herself. On the day in question, Elizabeth may have been treating the Babbs-in-laws' misbehaviors as a personal matter, as she had in the past, and may have been observing their trysts out of a strictly personal motivation. But she was interrupted by a married couple, and it may have been their moral outrage that drew Elizabeth into the suit while supplying her with a "cover" or respectable motive for her spying.

If Elizabeth's eavesdropping underscores the difficulty of separating intimate experience from personal power and social control, so does the case of Raymonde Testanière. Earlier we saw that in her thirteenth-century village in the Pyrenees, Raymonde overheard the whispered conversation of three heretics when she climbed up a dung heap and listened through a chink in an outer wall. One of the heretics was Guillaume Authié. When Raymonde told the bishop what she had seen and heard, she may well have been rewarded for helping to preserve control. But in a small village, business is rarely impersonal, and this incident was no exception. Raymonde's employer and provider, Bernard Belot, was an arch enemy of Authié. Belot had fathered at least two of Raymonde's children, but had thus far refused to marry her. Raymonde may well have reasoned that if she testified against Authié, this would please Belot, redounding to the benefit of her children and her as well as the village and church.

Gender and sex

I mentioned earlier that when I told friends I was writing a book about eavesdropping, men and women responded differently. The men either nodded in silence or asked a few technical questions, impassively. Women, by contrast, grinned, blushed, averted their gaze, or raised their hands in mock surrender, as if to say "You got me." Do the historical records confirm these casual impressions that proneness to eavesdropping is gendered? Do women show up in the court records more often than men?

Yes, they do. In Montaillou, Jacques Fournier's Inquisition Register details numerous instances of knothole and keyhole eavesdropping by women, along with a few more adventurous cases, and it is clear that the women of the village predominated where these kinds of *in situ* perceptual invasions were concerned. The men "were inquisitive enough," wrote historian Emanuel Le Roy Ladurie, who translated and interpreted the Register, "but their curiosity was nothing beside that of the women."[20]

Women predominate in the sort of normally concealed eavesdropping that one can do from one's home, like Margaret Browne, or while moving about one's village, like Elizabeth Tullett, but what explains this trend? One possibility—a boring one, but we cannot dismiss it out of hand—is that women eavesdropped more often than men simply because they were in a position to do it more often. Sexual misconduct, at least the type that produced arrests in early modern England, usually took place in a house. If it was detected at all, it would likely be picked up by someone who was also at home at the time, and that would usually be a woman. "The wife," wrote social sage William Gouge in 1622, "causeth many things to be espied, and so redressed, which otherwise might never have beene found out; for two eies see more than one, especially when one of those is more at hand, and in presence, as the wife is in the house."[21]

Of course, we still might wonder why the women provided such rich descriptions of the trysts they spied on, as when Margaret Browne testified to the color of Mrs. Underhill's underwear, and recalled, apparently verbatim, the words with which the adulterous wife teased and taunted Michael Fludd. There is little in the women's eye-witness testimony to indicate that they hesitated to describe before an open, male-dominated court sexual encounters that, even by today's standards, would be called "lurid."

But we still have a question on the table: did women more frequently eavesdrop about adultery and other things that took place in houses simply because they were home more often? Possibly, but there is a more basic issue here, one relating to the domestic ecology of England (and elsewhere): why were the women at home more than men? It is here, I think, that we are likely to locate a more compelling reason for the gender difference.

Of course we know that for various reasons, some cultural, others biological, women were more concerned than men with the stability of long-term relationships and the quality of child care, which fell mainly to them. Women have long worried about threats to these things, and have therefore been seen as moral gatekeepers, concerned—more than men—with a range of family matters, including marital fidelity. Except for daily trips to the market or village well, they were also expected to spend most of their time indoors, in private space, not in the public areas that were dominated by men.[22] For women to police the activities that went on in homes was, for the most part, to act in their own interest.

What are we to make, then, of Le Roy Ladurie's reference to the "curiosity" of the women of Montaillou? Was this a trivialization of women's more serious concerns? Surely he was not alone in using this term. In 1616 an English writer, Alexander Roberts, characterized women's sense of curiosity as overdeveloped. "They harbour in their breast," he said, "a curious and inquisitive desire to know such things as be not fitting and convenient." Nicole Castan characterized three centuries of French women, beginning in 1500, as "curious by nature." "Women of the lower orders shamelessly admitted it." One confessed that "she was 'obliged' to follow the movements of a passerby, another that she could not help overhearing a conversation or lying in wait for a neighbor."[23]

Exhibit 15 Wartime poster warning Englishmen about female eavesdropping

"Curiosity," of course, is what biologists would call the "proximate mechanism"—the appetite for intimate experience that was
installed in evolution, ensuring that the longer-term informational
needs of modern humans would be satisfied. This appetite provides
individuals with the experience or information that it will usually
benefit them to have, but which they might not actually acquire if
looking were only an obligation. Since "curiosity" makes it unnecessary to ingest needed information *dutifully,* it is not trivial at all
to identify this psychological mechanism as a relevant component—indeed, it is the critical outer perimeter—of our social intake
systems.

Intimate capital

Nicole Castan also commented that whatever French women noticed in centuries past "was *repeated.*"[24] In Castan's remark we find
another reason to suppose that *women would have* eavesdropped
more than men. Going back a good five hundred years, there is
evidence suggesting that women *gossiped* more than men. Recently
I summarized this evidence, which cuts across a number of different
cultures as well as time periods.[25]

If women gossiped more, then they surely would have done
more of what gossip entails, that is, would have spent more time
disclosing and discussing intimate behaviors. Since eavesdropping is
the necessary "intake" mechanism, it makes sense that women
would want to devote some amount of time to that activity.

It also means that they might *need* to gossip, at least if they wish
to achieve communion with other women. In the early 1970s,
sociologist Elizabeth Bott studied twenty families residing in London. She found that the women in these families comprised a
network—a gossip network. Mutual aid was extended to those
who belonged to this network, and the cost of membership was
willingness to gossip and be gossiped about. The rules were simple,
she wrote, "no gossip, no companionship."[26] But in such an

Exhibit 16 *"Slanderous gossip: it's beneath you."* Poster in a Berlin factory in the 1950s warning German women not to gossip

arrangement the reservoir of material that is used to negotiate companionship has to be refilled, from time to time, by fresh new acts of eavesdropping—a gossip network is an *exchange* network. One cannot expect to get the inside story on everyone else if one never takes a turn in supplying such stories. The message is clear: the indirect cost of mutual aid, at least in Bott's sample, was *mutual eavesdropping*. What the women comprised was an *eavesdropping-and-gossip network*.

Now discussions of gossip, as Oxford psychologist Nicholas Emler has pointed out, almost invariably call attention to degenerate and even malicious aspects of this activity. Gossip, Emler wrote, is regarded as "a rather vacuous, aimless activity which contributes little or nothing of value to human affairs, beyond a degree of entertainment and diversion for superficial and idle minds." But it gets worse, for gossip is also seen as "a form of mischief, a threat to the good order of society."[27]

Clearly, gossip has a terrible reputation. But let us put aside for a moment the cultural voices that tell us these things and think about the facts. Gossip occurs when two or more people talk about the people they know. The material that is exchanged is usually intimate, relating to personal events and relationships, because people are interested primarily in those things.

Now let us return to eavesdropping. It, too, is preferentially devoted to intimate activity. If eavesdropping involves the theft of intimate experience, the question naturally arises as to what the thief does with this stolen material. Is it merely to be held in one's mind and savored, or is it to be shared with others? I suggest that wherever the person eavesdropped upon does something that can be portrayed to another, the eavesdropper is likely to convert the residual images into a form of capital. This "intimate capital" is likely to be worth something to others, and may be given or traded away, and if it is, we will say that the eavesdropper has "gossiped." If this happens, and it often does, the time devoted to eavesdropping may be compensated many times over.

If eavesdropping involves the theft of intimate experience, and gossip its distribution, there may be an analogy between these practices and the theft and sale of merchandise. In her book, *The Fence*, Marilyn Walsh described the social arrangement and flow of goods in a typical larcenous network. The middlemen, or "fences," are familiar with the thieves and prospective buyers.[28] Knowing what sort of material is valued, the fence passes this information along to his suppliers, the thieves, and the thieves then set about to steal it. I use this analogy because eavesdroppers are more inclined to take in private activity that will interest their friends, who grasp it like a baton and relay it through their gossip networks.

English eaves

From an evidentiary perspective, adultery trials were gold mines, with the richest possible lodes. But there was another way that eavesdropping crept into court records. Recognizing that behaviors set in motion by eavesdropping could stir up tiny villages, societies enacted laws to address the problem at source. Toward the end of the 1300s, and possibly a century earlier, English villagers were already being arrested for going out at night and listening to their neighbor's secrets. In due course, the practice took on an architectural focus—the "eaves-drop," the area outside houses where rain fell from the eaves to the ground. Standing there, "eaves-droppers" were able "to listen secretly to private conversation."[29]

Note that the eavesdropping that was outlawed was *not* the opportunistic kind that could be done in the comfort of one's own home, or the area around it, or in the doctor's office, a restaurant, or the hairdresser's. It was *not* the embedded or social type of eavesdropping that people do while simply going about their business, in the place where that business is normally done. The kind of eavesdropping outlawed by the English was *not* the kind that is enhanced when a person like André Breton's detective adopts an "ultra-receptive posture," or puts himself "in a state of grace with chance." No, the kind of eavesdropping that was criminalized was more adventurous, for it involved leaving one's home, going to another person's residence, and taking up a position near an outer wall, well outside of any normal social or business context. It involved trespassing. The punishment was a small fine.

This invasive sort of secret listening clearly bothered the English, who were growing accustomed to the benefits of domestic life and private conversation. But listening was not the only, or even the most worrisome, thing. When the English passed a law against eavesdropping they forbade the *conjunction of two behaviors* (as in blackmail legislation), making it a crime to "listen under walls or windows, or the eaves of a house to hearken after discourse, *and thereupon to frame slanderous and mischievous tales.*"[30]

Unlike the separate elements of blackmail, either of these acts—eavesdropping or telling tales—would have been worrying, but this imprecision in the English law is discouraging, because it means we cannot easily tell from the arrest records who eavesdropped, told tales, or both. Fortunately, the language in some of the charges adds clarity. For example, Marjorie McIntosh turned up numerous cases where a person was charged with being "a listener at windows and *sower of discord* between the neighbors," or "a common listener at night who *followed the said listening by increasing disputes.*"[31]

Arrests for the criminalized kind of eavesdropping left behind a trail of court records going back over six hundred years. A careful look at this history—much of it nicely documented by McIntosh in her book, *Controlling Misbehavior in England*—provides insight into our ancestors' desire to observe and control the personal lives of others. McIntosh's tabulation of selected court records indicates that for a good two hundred years, beginning in the 1370s, the medieval cocktail of eavesdropping and tale-telling comprised about eight percent of all social crimes.[32]

In *court-welcomed* eavesdropping, the testimony of a single eye witness goes on for pages and pages. By contrast, court records in a typical case of *court-punished* eavesdropping are limited to the charge itself. For example, in 1425 John Rexheth was charged with "listening at night and snooping into the secrets of his neighbors." Nearly a century later, Agnes Nevell was accused of disturbing Edward Node by lying under his windows, where she "hears all things being said there by the said Edward." In 1578 a court ruled that Philipp Bennett was "an Evesdropper, and doth harbour under the wall and windows of his neighbours."[33]

Reasons for the concern about listening are obvious. In the privacy of their own homes, people were clearly entitled to engage in intimate conversation. But there was real fear that if the eavesdroppers *talked*—a temptation if wrong doing was suspected—they would undoubtedly do so in conspiratorial tones, or a state of rage, and this would stir up trouble. Neighborhoods, it was feared, would become unruly; villages would become difficult to govern.

I have yet to encounter in court records one piece of overheard conversation that caused problems when passed on. Possibly it was what they saw and heard the people do, not what they said; or perhaps the courts were attempting to keep the content of invasively eavesdropped conversations from going further.

In the U.S. there were fewer eavesdropping arrests but similar concerns with eavesdropping as a *cause* of social disturbances. In June of 1886, Louisa Ehrline was indicted for eavesdropping in Pennsylvania. The indictment alleged that she "was and is a common eavesdropper," and that she "did listen about the houses and under the window and eaves of the houses of the citizens then and there dwelling, *hearing tattle and repeating the same in the hearing of other persons*, to the common nuisance of the citizens of this commonwealth, and against the peace and dignity of the commonwealth of Pennsylvania."[34]

Flimsy architecture

If a person were to stand under the eaves of a modern house, it is unlikely that it would be possible to hear much "tattle." The walls are too thick and insulated, and even where a bit of speech might leak out, it would quickly be lost in the ambient noise. But in early modern England the acoustics for eavesdropping were ideal. There was virtually no background noise—no cars or trucks, or noisy lawn equipment—and the walls were just as eavesdroppers like them: holey, cracked, and paper thin.

In her book, McIntosh wrote that in Romford, a market town, the sound of a domestic argument "was magnified because the narrowness of the streets and walls meant that words spoken in or near one house might be heard in *several other buildings*." In a trial held in 1613, Elizabeth Hunter, a thirty-three-year-old widow, testified to the effect "that while in her own house one morning she heard two women 'chiding.'" Elizabeth went to her door and saw Grace Patient and Alice Flud, across-the-street neighbors, standing in their own doorways, arguing. Two other witnesses, young women who worked in a shop behind Alice's house, testified that "Grace called Alice 'a hedge whore,'" according to McIntosh's trial notes, "and that Elizabeth had joined in the argument, while still standing in her doorway across the street."

In abutting houses it was not even necessary to go outside in order to hear what the neighbors were saying. In 1586 Margery Oliver took her laundry to Agnes Bolter's house in Romford so that they could talk while Margery dried and smoothed the clothes. "As the two women chatted, Elizabeth Stevens, *a neighbour in an adjacent house*, overheard them and thought they were discussing her. She began to shout slanderous comments *through the wall* about Margery, calling her 'a bridewell bird' and 'an errant whore,' saying that she had an illegitimate child." These insults, according to McIntosh, were heard by the two women folding the laundry on the other side of the wall, but also by Agnes's husband Thomas, who was working somewhere else in the house.[35]

In certain respects, a stroll through early seventeenth-century Romford, and countless other villages throughout England, Europe, and colonial America, was like the "stroll through the worlds of animals and men" envisaged by Jacob von Uexküll. For inside the ecological "bubble" of these places there was the resonance of countless human sounds and signals, many given off incidentally by people as they went about their daily business, allowing each to note the whereabouts and actions of every other villager. Whether the actors liked it or not, every disturbance of the sensory landscape was treated as a "To whom it may concern" message, and everyone was concerned.

Normally, this sort of awareness is helpful in small, interdependent communities, but something else was happening in Romford. The villagers were blaming each other, shaming each other, fighting to expose wrong doing, and doing everything *ferociously*. What was going on?

One thing that was going on was staggering population growth, a change that, as mentioned earlier, would cause the social landscape to restructure on a massive scale. In the year 800, the population of the British Isles was estimated at 1.2 million, a figure that had grown to 2.8 million by 1200, with a further increase to 5.3 million in 1340.[36] These changes produced strangers where there had been friends and acquaintances, with heightened competition for the same small slices of economic action. The result was an "extraordinary amount of back-biting, malicious slander, marital discord and unfaithfulness, and petty spying," according to historian Lawrence Stone.[37] "If new arrivals and established families were being forced into closer contact in housing, commerce, and employment," wrote McIntosh, "harmonious social interactions may well have been jeopardized. The spread of quarreling, malicious gossip, and invasions of privacy could thus all have been magnified as population levels increased."[38]

Trouble was bubbling up but there was no one at higher levels who could bat it back down. Lacking an effective constabulary, the citizens of tiny villages would just have to operate their own system. Not that there was something missing here. In this and practically everything else, the order of the day, literally, was *posse comitatus*—"the power of the county." This is all there had ever been. Like the Athenian citizens, the English had their own system of social control.

Gender redux

In the arrests for eavesdropping there is generally less detail than in the court-welcomed cases, as indicated, but the records reveal one thing about the people who were caught under the walls and windows of their neighbors' houses—their gender. McIntosh has reported that for a good two hundred years, beginning in the 1370s, about eighty percent of the courts having some incidence of eaves-dropping (blended with nightwalking) happened to *hear male cases only.*

McIntosh never actually counted the number of males and females who were arrested for eavesdropping—it was the number of courts reporting only one sex or the other, or both—but there must have been a fairly strong difference between the sexes for her to get such lopsided figures; and this presents us with a conundrum. If court-welcomed eavesdropping was so frequently carried out by women, why were so many men charged with this other kind of criminalized eavesdropping? In fact, we will see that it makes more sense to ask why *so few women were arrested.*

To appreciate my reasons for reframing the question, it helps to consider a fact about the architectural type of eavesdropping. It was best done under the cover of darkness. If one was detected *before* eavesdropping, the desired perceptual experience was unlikely to be forthcoming. If discovered *afterwards,* the eavesdropper might be reported. If eavesdroppers wished to avoid detection, and to escape prosecution, they needed to take up their under-eaves position at night. With poorly lighted streets, there was a chance that they might be able to do it *and* get away with it.

Earlier we asked who was home more often. Now it is necessary to ask: who was out at night? Out at night was not where respectable women would normally be found. Being seen out after dark posed a physical danger to women, and to their reputa-tion, since they would have been suspected as "nightwalkers," or prostitutes. "Merely to walk unescorted at night rendered a woman liable to be *arrested for immorality,*" wrote Sara Mendelson and Patricia Crawford. "Women, but not men, were subject to a *de facto* curfew after dark."[39]

The English had a term for out-at-night individuals. They were *noctivagators*. The root *vagor* implies that nightwalkers were seen as vagrants, or wanderers, with no discernible reason for being out.[40] There are indications that the "nightwalker" label was already in use in fourteenth-century London. Three centuries later, a justice ruled that it was lawful to arrest nightwalkers in order to *prevent* "malfeasance."[41] Since women were not supposed to venture outside at night, it was unlikely that many would be seen or arrested for eavesdropping. McIntosh reported that between 1370 and 1600 over ninety percent of the arrests for nightwalking were men.

But were men out just because they could get away with it, or were they out for a reason that was functionally related to the eavesdropping for which they were arrested? Were they investigating? Were they patrolling what they took to be the boundaries on their own territory? Were they attempting to keep their neighborhoods safe? Or were they on their way home from a public house, and in a mood for mischief?

As we saw earlier, there appears to be a rather general relationship between sex and territoriality in the animal kingdom. Males generally spend more time looking for predators, and defending their territory, than do females. Among primates, adult males are distantly vigilant, focused on the periphery of the troop's occupied territory. Adult females are proximally vigilant—more concerned than males with the welfare of infants. I assume that medieval English men were out, in part, because they were attempting to keep the outsides of homes—their neighborhoods and villages—safe by protecting the outer perimeters, trusting women to police internal spaces. But in the next chapter we will see that the prevalence of male eavesdroppers was not merely due to a difference in opportunity, for men have long been the ambient strollers who kept an eye on strangers, even where women had equal opportunities to participate.

Eavesdropping led to "slanderous and mischievous tales" which, as we have seen, could get one arrested for a violation of the "eaves-dropping" law. But what is concealed here is the fact that irresponsible accusations, or any charge that was rendered loudly, stridently, and persistently could—*by itself*—get one arrested for a different crime, one that was *implicitly female*. It was called "scolding."

Scolding

The legal statutes of 1675 defined a scold as "a troublesome and angry *woman*, who by her brawling and wrangling amongst her Neighbours, doth break the publick Peace, and beget, cherish and increase publick Discord."[42]

Laws against disturbing the peace make sense, but a crime that could only be committed by women? How can there be a law that is only breakable by females? Even modern rape laws are gender-neutral. But the reference to angry women is no illusion. In his *Commentaries on English Law,* Sir William Blackstone wrote of the charge of scolding, "our law confines it to the feminine gender."[43] Why associate brawling and wrangling with women; and who were their victims?

Scolding was a public attack on a person, to her face. It was usually set in motion by information, which may or may not have been reliable. If even marginally credible, scolding—like every case of garden-variety slander—could seriously injure the reputation and social standing of the victim. If such an invaluable asset could be damaged by scolding, one would hardly need to cast around for reasons to prosecute it.

Scolding consumed a lot of court time. In the two centuries beginning in 1370, scolding was the most frequent of all social offences, and in the typical case, the accuser and the accused were both females. In the vast majority of scolding cases—over nine in ten—the charge was of a sexual nature, according to Laura Gowing's analyses. In over a third of these sexual allegations, it was lexically specific: "Whore!"[44]

In the winter of 1610 Alice Rochester hurled a whore charge at Jane Lilham in earshot of their neighbors in London. "Thow art a whore and an arrant whore and a common carted whore," Mrs. Rochester said. But Mrs. Rochester had something more specific on her mind that day—something more personal. For she continued, more pointedly, *"thow art my husbandes whore."* Her husband, Mrs. Rochester screamed at Miss Lilham, "hath kept thee a great while at Newcastle and all that he got he spent on thee . . . *thow has lyne oftener with him then he hath done with me."* Miss Lilham took Alice to court six months later, and five female ear witnesses testified on her behalf.

Mrs. Rochester believed, and may have known, that she was losing her husband—his affections, his earnings—to a competitor. The female scold's accusation of whoring undoubtedly attracted some measure of sympathy, at least from other married women, who potentially faced the same threats.

In some cases of whore-scolding, there was no reference to a husband. In 1495 court records in Waddesdon, England indicate that one Elizabeth Godday was charged with calling Katherine Walrond a whore, and the charge did implicate a man. But it was not Elizabeth's husband, if indeed she was married, but Sir Thomas Couley, a chaplain, whom Katherine was allegedly tempting into a sexual relationship. The case against Elizabeth was dismissed when she "purged herself" of the accusation. Ten years later, Agnes Horton and Joan Whitescale were summoned to court, evidently to receive judicial rebuke, for calling each other a "strong whore." In 1521 Agnes Yve, of Chesham, set a new record of sorts. She hurled the whore charge so often that *forty women* turned up in court to support the accusation of scolding.[45]

Anxieties about reputation and discord were sufficient to prosecute charges of scolding, but that doesn't mean they were the sole basis for such charges. Indeed, these were just the tip of a more complex and interesting iceberg. In the submerged portion were two freedoms. One was single women's freedom to poach a married man. The other was married men's freedom to engage in extra-marital sex.

The first and most direct targets of scolding were other women—single women. These women were loudly and publicly "addressed," and this was overheard by others at home, usually women. This was no accident. The scold intended that her insults and charges become public knowledge.

The typical scold was a married woman. Her marital status was well worth preserving; early modern women had few ways to make money. Their financial security was no stronger than their marriage. Anything that might loosen marital bonds was a serious threat. The single greatest threat was mate-poaching—competition for the husband's affections—and in the typical case of whore-scolding a wife was claiming that another woman had engaged in sex with her husband, or at least attempted to alienate his affections. This is understandable: adultery was considered sinful and this undoubtedly emboldened the wife to make a fairly public sort of charge. But an implication of the charge was that her husband may have already become involved in an extra-marital relationship. If so, she was indirectly charging him with something.

This could not have gone down well with many of the men in the community, and it is a major reason why female vocal abuse would have been prosecuted by the male-dominated courts with unusual vigor. When forty women file into court to support a friend, men have grounds for fearing the power of scolding. An isolated case of whore-accusation is one thing, but a recurrent pattern might well have consolidated to form a clear and present threat to men's biological imperatives, at least those that involved extra-marital sex.

There is a timeless quality to these events, as timeless as human biology. I have taken a look at the titles of the Jerry Springer show for the three television seasons beginning in 1991, 1996, and 1997. Of over five hundred titles, 39 percent were explicitly about some aspect of sex. In the final year, 63 percent involved this subject. Breaking down "sex" into ten categories, I found that the single most popular topic on Jerry Springer was *sexual competition and adultery.* Overall, one out of three programs involved this topic.[46]

The sexual competition category is interesting. By itself, this category comprised 20 percent of all the sex-linked programs. Some of the titles include:

"Back Off... He's Mine"   "Hands Off My Lover!"
"He Doesn't Want You! He's Mine"   "Get Away From My Man!"
"Stop Stalking My Man"   "Stay Away From My Lover"
"Leave My Man Alone"   "You Won't Steal My Lover"
"You Can't Have My Man"   "Get Your Own Man"

Medieval men obviously did not want the whole community to know the content of their private life. They also did not want women to have the authority to decide what others would know about them. This second concern would have been less acutely felt if women had been ignorant or privileged, but they were neither. Married women had a great deal of knowledge about the details of their husbands' private lives, which could be divulged at any time. This placed men perpetually on notice. If they did anything that crossed the lines drawn by their spouses, there could be ruinous consequences.

Men value their autonomy. Intimacy is a form of vulnerability and is therefore a threat to autonomy. If married women talked to their friends about intimate experiences, including their own, men would surely panic at the thought that aspects of their own sexuality were being broadly, if quietly, cast around their tiny villages. In a short essay published in 1678, a scold was caricatured as "a Devil of the feminine gender; a serpent, perpetually hissing, and spitting of venom; a composition of ill-nature and clamour... animated gunpowder, a walking Mount Etna that is always belching forth flames of sulphur... a real purgatory."[47] Nearly four hundred years ago, Alexander Roberts wrote that women "are of a slippery tongue, and full of words." If they know of "wicked practises," Roberts wrote, they "are not able to hold them, but communicate the same with their husbands, children, consorts, and inward acquaintance; who not considerately weighing what the issue and end thereof may be, entertaine the same, and so the poyson is dispersed."[48] In 1653 *A Brief Anatomie of Women* identified the tongue, "that stirring and active member," as one of women's greatest liabilities.[49] It's hard to see how men could have expressed more emphatically their fear of vocal women, a fear that the men themselves would have failed to comprehend.

The literature of the seventeenth century contains clues to gender concerns in the hurtful use of speech. One of the poems published in that period—Robert Harper's *Anatomy of a Woman's Tongue*, published in 1638—likened women's speech to a poison:

> A Man that had a nimble-tongue Wife,
> With whom he liv'd a discontented Life;
> For she would tell all that her Husband did,
> And from her Gossips nothing should be hid.
> If he sometimes did come Home drunk to Bed,
> About the Town it should be published.
> If he a Woman do salute or kiss,
> Why all the Town forsooth must know of this.

Harper concluded his poem with a plea:

> O Women, be not cruel unto Men,
> Ill Words are worse than Poison now and then.

The worry embedded in Harper's poem was explicit—that women would broadcast harmful information about men's intimate activities. An indication of how far men were prepared to go to limit the communicative power of women is in the punishments they invented, and meted out, for exercising too much of it.[50]

Punishment

The penalty for eavesdropping was often a small fine, but there were two rather severe punishments for scolding—the behavior that was frequently set up by eavesdropping. The legally prescribed one was dunking, which dated back to the twelfth century. In dunking (or "ducking"), the guilty party was placed in a "scold-cart" or "ducking stool," sometimes called "cucking" stool from the semantic association with "cuckquean," the female equivalent of "cuckold." In essence, the stool was an armchair fastened to one end of a long pole. The pole was hinged to a pedestal that was dug into the ground, affixed to the side of a bridge, or mounted on a trolley. It worked like a seesaw. Men raised the opposing end of the pole, dunking the scold. One stool had such a long pole that the scold could receive her dunking "while the administrators of the Ducking stand on dry land," gushed one admiring (male) narrative from the time.

Dunking was not the most practical means of punishment for a speech-related crime. An Oxford don noted in 1686 that dunking, whatever its other virtues, "gives the tongue liberty, 'twixt every dipp."[51] But this may have been construed as an advantage, for it gave the "administrators" the opportunity to repeatedly dunk convicted scolds until all signs of hateful speech were extinguished. "If the confirmed termagant vented her angry clamour as soon as she recovered her breath after the plunge," wrote Leominster's local historian, F. Gainsford Blacklock, "the Ducking was repeated till exhaustion caused silence."[52]

A popular alternative to the stool, dating to about 1620, was the scold's bridle, a helmet-like structure made of thin iron bars and secured by a padlock. The offender's nose was held by an opening in the front, just above a long metal bit or "tongue depressor" that lay flat on the tongue. The bits ranged from 1½ inch to 3 inches in length. "If more than 2½ inches," wrote T. N. Brushfield, who examined a number of bridles in the mid-1800s, "the punishment would be much increased," for "it would not only arrest the action of the tongue, but also excite distressing symptoms of sickness, more especially if the wearer became at all unruly."[53] In some bridles, the bit terminated in a bulb that was covered with iron pins. In practice, these often punctured the victim's tongue.

As barbaric as the bridles were, some level of admiration was expressed both for the form and function of these "engines," at

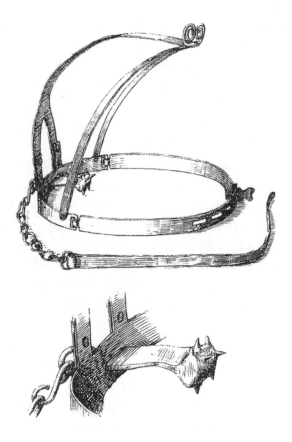

Exhibit 17 Scold's bridle

least by men. It was "a very ingenious contrivance," wrote one gentleman, James Lackington, in his late eighteenth-century memoirs. Lackington advised any would-be manufacturers, however, "to be cautious in offering them to public sale, and by no means to advertise them, especially if a married man, or having any views towards matrimony."[54]

A rare first-person account of bridling, dating back to 1656, survives. Earlier on the day in question, Dorothy Waugh, a Quaker, had spent some time in the town market of Carlisle, railing against sin. At some point a town official appeared and hauled her off to jail, where the mayor subjected Miss Waugh to interrogation. Dissatisfied with her responses, he decided it was time to take the town bridle off the shelf. There were "three barrs of Iron to come over my face," Miss Waugh later wrote, "and a peece of it was put in my mouth, which was so unreasonable big a thing for that place as cannot be well related, which was locked to my head, and so I stood their time with my hands bound behind me with the stone weight of Iron upon my head, and the bitt in my mouth to keep me from speaking."[55] Miss Waugh endured this for three hours, after which she was unbridled and held in jail for a period, then rebridled and whipped out of town by the constable.

To some degree, what posed as a community control problem was, in actuality, a desire by men to bridle "inconvenient women." Men were concerned with vocal abuse purely as a woman-out-of-control problem. But if whore charging was taken seriously, male sexual behavior outside marriage would surely be curtailed.

For insight, let's envisage a different situation. Suppose that middle-aged married women were stridently charging young mothers with child-rearing practices that fell below a culturally approved standard—not an unreasonable supposition given the high rate of infanticide in medieval days. Let us further imagine that young mothers were charged, more specifically, with spending too little time with the children, and failing to offer sufficiently strict discipline, or to impart solid moral values. Would the men of the community, including the judges, police, lawyers, and other court officials, have rushed to silence the middle-aged women with a charge of scolding? Would they have towed them around town in a cart, taken them to the nearest body of deep water and repeatedly dunked them until they professed regret for their intemperate words? Would husbands and town mayors have clamped these advocates of more stringent child-rearing standards in iron bridles until their tongues bled?

Charivaris

If dunking and bridling were the punishment for scolding, a behavior frequently set in motion by eavesdropping, how did citizens respond when a citizen merely *reported* wrongful acts that were detected by eavesdropping?

Beginning at least seven hundred years ago, the French put on public "roasts" for ordinary people—none famous—who had committed various kinds of transgressions. Most of these misdeeds were legal, even if forbidden or frowned on by the church. Some merely involved lifestyle choices that were upsetting to community members. The roasts were called "charivaris"—the origin of American "shivarees." The English had "skimmingtons," and the Italians and Germans had *scampanate* and *katzenmusik*.

Skimmingtons have been lucidly described. After the original observation, information was then circulated among the remaining villagers by way of gossip. When some number were fed up enough to take action, a public ritual was scheduled. Typically, the "victim" was dragged from his or her house and made to sit backwards on a horse or donkey, less commonly a wooden ladder or pole (the "stang") that was shouldered by brawny celebrants. If the victim could not be found, a neighbor might be substituted—and fairly so, in the eyes of the organizers, since he was in a position to witness the misdeed but had done nothing to prevent it.

The guilty party, often bearing a banner that identified the offence, was then led through the village in a lively procession. The procession was accompanied by a number of cacophonous townsmen—including boisterous children—who blew horns and whistles and clanged together all manner of things metallic, from pots and pans to skimming ladles (hence the name "skimmington"), which were used by wives, like the proverbial rolling pin, to punish husbands who came home drunk. Occasionally there were gunshots and fireworks. After a thorough shaming, victims were occasionally thrown into the town stocks or a local body of water.

What had the guilty parties done that merited the level of public humiliation involved in these spectacles? Clearly, the adults of the town, and their children, were being force-fed a list of things to avoid, or to do secretively, or advisedly, in the future. What was on the list?

The answer can be stated simply: sex and marriage. The leading cause of French charivaris, according to a tally by Violet Alford, was remarriage of a widow or widower, especially where there was a vast difference in age. The second most frequent cause was husband beating, followed by adultery by a married woman. The fourth cause of French charivaris was, simply, marriage.

Evaluation of a different sample indicated that over ninety percent of the charivaris were provoked by remarriage. In some cases the betrothing parties were of disparate age or wealth, or were simply old. In a charivari held in Aubais in February of 1745, a sixty-four-year-old tanner named Baudran married Thérèse Batifort, aged forty-four. The bride, it was claimed, had twenty-two teeth, including all canines and molars. Her sexagenarian groom had just fourteen, "age having claimed those that might have been serviceable."[56]

In other cases the remarriage was preceded by a period of "improper conduct during widowhood." Natalie Davis turned up a sixteenth-century charivari against a newly wed husband who failed to consummate his marriage until the third night (one wonders how they knew).[57] Other reasons included the rejection of a reputable male suitor in favor of one who was richer, much older, or foreign, and pregnant brides who marched down the aisle in white. Charivaris were also held when a young man married for money, or the bride and groom were literally kissing cousins. In some cases, fun was made of newly weds who had not produced a baby "soon enough."

Just why the youths of the community cared about the marriage of a younger woman to a dentally challenged senior citizen was the subject of some speculation. "Men stimulated by the desire to bind their destiny to a woman," wrote one Captain Deville in 1818, "must have found it difficult to watch one of their number, who had already claimed his tribute from the fairer sex, aspire to take another at the expense of those still animated by this fond hope."[58]

Exhibit 18 *La Croisée*
(The casement window)
I, Philibert-Louis
Debucourt, 1791

In England, accounts of shaming spectacles mention husband-beating, marriage of a nagging wife and submissive husband, and marital quarrelsomeness. Most of the other "offences" were like those charivaried by the French . . . with one conspicuous exception. According to separate reports by Edward Thompson and Martin Ingram, cuckoldry was very frequent, perhaps even more frequent than adultery.[59]

The focus of these shaming rituals for cuckoldry was usually women's defiance of male authority, but the typical charivari, according to Anthony Fletcher, "was always directed primarily, if only implicitly in some cases, against the husband and . . . its message was directed at other husbands. The crucial issue was his personal and sexual control over his wife."[60]

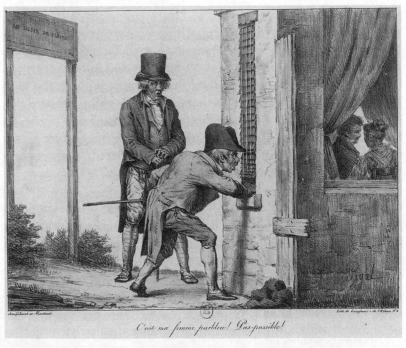

C'est ma femme parbleu! Pas-possible!

Exhibit 19 "C'est ma femme parbleu! Pas-possible!" ("Damn! That's my wife!), Edme-Jean Pigal, 1822

Charivaris demarcated moral property lines for anyone wishing to test the limits in their own lives or impose them on others. Charivaris also gave individuals a sense of their own power in relation to that of the community and, according to Martin Ingram, supplied villagers with a conceptual framework that could help them organize their experiences.[61]

It is significant that in most accounts of these spectacles, there is frequent mention of mime and mockery, and especially derisive or explosive laughter. The events were thus, at the same time, punitive and festive, though there may have been a nervous quality to the laughter. Some historians, attempting to understand the nature of the laughter, referred to "cathartic release."[62] It's as though the people were simultaneously trying to discourage what was going on in their community and reconcile themselves to it.

Concerns about the moral tidiness of small villages would continue, but people were streaming into cities. London and Paris were bursting at the seams. The world, if anyone cared to notice, was individuating rapidly. There were now many humans, and many different types of humans. It was time to take stock of who was out there. Fortunately, the human types were all too ready to help.

CHAPTER SEVEN

Passionate Exhibitors

[In] Paris...one gladly exteriorizes one's self. We find it tiresome to live and die at home...We require public display, big events, the street, the cabaret, to witness us for better or for worse...we like to pose, to put on a show, to have an audience, a gallery, witnesses to our life.

Alfred Delvau

I N the public spaces of nineteenth-century Paris there was a continuous parade of passionate exhibitors, ordinary people with an urge to "exteriorize" themselves, as writer and lexicographer Alfred Delvau said, to display the most compelling form of their public selves to an appreciative audience.

Fortunately for the exhibitors, the bleachers were filled with passionate spectators. "[P]aving-stones have ears," wrote Balzac, "and doorways have tongues, the window-bars have eyes: there is no greater danger than gossiping at front entrances. The tail-end of a conversation, like the postscript of a letter, may be as dangerously indiscreet both for those who let themselves be overheard as for those who overhear it."[1]

If every message on the cobbled streets of Paris was marked "To Whom It May Concern," or at least interpreted that way, there was one spectator who was unusually concerned. This individual navigated public space alone and was—or at least considered himself to be—superior to the crowd. Known as a *flâneur*, a stroller, he moved about with aristocratic bearing, in embroidered vest and velvet coat, and was studiously, almost scientifically, investigative.

Just as a feature of domestic architecture produced the "eaves-dropper," so did an adventure in urban architecture attract and mold this intensely empirical Parisian. Two centuries ago, the citizens of Paris had grown weary of the city's dark and dirty streets, equally lacking in sewers and sidewalks. The streets, moreover, were clogged with several forms and species of traffic, offering "a frightful spectacle," according to architect Johann Geist, with "constant pushing, shoving, crushing . . . as if one-half of the population were paid to gallop incessantly behind the other."[2]

Clearly, something had to be done. A solution appeared in the form of arcades—iron-framed, glass-domed, marble-paneled passageways lined with elegant shops.[3] Arcades, it was thought, would save pedestrians from getting run over by carriages and carts. Furthermore, these new venues were spacious, dry, and bright—features ensured by glass domes and gas lamps—and an agreeable temperature all year around.[4]

Humans under glass

The arcades had a variety of shops that specialized in linens, knitwear, silks, lace, glass, tapestries, furniture, and other goods, drawing a broad range of patrons, from the hoi polloi to the upper crust, and all were able, finally, to move about unpaced by the sights and sounds of city traffic. For a time, it was fashionable to take turtles for a walk in the arcades.[5]

The human spectacle was absorbing. If someone wanted to study Parisians, there could not have been a better place to do so, and *flâneurs* did. Outside, one *scampered* along the narrow and

Exhibit 20 *Galerie Colbert, Rotunda*, lithograph by Billaud, 1828

dangerous streets of Paris, ever alert to the encroachment of speeding cabriolets. Inside, this new and more leisurely way of ambulating, according to Walter Benjamin, a German literary critic and philosopher, "could hardly have assumed the importance it did without the arcades."[6] What was so interesting about these strollers?

Clues began to surface almost immediately. In 1806—several years after the first arcades were built—a pamphlet appeared under the title *Le Flâneur au salon ou M. Bon-Homme*. It called attention to the *flâneur*'s detachment from ordinary people, and his appreciation of all things visual.[7] In time, other characteristics became evident. An important one was the intensity of the *flâneur*'s desire *to inspect everyone*. In words that are now familiar, the poet

Charles Baudelaire wrote about this "'I' with an insatiable appetite for the 'non-I.'"[8]

Although it was not immediately understood, many of the *flâneurs* were also motivated by a second desire, one that was not initially apparent. It was the Asmodean urge *to expose everyone*. But it was not a desire to illuminate them *individually*. Nor had that been the purpose of Asmodeus when he removed rooftops from the better homes in Madrid more than a hundred years earlier. True, the limping demon had taught his student, Cleofas, about the secret thoughts and actions of the *humans* inside, but in reality his focus was on the revelation of *human types*. So was the *flâneur*'s.

Was the *flâneur* an extrovert, a people person? Some period descriptions suggest so. "The crowd is his element as the air is that of birds and water of fishes," wrote Baudelaire, in reference to one *flâneur*, the painter-illustrator Contantine Guys. "His passion and his profession are to become one flesh with the crowd." But the *flâneur* had no interest in *connecting* with anyone in the arcades, no desire to *interact*. A glance at the personal correspondence of the early eighteenth-century English poet Joseph Addison provides a partial explanation. After a spell in the country, Addison wrote a friend that he was sick of people prying into his personal affairs. He planned, he said, to "get into the crowd again as fast as I can, *in order to be alone*." Multitude and solitude were one and the same, wrote Baudelaire. The man who wants to be alone must be able "to *people his solitude*."[9]

But *flâneurs* were not the only curious citizens in Paris. There was a second class of individuals, *badauds*, commoners who were given to idle observation, with exaggerated reactions and little real understanding of anything that they witnessed. The typical *badaud* was drawn to things that happened in the streets. He "is astonished by everything he sees," went the entry in a contemporary dictionary, "he believes everything he hears, and he shows his contentment or his surprise by his open, gaping mouth."[10]

Accounts indicate that *flâneurs* were more independent than *badauds*. The *flâneur* "is always in full possession of his individuality," wrote Victor Fournel in 1858, reinforcing what *Le Flâneur* had said a half century earlier, whereas the *badaud* "is absorbed by the outside world, which intoxicates him to the point where he forgets himself."[11]

There was another difference between these two kinds of spectators. The *badauds* were observing things that happened in the arcades. The *flâneurs* were not. They were observing the *badauds*. In a moment we will see why, but there is a characteristic of *flâneurs* that needs to be considered first: their sex.

Flâneurs were men

Considering their desire to gaze upon human scenes, and to use the crowd "to people their solitude," it may come as little surprise to know that the Parisian *flâneurs* were men. What does this mean, and how does it fit with other facts about vigilance and eavesdropping that we have seen?

Sex differences appeared in the eavesdropping data that we examined earlier, and it was a challenge to interpret them. We saw, for example, that four and five centuries ago English men were arrested for eavesdropping far more often than women. Although it was tempting to attribute this disparity to biological factors, we reasoned that some of the difference may have come from a cultural fact: the invasive, under-the-eaves type of eavesdropping that was outlawed typically occurred at night when women were unlikely to be out. We also noted that women, more than men, testified in court to things they had seen in the vicinity of their home, but then we recognized that the home was a place where men spent less time. True, we did see deeper reasons why men and women might have preferred to observe and investigate as they did, but our question about *flâneurs* still remains. What caused the sex bias in *flânerie*? Were the arcades sex-biased as well?

Certainly most of the public spaces in mid-nineteenth-century Paris belonged to men. They dominated the coffee houses, the theatres, and the streets. But women did frequent the arcades. Indeed, it was planned and fervently hoped that they would do so. The arcades were lined with boutiques that specialized in women's things, and many of the staff were female. Moreover, unlike the streets, the arcades were *intérieurs*, and bore few of the taboos of public areas. Lithographs of the period also show plenty of women in the arcades (even if few were depicted alone, as some men were). So there could have been the odd *flâneuse* here and there, but accounts agree that the *flâneurs* were uniformly male.

But there are other reasons to suspect that a masculine noun for the arcadian "stroller" was appropriate. For one, if plunging into the arcade was a way of achieving solitude, is this something that women would have wanted? Men more nearly fit the description of the loner, the hunter, the autonomous being who feels he can easily survive on his own.

It is also the case that *flâneurs* were highly visual, like the artists they admired (some, like Constantin Guys, actually were artists), and we do not have to look far for connections between maleness and vision. Various authors have written about the "male gaze;" none, to my knowledge, has written about a female equivalent. Scopophilia, a love of looking, is strongly associated with males. Men are often thought of as voyeurs; it is hard to find any uses of the word "voyeuse." There are Peeping Tom laws, but no statutes that specifically forbid Peeping Tammys. In the 1950s Alfred Kinsey and his colleagues, following on from Gilbert Hamilton, found that men were far more drawn to, and excited by, visual sex than are women.[12] Nearly ninety percent of modern American stalkers— many of whom are merely seeking to maintain visual contact with their victim—are men.[13]

Female (and feminist) scholars do not doubt the male advantage in *flânerie*. "Moving through public spaces emerges as a uniquely gendered practice," wrote Anke Gleber.[14]

How did the flâneurs get away with it?

Flâneurs were hunters of human images. Like other kinds of hunters, including Cartier-Bresson and the other photographers who patrolled the streets of Paris a century later, they had found a way to observe their prey without their prey observing them. How did the *flâneurs* get away with this? After all, the prototypical *flâneur* was dressed like a dandy, often seen with an umbrella over one arm, or hands crossed behind the back. Some were depicted with opera glasses. Are these ways to *avoid* attention?

Exhibit 21 *A flâneur* (from Louis Huart, *Physiologie du flâneur,* 1841)

One way that *flâneurs* were able to observe arcadians in their natural state was by moving slowly and deliberately. Moreover, the *flâneurs* were not actors, not reactive or labile, not swept up by urban events like the *badauds*. Even if their clothing attracted attention, this attention was directed at the *flâneurs* as *exhibitors*, not as investigators.

Flâneurs also situated themselves in areas where they would attract little notice. A drawing by Edouard Traviés depicts a *flâneur* standing behind a crowd, which is looking in the opposite direction at a puppet show.[15] More often, *flâneurs* mingled with the other arcadians, gravitating toward the center of some assemblage. From there, attention would naturally fan outwards, toward some thing or event at the periphery. The principle was articulated by Addison. In a crowd, he wrote, *"I can there raise what speculations I please upon others without being observed myself."*[16]

What was the flâneur's real purpose?

The *flâneur*, wrote sociologist Christopher Prendergast, was "an expert at converting the city into a fund of interesting 'sensations.'"[17] In fact he was a closet taxonomist, but he was not applying his perceptual and interpretive skills to butterflies or birds or plants, as other taxonomists do. The *flâneur* was sorting through the different classes of his own species. He was categorizing the people of Paris. Walter Benjamin understood this, writing that the real mission of the *flâneur* was *"botanizing."* In 1841 Albert Smith referred to the various categories of beings seen on the streets of London as "social *zoologies.*"[18]

But why go around classifying Parisians? What could this possibly accomplish? Clues are to be found in the demographics of Paris. In the mid-1800s the population of Paris was just over one million, having tripled since the turn of the century. This was more strangers than many Parisians—especially the newly urbanized—had ever seen, and there was, according to literature professor

Richard Sieburth, an "uneasiness associated with the emergence of the modern urban crowd." Embedded in that crowd were pickpockets, thieves, and confidence men. They would have to be identified if pedestrians were to avoid what Sieburth called the "potentially threatening exteriority of the city."[19]

But there were other demographic factors at work here. Psychologists have long known that when people are overloaded with anything, they either withdraw or begin to look for similarities and patterns. This reduces a cumbersome number of separate entities to a manageable number of recognizable categories. One million individuals cannot be intelligible, but according to unconscious assumptions that were operating at the time, a fractional number of categories might be.[20]

The citizens of Paris were also diversifying, making their actions harder to predict. The individuation of city folk was described eighty years ago by a Parisian psychiatrist, Eugène Murkowski. "I go into the street and meet a number of people," he wrote, "but each of them, while forming a part of a whole, follows his own path and his own thoughts; we go in opposite directions."[21]

"We are a society of selves," wrote Nicholas Humphrey. "*We* are a set of *I's*," he went on, echoing the words of Baudelaire, "individuals who due to the very nature of conscious selfhood are in principle unable to get through to one another and share the most central facts of our psychical existence."[22]

In *Paris, A Rainy Day*, painted by Gustave Caillebotte in 1877, pedestrians are seen following their own paths. Each is heading in a different direction, inspired, one assumes, by a strictly private goal or plan.[23] In their distance from others, and different trajectories, the strollers seem to express a desire to be regarded as unique individuals—individuals with minds of their own.

If there was a visual conversation in the streets of Paris, what Renoir and other artists were recording was each stroller's individual, and oblique, "comment." As passionate spectators, *flâneurs* intercepted these comments, these individual contributions to the

Exhibit 22 *Paris: A Rainy Day*, Gustave Caillebotte, 1877

Parisian buzz, but how did their interpretations become public? How did all the "botanizing" affect the people of Paris?

Physiologies

To have any effect on the people of Paris, the lessons of *flânerie* would have to be conveyed in some form—and they were, thanks to *physiologies*. These were satiric ethnographies in the form of paper-bound, pocket-size books. *Physiologies* offered citizens and tourists information that would be needed to negotiate the city of Paris but, unlike other guidebooks, made no mention of restaurants and public monuments. Their sole focus was anthropological, a description of the people one was likely to encounter in the streets. "From the itinerant street vendor of the boulevards to the dandy in the foyer of the opera-house," wrote Benjamin, "there was not a figure of Paris life that was not sketched by a *physiologie*."[24] There were *physiologies* of the adoring lover, the English tourist, the bluestocking, the prankster, the Bourbonnais, the bourgeois, the drinker, the bachelor and the spinster, the hunter, the cuckold, the creditor and the retailer, the country priest, the stevedore, the salesgirl, and—inclusively—the *flâneur* himself.[25] In London, Albert Smith came up with the gent, the ballet-girl, the mooner, the Regent Street idler, the lounger, and the flirt, among others.

At one franc, *physiologies* sold for less than a third of other books' cost, and they were clearly designed to be sold in the streets. The *flâneur* who produced them, wrote Christopher Prendergast, "makes the city safe and innocuous by classifying its population in the form of picturesque character sketches, giving a picture of Paris as 'harmless and of perfect bonhomie.'"[26]

The public couldn't get enough of these whimsical guides to urbanized *Homo sapiens*. Between 1840 and 1842, at least 120 different *physiologies* were sold. It is estimated that half a million copies were printed—approximately one for every Parisian who could read.

So now we see. These mysterious characters, strolling impassively through crowds, savoring their solitude, speaking to no one, and giving no clues to their purpose, were interpreters of the human condition. They, like other naturalists, were conducting research on living beings. Because of their orientation to visual scenes, and their disposition to categorize people, they were, in their own quirky way, dealing with the stranger problem. Those who shelled out one franc could go around Paris like amateur ornithologists with their field guides in one hand and a pair of opera glasses in the other.

That the *flâneurs* were planning to tell a story about their perceptual experiences suggests another reason to suspect a male bias in *flânerie*. "Urban stories," wrote sociology professor Priscilla Parkhurst Ferguson, "can be told only by those immune to the stress and the seductions of the city, who can turn those seductions to good account, that is, into a text that will exercise its own seductions."

This, she argued, would have been men, women being "components of the urban drama that the *flâneur* observes."[27]

Did the *physiologies* accomplish their purpose? It's difficult to tell, but the public's reading of them, according to Benjamin, "served to reduce the crowd's massive alterity to proportions more familiar, to transform its radical anonymity into a lexicon of nameable stereotypes." This, he said, gave readers "the comforting illusion that the faceless conglomerations of the modern city could after all be read—and hence mastered—as a legible system of differences."[28]

Paris was not the only great city in Europe to build arcades, nor was *flânerie* impossible without them, especially when the viewer was stationary and his subjects on parade. In 1840 Edgar Allen Poe wrote a detailed account of his own experience as a *flâneur* in the city of London.[29] In "The Man of the Crowd," one encounters Poe sitting in the window of a coffee house, nursing a cold, observing pedestrians. When he first looked out the window, Poe saw the passers-by as undifferentiated masses, but he quickly began to focus on details, examining "the innumerable varieties of figure, dress, air, gait, visage, and expression of countenance." One class of Londoners that caught Poe's eye was a tribe of junior clerks, "young gentlemen with tight coats, bright boots, well-oiled hair, and supercilious lips." Poe also noticed pickpockets, gamblers, clergymen, peddlers, street beggars, feeble and ghastly invalids, modest young girls, and women of the town. In a perfect statement of the *flâneur's* purpose, Poe wrote, "It was impossible to keep track of what everyone was up to, but one could determine whether individuals belonged to categories that required evasion or embrace."

In Paris, the days of the arcadian *flâneur* were numbered. The first nail in the coffin was driven by the police, mid-way through the nineteenth century, when the prefect ruled that no arcade on private property could be made accessible to the public without permission of the police. Around the same time, Napoleon III commissioned Georges-Eugène Haussmann to rebuild Paris. This meant, at a minimum, replacing many of the narrow streets with broad boulevards. These boulevards were to be lined by sidewalks along with gutters and underground drains. Pedestrians would be able to walk along the sides of boulevards, undisturbed by vehicles and animals. In the 1850s, three thousand new gas lamps were installed in Paris, and many of these were kept burning all night. Paris had become a good place to walk, and the new strolling venues lured people out of the arcades. After a half-century of applied anthropology, the *flâneur* was losing his natural labora-tory.[30] About to make her debut was a new sort of spectator, one with an entirely different purpose and style. It was the *flâneuse*.

The flâneuse

With streets that were cleaner, drier, and safer, there were diminish-ingly few reasons why women would feel it necessary to avoid them. But there were also some significant new *intérieurs*, and these ushered in new reasons to spectate, reasons that appealed particu-larly to women.

In boutiques, women could only see and touch things that were kept behind glass, and one had to be cautious. The price had to be negotiated—one could easily make a bad deal—and shop policy often forbade refunds and returns. All this changed in 1869, when Aristide Boucicaut opened Bon Marché, the first major department store in Paris. It took up an entire city block.[31] Like the arcades, it was an indoor-but-public space, and it was designed especially for women.[32]

In Bon Marché the merchandise was on the floor, and women were encouraged to inspect everything. In *Au bonheur des dames*, a novel published a dozen years after Bon Marché opened its doors, Émile Zola wrote about the allure of this new experience. Undoubt-edly the *dames* were amazed at the large volumes of merchandise, but Zola suggested that the shops were also "selling aspirations, status, dreams and yearnings." Zola understood that stores like Bon

Marché had erotic connotations for women, that "the bright, subtly designed emporia 'seduced' them into buying the goods on offer."[33]

In Bon Marché women could touch women's lingerie, even, if they chose, fondle it. This, as Valerie Steele has written, evoked feelings of sexual intimacy.[34] In *Les Grands Bazaars*, published in 1882, Pierre Giffard wrote of the woman who, "prey to the seductions of lace," empties her purse, "her eyes on fire, her face reddened, her hand shivering."[35] The texture of silk, wrote one woman, "gives me voluptuous sensations even stronger than those I feel with the father of my children."[36]

"The female *flâneur*, the *flâneuse*, was not possible until she was free to roam the city on her own," wrote media theorist Anne Friedberg, a freedom that "was equated with the privilege of shopping on her own."[37] In the late nineteenth century, department stores were built in London, New York, Philadelphia, and Chicago. Immediately, window-shopping became a popular pastime. In 1902 a writer for *New York Sketches*, Jesse Lee Williams, grumbled about the magnetic allure of shop windows, "which draw women's heads around whether they want to look or not."[38] Shop windows feminized the sidewalks, adding a feminine component to *flânerie*.

Parks, promenades, and sidewalk cafés

Eventually, the onslaught of cars and trucks on the boulevards of Paris made streetwalking less desirable than it had been in the past.[39] Fortunately, Haussmann not only built boulevards and sidewalks. He built parks. By 1870 Paris could claim about 4500 acres of municipal parkland, nearly one hundred times more than the city had on offer twenty years earlier.[40]

Like the arcades, beautifully ornate city parks encouraged leisurely displays of men and women. They became a human pageant, a stage for all human activity, from work and play to love and death.[41] These promenades provided citizens with opportunities to see and be seen while garbed in their finest clothes.

"The urban promenade," wrote history professor Penelope Corfield, provided the perfect venue "for the citizens to sally forth to view the sights and each other." Participants enjoyed "the pleasure, puzzle, and necessity of scrutinizing each other discreetly."[42] Adding to this pleasure and puzzle was the fact that everyone was not exactly as they seemed, or wanted to seem.

Promenades were not just for men or women. They were for couples, and for families. These familial promenades performed an instructive or regulatory function. When a family went out for an evening stroll, it was assumed that the husband would "see himself as others saw him," according to architect Galen Cranz, "the head of a family, wife on arm, children in tow, all in Sunday best. Reformers reasoned that he would experience this as pleasurable and resolve to make it the mainstay of his life." In 1890 the commissioners of Boston's parks department saw public viewings as a course of moral instruction. The mere sight of "good women and dutiful children" was expected to exert "a wholesome influence" on other patrons, and to do so far more effectively than laws and police ever could.[43]

In the early 1970s the patrons of two parks in Portland, Oregon were questioned. A fifth or fewer of the interviewees said they went to the parks to wade, eat, talk, read, or engage in crafts or hobbies, or to exercise. The majority of patrons—fifty-five percent—said they went to the parks in order to "watch other people."[44] Around the same time, professor of landscape architecture John Lyle studied the great parks of Paris and several neighborhood parks around Los Angeles. He found that the favored places "were usually in the hearts of the parks, where crowds of people often would promenade along major paths or around bodies of water, while others sat watching them."[45]

There is a huge dramaturgical component here. Like a theatrical production, public life "requires actors and audience, a stage and a theater," wrote Suzanne and Henry Lennard. "Some persons sit or walk in public in order to be seen, to display particular attire, and thus to impress an imagined or real audience. They wish to be identified as a member of a group, or try out a special role or a new identity. They seek an audience." Responsively, we, the other exhibitors, "fantasize about their origins, purposes, and possible relationship to us."[46]

Outdoor bars and cafés have been popular in Europe for many decades, but people watching and social displays may be growing in popularity, at least if Dutch sidewalk cafés are any indication. In the city of Utrecht, the amount of space devoted to sidewalk cafés tripled between 1970 and 1975, and had doubled again by 1991. Similar growth occurred in other cities in the Netherlands. In the early 1990s, Dutch urbanologist Jan Oosterman wrote that the main reason people sit and sip coffee in sidewalk cafés is to "watch people go by." "The chairs," he noted, "are always placed towards the street, as the chairs in a theatre are placed towards the stage." The patrons don't want "to get involved with anybody passing by," wrote Oosterman. "It is mainly the spectacle that people come for."[47]

We are all exhibitors and spectators. We display ourselves and check out each other's displays—as though we were attending a continuous costume or masquerade ball. These dispositions, as we have seen, are linked to facts about human biology, but their timing and appearance are sensitive to cultural factors. Places, like walls and arcades, are important. So are laws, religion, and social and economic competition. One dramatic factor, acutely felt by the rich and famous owners of manorial homes, was the ubiquitous presence of servants—individuals who were paid to keep an eye on their master and mistress but frequently saw too much.

CHAPTER EIGHT

What Will the Servants Say?

I declare, having served in the capacity of manservant to his excellency Marquis Francesco Albegati for the period of about eleven years, that I can say and give account that on three or four occasions I saw the said marquis getting out of bed with a perfect erection of the male organ . . . and this I saw and observed with complete certainty and without being deceived, because I was in a position to observe it and see it at my ease because of my employment.   A servant, in his testimony, 1751

ENSCONCED in their mansions and stately homes, the rich and famous were a cause of curiosity. Everyone wondered how they lived. Remarkably, opportunities to find out were freely available to a class of people who were poor and ordinary. They worked and slept under the same roof, and were expected to linger outside bedroom and parlor doors in case they were beckoned. With eavesdropping in their job descriptions, these domestic servants—generally young and vulnerable—saw and heard things that normally occur, and did occur, behind closed doors. If the mistress of the house was charged with adultery, or the master was accused of sexual neglect, butlers and maids—usually the only witnesses—were called to testify. Telling the truth could fortify their employment, or threaten it. So could lying.

Servant testimony was rich in intimate details—of morning erections in allegedly impotent husbands, beds that were "tumbled" and stained, sofas indented by the backs of unfaithful wives, and gentleman callers struggling to regain their composure as they buttoned up their breeches. The stories of servants and their masters read like novels, with characters truly named Munnings Capp, Clotworthy Dobbin, and Wortham Hitch, and virtues like obedience, loyalty, and honor juxtaposed with contempt, betrayal, and shame. Inevitably, the possibility of bribery and blackmail lurked. Life in a stately home was problematic. Servants knew too much.

On May 15, 1776, John Potter Harris, twenty-six, of Basinghurst, England, brought suit against his wife, Elizabeth, twenty-three. She was "vicious and lewd," he claimed, and had forgotten her conjugal vows.[1]

Several witnesses were called. Three were servants in the Harris home. The first to testify was Sarah Simmons, twenty-five, a servant to Mrs. Harris. She began by recounting a Sunday evening in April, 1775, when her mistress came into the kitchen and ordered the servants to bed. Why? It was an odd request since there were always things to be done after dinner. Sarah was also told that her personal services would not be needed that night. Mrs. Harris would undress herself. Confused, and somewhat suspicious, Sarah went to her room.

But she did not go to bed. Nor was Mrs. Harris planning to undress herself.

Sarah and her roommate, Catherine Durnford, tried to interpret Mrs. Harris's actions. They surmised that Mrs. Harris was planning to spend the night with a man who, in previous visits, had displayed inappropriate affections toward Mrs. Harris, and she toward him. It was the Reverend John Craven, the rector of Woolverton, a parish adjoining Basinghurst. He had been given a room down the hall.

Sarah told Miss Durnford that she intended to catch her employer in the act. Donning a nightgown, Sarah blew out the candle, cracked opened the door of her room, and listened. She heard Mrs. Harris enter her bedchamber—which was directly across the hall—and about fifteen minutes later heard Mr. Craven leave his room, walk down the hall, and open Mrs. Harris's door.

Sarah was careful to note the time. It was midnight.

Sarah crossed the hall and stood outside her mistress's door, where she "listened at the key-hole" and "heard Mr. Craven and Mrs. Harris whispering together, and heard them kiss each other." The room was dark, but Sarah was able to make out some incriminating sounds—first the "movement" of bed clothes, and then the "cracking" of the bed. This continued for about two or three minutes, Sarah testified, "and immediately afterwards every thing was quite silent," and remained so for the next half hour.

When she returned to her room, Sarah discussed Mrs. Harris's adulterous activities with Miss Durnford. Perhaps, Sarah suggested, she should tell her mistress that Mr. Harris had come home and was bound to discover her in bed with Mr. Craven. Mr. Harris was a sympathetic character. Nothing in the court records suggests that he knew about his wife's misdeeds—misdeeds that were carried out under his own roof, some, even, in the marital bed. Miss Durnford tried to talk her out of it, arguing that the better course, considering what Sarah had already seen and heard, was simply to confront Mrs. Harris the next morning. It was a suggestion that Sarah would follow, but not until she had completed her investigation. Sarah made her way down the hall and looked into Mr. Craven's room. His clothes were missing.

Later, at about two o'clock in the morning, Sarah heard Mr. Craven walk back to his room. Remarkably, she was able to hear him blow out his lamp "at two or three puffs" before he returned to his assignation with Mrs. Harris. Sarah resumed her keyhole vigil, now in its second hour, "and heard Mr. Craven get into, or upon the bed, and heard Mr. Craven and Mrs. Harris whispering together, and kissing each other; and she also heard the bed crack, and make a noise; and such cracking, or rustling of the bed continued for a few minutes" until, for the second time that night, "all was silent again."

Sarah crept up and down the hall for another hour or two, waiting for something to happen. At about four o'clock, she told the court, Mr. Craven left Mrs. Harris's bed and returned to his room.

The next morning, after half a night of eavesdropping, Sarah entered her mistress's room. She was there to dress her, but Sarah used the opportunity to recount what she had seen and heard the previous night. Mrs. Harris first denied it, then admitted that Mr. Craven had been in her room for "a little while." Sarah said it had actually been "a great while," noting that Mr. Craven's stay had lasted until four in the morning. Mrs. Harris asked Sarah if she could swear to it, and she answered that she could. At this point, according to Sarah's testimony, Mrs. Harris became visibly "confused and agitated" but made no reply.

After Mrs. Harris went down to breakfast, Sarah and a fellow servant, Elizabeth Holden, fifty, entered Mrs. Harris's room. They found the bed "very much tumbled," with "several marks or spots upon the sheets." Since the sheets had been changed the previous night, the marks and spots, Sarah told the courts, must have been made by Mr. Craven and Mrs. Harris "having lain together that night, and having had the carnal knowledge of each other."

At the end of the day, Mr. Craven left the Harris house, first calling Sarah to help him on with his great coat. She was rewarded with a guinea. Was this hush money, Sarah wondered?

Something happened the next day to suggest that it was. Mrs. Harris offered her a gown and petticoat, and other things, and asked Sarah "not to tell tales." As a servant, Sarah was instructed, she was not in a strong position to do so.

Two months passed before Mr. Craven visited the house again. On that occasion John Appleton, a servant to Mr. Harris, told Sarah that Mrs. Harris was in Mr. Craven's room. He asked her to join him in a vigil outside the rector's room. Once again, the rustling of clothing and the sound of whispering could be heard through the keyhole. When someone started to unlock the door, the two eavesdroppers raced back to their rooms.

Later in the proceedings, Elizabeth Holden and John Appleton testified to two other trysts. In each case, the two servants had stayed up much of the night, hearing the sounds of whispering, clothes rustling, bed cracking, and silence, and discovering stains on the sheets the following morning; and in each case they, like Sarah, were specific as to the date, day of the week, and time.

The court had heard enough. Under the law, two witnesses were required, and the court had heard from three servants, with almost identical testimony provided, remarkably, by Mrs. Harris's younger sister. The verdict? Guilty. By committing adultery, Mrs. Harris had broken her conjugal vows. Her marriage to John Harris was over.

Dilemmas

The Harris case raises interesting questions about privacy, intimacy, and morality; and offers new insights into the motives and benefits, and consequences, of perceptual trespassing. Why the all-night vigils, keyhole-klatches, morning-after bed inspections, and behind-the-scenes talks about what was going on and what to do about it? It was one thing to seek out entertainment, or erotic experience. The servants were young and single, and life in a large country house could mean long spells of boredom and drudgery. But there was personal danger here. Why did a servant risk losing her livelihood by confronting Mrs. Harris, even after she had been told that her position, as a servant, was not that secure? Why would three servants testify in a court of law to activity that, if believed by the court, would terminate Mrs. Harris's marriage? If the household broke up, perhaps these servants would no longer be needed. If, on the other hand, their testimony was unconvincing, their mistress would be in a clear position to strike back. They could lose their jobs in this scenario, too.

One possibility, of course, is that Mr. Harris had assured them that if they testified against his wife, their jobs would be safe, perhaps even upgraded. Servants were usually loyal to the master of the house, less frequently to the mistress, and the house was almost certainly his property. A proved charge of adultery was equivalent to an instant divorce, but Mr. Harris would still require some number of (loyal) servants to remain in their posts. By testifying to what they had witnessed, the servants would be, or be seen as, loyal and virtuous, and their employment in the Harris household would continue.

Of course there was plenty of room for moral indignation. Mrs. Harris's behavior was in clear violation of biblical injunctions and English law. Besides, to carry on so flagrantly was shameful, occurring not just once, but repeatedly; happening not spontaneously, but by prearrangement; and it took place just a few feet from the quarters of young women who would have placed a high valuation on their own personal virtue. Even Mrs. Harris's younger sister testified against her.

Sarah and the other servants were precise about the month, date, day of the week, and time of each act or scene to which they testified, even though some had occurred several months before the trial. They must have kept written records. Had they planned from the beginning to "get" Mrs. Harris? If so, were they respecting what they believed to be Mr. Harris's wishes in the matter; or were they following his orders?

Domestic service

As many as five hundred mansions, or "stately homes," were built in Britain between the sixteenth and twentieth centuries, and they could not be managed without a great deal of domestic help. In an analysis of English communities it was found that just over *thirteen percent* of the population worked as servants.[2]

From the standpoint of home maintenance, some of the servants may have been superfluous, but any extra ones would have carried a symbolic value, signalling that the owner was rich. This was a message that many landowners wished to send. The best way to

Exhibit 23 *The Washing Tub*, Pierre Vidal, from an engraving by F. Masse

distinguish oneself from laborers, wrote Eric Hobsbawm, "was to employ labor oneself."[3] Nearly ninety percent of the homes that employed servants had between one and three. But many went beyond the basal rate, and there may have been the equivalent of an arms race going on. "The chief use of servants," wrote Thorsten Veblen in 1899, "is the evidence they afford of the master's ability to pay."[4] The larger homes had as many as sixteen.[5]

For reasons that we will see later—eavesdropping chief among them—the use of servants eventually fell off. By the end of the nineteenth century, the figure had dropped to about five percent, but domestic service was still one of the largest employment groups in Britain.

It is interesting that the servants, who were culturally positioned to eavesdrop on intimate behaviors, were preponderantly young women, who were biologically disposed to do so as well. From eighty to ninety percent of all those in domestic service were female. About three-fourths of all servants were between fifteen and twenty-four years of age; nearly one in twelve servants were between ten and fifteen.[6]

Domestic service was highly specialized. If a family member needed something, there was a servant to do it. Some servants worked as maids, governesses, butlers, waiters, or grooms, others as escorts, cooks, stewards, or chambermaids. All were expected to be on hand, night and day, and many slept near the person or thing that they were expected to service. In seventeenth- and eighteenth-century Europe, as in the plantation households of Athens many centuries earlier, valets and chambermaids had bedrooms adjacent to the master or mistress. Others slept in the same room. Some maid servants shared their mistress's bed.[7]

If such an arrangement seems unusually cozy, it could also be unusually safe—for the mistress—at least if she intended to remain loyal to her husband. For this would guarantee her a witness—undoubtedly a loyal one—should doubts arise as to her marital fidelity. In ancient Athens, when husbands went away on business the wives would check themselves into a *gynaecaeum*, a "monogamous harem" where no men were allowed, for the same reason. In a moment, we will see how serious this concern actually was.

If intimately situated, personal servants were also intimately involved. Waiting maids, like Sarah Simmons, helped to dress and undress their mistress, and to bathe her. It was not unusual for servants to see their master or mistress naked or even, on occasion, to see them having sex.[8]

The intimacies, privileges, and trust between masters and servants all point to the existence of *relationships*, ones that figured significantly in the lives of both. William Blackstone wrote that the contract between employer and servant embodied the first of the "three great relations of private life."[9] The others, he wrote, were between husband and wife, and parent and child. In a *Familiar Summary of the Laws respecting Masters and Servants*, published in 1831, the anonymous author wrote that the relationship between master and servant, was "one of the most important and universal relations of the ordinary affairs of life."[10]

Hard evidence

Sometimes the intimacies between employers and their servants proved unexpectedly beneficial. In 1751 the wife of Marquis Francesco Albergati Capacelli asked a court to annul her marriage. The Marquis, she said, was impotent, and therefore unable to consummate the marriage. In defense of his virility, the marquis introduced what can only be called "hard evidence." He was seen "getting out of bed with a perfect erection of the male organ," according to one valet. Another servant stated that he had seen the marquis "with a hard and perfect erection" while he was putting on his shirt. One evening, Albergati and his friends romped around in the nude, leaving several servants impressed with the marquis's endowments. One noted that he had "excellent assets." Another that he had a "fine thing."[11]

Exhibit 24 *Le Toucher*, Abraham Bosse, 1638

When viewed against prototypical eavesdropping, where psychological and other boundaries separate the viewer and the viewed, the situation in stately homes seems incredible. Everyone was passionately curious about how the rich and famous lived, and a significant minority were there to see, hear, and smell them twenty-four hours a day. They knew how their employers lived, partly because it was *their job* to know. Spending so much of their time under the same roof, these privileged insiders knew what the aristocracy ate and drank, when and with whom they slept, how often they bathed, what clothes they wore at home, and how they spoke to each other. The servants knew what made their master and mistress laugh, what ailments they suffered, and what kinds of music and entertainment they enjoyed. They knew who visited the home, and who their masters' friends were.

Beyond their natural curiosity, young servants had reasons to soak up all these details. Many were fiercely ambitious. Domestic service was regarded as a transitional career. The young men hoped that someday they, too, would become important members of society. Domestic service would teach them how to behave like gentlemen.[12] Practically everything on display was emulated, from ways of gesturing and speaking to a fondness for tea and snuff, and particular ways of dressing. The servants also embraced their employers' ideas and moral values. "A new attitude towards church or state," wrote J. Jean Hecht, "was as likely to be passed on as a new way of cocking a hat."[13] These new behaviors positioned servants for better things and served as an important means of cultural diffusion from the upper classes to the lower ones. For female servants, it is thought, additionally, that household service served as an "apprenticeship" for marriage. In nineteenth-century France about a third of all young women worked as domestics before they married.[14]

Since house servants were physically close to manorial life in all its forms, they were routinely exposed to intimate scenes. But proximity was not the only reason why they saw and heard as much as they did. Their ubiquity caused them to be regarded as household fixtures. It was easy for the family to forget about them. Some masters and mistresses seemed to *look through* the servants. Their disregard could be seen as a form of display, one that would keep servants *in their place*, reminding them of the disparity in social rank that existed. Intentionally exposing the staff to personal intimacies could be seen as granting them a special privilege, wrote Rafaella Sarti, but it could also be seen as a "theatrical representation of power."[15]

It is astonishing to consider that nearly one in ten English people— and, we may suppose, a much higher ratio in the underclasses—made their living in places where benign forms of eavesdropping were *required*. Without eavesdropping, how would the servants know that more wine was needed, a horse should be saddled up, or a log added to the fire? But there were invisible property lines that domestic workers were not to cross. How were they to respond to subtle requests, or to anticipate familial whims, without witnessing *too much*? What if, while looking for one legitimate thing, they discovered an illegitimate other? What if they stumbled upon things that were, literally, *too intimate for words?*

Clearly, these situations required maturity, judgment, and discretion. Servants regularly found themselves in possession of highly reliable information about their employers—regionally or nationally important people—that no one, not even other gentry, would have known; and some of those things, if made public, could radically restructure their master's and mistress's lives, even affect the larger social or moral climate of their community. How was the typical servant, a young woman or adolescent—or preadolescent—female to know how to evaluate, much less react to, the information she possessed? Should she discuss intimate, possibly sinful, behaviors with her fellow servants? How, in the work and sleeping rooms that she shared with older and more experienced servants, could she *avoid* doing so?

Fear of exposure

In an attempt to ward off problems—feeble as it was—servants were instructed. In *The Complete Servant*, published in 1825 by Samuel and Sarah Adams, who had over fifty years of domestic service, servants are advised to "Avoid tale-bearing, for that is a vice of a pernicious nature, and generally turns out to the disadvantage of those who practise it."[16] In 1873 the Adams' advice was repeated in *The Parish Magazine.*[17] Knowing that servants went to the market each day, and compared notes with other servants, made the fear of tales real. Gossip, true or false, could travel around a small village in minutes. Worse, perhaps, household secrets would end up in other stately homes, in the hands of the employers' *closest friends*.

There was a massive paradox here. The owners of great estates had countless luxuries, and assistants to anticipate their every need. As major landowners and employers, they held a commanding position in the region, and contributed heavily to the local economy. They were positioned to be heard and respected. If they behaved themselves, and treated people fairly, they were likely to be admired.

Exhibit 25 *Curiosity*, 1817

And they lived in constant fear. If their misdeeds came to light, or their dalliances were exposed, they could lose everything.

In *Aurora Floyd*, published in 1863, Mary Braddon asks why servants are so "feverishly inquisitive" about every action and feeling of their employers. She wonders if it is because they "abnegated for themselves all active share in life."[18] Long before,

Exhibit 26 *Madame is Receiving*, Remy Gogghe, 1908

an article in a 1778 issue of *Town & Country Magazine* observed that "servants are domestic spies." If a woman of fashion "yields to the impulses of her passions," the article said, she "must live a very

Exhibit 27 The lady's maid tries to read her mistress's letter," from *The Servant's Magazine*

disagreeable life with her waiting-maid . . . Her fate is determined, her reputation is in her domestic's hands, and she [the maid] can dispose of it at pleasure."[19]

In 1852 Geraldine Jewsbury wrote her friend, Jane Carlyle, with some advice about a curious servant. "I would not keep her if I were you," she told Jane, "such a development of curiosity will surely be fatal to any mistress under the sun. It will not confine itself to inspecting letters, and all that, but it will show itself in listening to private conversations, and in prying into all your comings and goings." Geraldine reminded her friend that "servants are so coarse in all their thoughts that they can understand nothing they see, but put the most abominable construction on all that passes."[20]

One hundred and fifty years later, the author of a legal handbook offered a warning. "The testimony of discarded domestics should be received with great caution, and the most sifting," he wrote, "otherwise our position is fearful, our tables and beds would be surrounded with snares, and our comforts converted into instruments of terror and alarm."[21]

Collaboration

Of course not all situations between masters and servants were antagonistic. In long-term relationships there was often a good deal of empathy, trust, and mutual fondness. Some masters and mistresses formed alliances with their domestic staff. In *The Art of Keeping Wives Faithful*, first published in 1713, members of the upper classes were advised to *buy* the loyalty of their servants. If a husband wanted to find out what was going on in his household when he was away, *The Art* advised him to use the valets and servants to his advantage, for "it is through them that nearly all the intrigues of wives are conducted, or at least they always know about them."[22]

This particularly applied to house maids, who could be unusually close to the young ladies of the household. In long-term situations the maids may have nursed them and played with them as children. Later they became confidantes.[23] "When asked by her mistress to conspire to facilitate a sexual liaison," wrote Lawrence Stone, the seventeenth-and eighteenth-century maid tended "to put her duty to her mistress first and that to her master second."[24]

In cases of adultery, the servants were often faced with a morally ambiguous, personally dangerous, and financially risky choice. "What was the moral obligation of servants who detected their master's wife in adultery," asked Stone. "Should they warn her to stop, and themselves keep silent, thus saving the marriage and preserving the household? Or should they tell their master and bring the whole household down in ruins?"[25]

As we saw in the life of the courtesan Harriett Wilson, individuals who are fairly low on the social ladder may have a great deal of information that is potentially damaging to others and elevating to themselves. If women had little or no power, but copious quantities

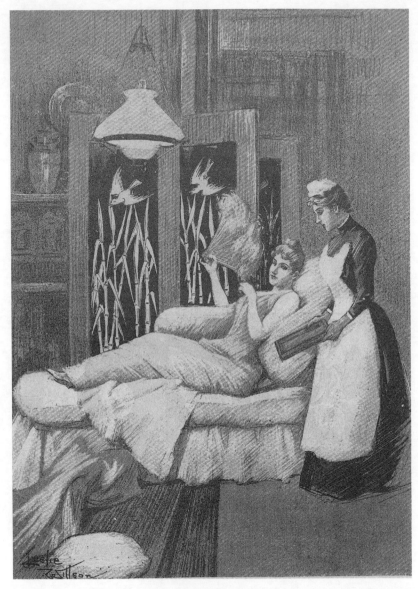

Exhibit 28 *What's in a Name?*, 1892. Mistress: "Didn't the gentleman leave his name?" Maid: "Yes, ma'am; he said it was Immaterial."

THE PRIVATE LETTER DRAWER.

Exhibit 29 *The Private Letter Drawer*, photogravure by Attilia Simonetti

of intimate knowledge, the solution to their problem was staring them in the face: publicize, or threaten to publicize, the knowledge. Status could easily be changed with information, particularly the explosive kind that women had.

The motive behind a great deal of eavesdropping was to store up information for possible profit later. By the latter half of the eighteenth century most of the higher servants were literate, and a number of them made careful written notes of the times, days, and places when they saw or heard anything suspicious. They clearly kept these notes either for possible use when testifying in court some time in the future when the scandal broke, or else for money in return for withholding the evidence. It was possible that the mistress might be willing to give servants as much as a year's wages to buy their silence, and that the master might be willing to pay even more if they testified to the things that they had seen.

Looking for clues

One tends to think of eavesdropping as a process that is applied to people, but as we have seen previously, the Asmodean impulse also leads people to search places where others have been. Intimate behavior left a trail of clues, and the servants were very alert to them. Indeed, their job included putting rooms back in good order after each use, or abuse. It is hardly surprising that servants would have noticed rumpled sofas, stained beds, and other telltale signs of love-making.

In 1771 three menservants to Lord Ligonier of Cobham, a village south of London, went to their master's bedroom to inspect the scene. The carpet at the foot of the bed was found to be "much rumpled," and there were "two large dints at the bottom of the bed, as if two persons had been sitting on it, and the bed in the middle appeared as if somebody had been laying on it, and a little above the middle of the bed, was a round place, about the size of a person's head, covered with powder."[26]

The next day, two servants inspected the house gardens to see if they could find any additional evidence. Reminiscent of the Mehinacu tribesmen, who identified each other's activities from their foot- (and other) prints in the forest floor, Lord Ligonier's menservants inspected the sandy paths, which had been recently swept. There, according to court testimony, they found "prints of the feet, as well of the lady as of the man, at the garden-gate that opens from the lawn to the road."[27]

Sometimes the servants, working with the master of the house, set a trap for the mistress and her lover. In March of 1770, Richard Grosvenor, of Halkin, North Wales, sued his wife, Henrietta, for adultery. A key witness was Matthew Stevens, thirty-six. He was likely to have felt some loyalty to Lord Grosvenor, having served as his butler for sixteen years. The two conspired that Matthew should catch his master's wife *in flagrante delicto*.

In court, Matthew described how he had gone to the White Hart Inn in St. Albans and taken a room adjacent to where Lady Grosvenor was entertaining the Duke of Cumberland. It was a quarter to eleven in the evening. Matthew intended to monitor the activities in Lady Grosvenor's room.

He began by boring two holes in the door when Lady Grosvenor was out dining. Later, when she had returned, Matthew and his brother John were able to make out the "murmuring" tones of the suspected adulterers, which came from the direction of the bed. Though the bed could not be seen, Matthew could see all other places in the room, and they were not in any of those. Matthew drew the conclusion, and would later offer it in his testimony, that Lady Grosvenor and the Duke of Cumberland were "in or upon the bed."

After listening for an hour or more, the Stephens brothers decided that it was time for more invasive action. With the help of other servants, they attempted to break in. First they rammed the door, but when this failed they decided to pry it open with a poker. By the time Matthew and John had finally crashed into the room, the lovers had collected themselves and moved away from the bed. Having lost the chance to catch them in the highest degree of criminality possible, Matthew shifted his attention to the bed. It appeared to be "very much flatted, as if persons had lain upon it, and the sheet that turned down upon the bed was very much tumbled." He also "observed a dent in the further part of the bed" which, he surmised, had been caused by "the pressure occasioned by the back part of the head." To buttress the case, John consulted the chambermaid. She said that she had not left the bed in that condition—would have been ashamed to—and that she, like the Stephens brothers, "thought that some person had lain upon it."[28]

Public servants

That servants were allowed or encouraged to testify against their employers is an indication of several things. First, and most obviously, it indicates that the courts knew the only way many cases of adultery could be prosecuted would be through servant testimony. But there was a larger and more subtle issue. How, in *societies* that were increasingly privatized, would there ever be any knowledge of—or control over—what went on in homes without someone on the inside representing the public's interest?

As we know, the domestic walls wrought by sedentism and settlements were resisted in many places, mainly because they blocked perceptual access by outsiders. Over the generations, concerns about secrecy tended to abate, without completely disappearing, but in mansions and great estates the public's interest in domestic privacy, and the activities it allows, may even have grown. In England, according to Anthea Trodd, the mid-Victorian home was seen as "a private domain unregulated by public opinion."[29]

If anyone was to expose, hence to control, the behavior of wealthy people it would have to be the servants. In a sense, they became *de facto* journalists, shining a light on misbehaviors of the upper crust purely because of their inherent desire to investigate and report, fueled, perhaps, by feelings of resentment at what they should have to endure on a daily basis. With first-hand knowledge of wrongful things that no one else knew about, some may have felt a responsibility to get the word out, to say nothing of the personal power that would be gained by doing so. Since the masters and mistresses were not visible to anyone else, the servants were actually needed—in an investigative capacity.

We see this in seventeenth-century art. The Dutch, according to Simon Schama, were the first to satirize disruptions of family values.[30] Working in the style of Rembrandt, Nicholas Maes produced six paintings mid-way through the century that depict a servant or family member eavesdropping on an erotic encounter in the home. In each painting the eavesdropper looks directly at the viewer with a look of bemused disapproval.[31]

Exhibit 30 *Die Lauscherin* (The Eavesdropper), Nicholas Maes, 1657

Although Maes used servants to call attention to immoral behaviors through the medium of paint, they also came to play that role *in real life*. Just by being there, the servants' presence would have suppressed some misbehaviors. But everyone knew that the servants doubled as investigative reporters and gossip columnists. Their material was credible, which added to its inhibiting effect. The eavesdropping of servants was indispensable to societies that sought to maintain some standard of moral behavior. Prosecution of adultery and other domestic crimes was almost impossible without servants' testimony. That the upper classes would seek relief was predictable enough.

In the privacy of one's home

The more that servants were seen as enemies within, the more unnerved their masters and mistresses became, and servant fears were palpable. In *Aurora Floyd* the Victorian home was seen as a war zone. "Your servants listen at your doors," wrote Mary Braddon, "and repeat your spiteful speeches in the kitchen, and watch you while they wait at table, and understand every sarcasm, every innuendo, every look, as well as those at whom the cruel glances and the stinging words are aimed. They understand your sulky silence, your studied and over-acted politeness. The most polished form your hate and anger can take is as transparent to these household spies as if you threw knives at each other, or pelted your enemy with the side-dishes and vegetables, after the fashion of disputants in a pantomime."[32]

Eventually, the upper classes found ways to staunch the flow of incriminating information. The solution was not to get rid of the servants, but to isolate them.

In the sixteenth and seventeenth centuries, servants occupied rooms that were adjacent to the individuals they served, or lingered outside their doors so as to hear requests for service. This gave them access to things they didn't need to see and hear. A solution was to install bells outside of the bedrooms so the servants could be summoned from further away. In the last half of the eighteenth century, this arrangement was further improved by installing wires between family rooms and the servants' area, which could now be in the basement or other distant part of the house.[33] No longer would servants need to hover.

Nor would they need to intrude upon intimate dinners. A second invention, the dumb waiter, eliminated constant interruptions by servers of food and drink. In May of 1775, James Boswell wrote to a friend that while dining with his "wife's dearest friend" they were able to flirt "with unreserved freedom" because a dumb waiter was in use and they "had nothing to fear." In 1784 Mary Hamilton dined with her cousin at a friend's house. "We had dumb waiters," she wrote, "so our conversation was not under any restraint by the servants being in the room."[34]

Exhibit 31 Key escutcheon with swinging cover

These inventions were communications technologies. They made it possible to maintain the pre-existing system of domestic service, and to do so without relinquishing control over personal information. The use of bell ropes and dumb waiters thus marks a major development in the evolution of privacy *within* homes. By the mid-nineteenth century, architects had found additional ways to isolate the servants from the family—and the family from the family—including corridors, stairways, and sound-proofing.

There is one other bit of privatizing technology that, like whispering, seems to have emerged purely in the interest of thwarting eavesdroppers, and it was used in many homes, not just those that had servants. I refer to the key escutcheon, a metal plate that was used on doors that had skeleton key locks, hence keyholes that were large enough for someone to look or listen through. Escutcheons could be quite ornate, but the swinging cover—a tiny piece of metal, often teardrop in shape, used mainly on the inside of escutcheons installed on bedroom doors—was strictly functional. When hanging in place, the cover prevented outsiders from peeking through the keyhole.

So we come to a stand-off. Our not-so-distant ancestors were prepared to do what they could to ensure personal privacy, and the desire to invade it was not about to go away. But there was an alternative, a compromise of sorts. In a species with so rich an imagination as ours, not every experience has to be lived. In precisely the period that domestic technology was appearing, so were other forms of technology, ones that would enable people to acquire some of the same invasive experiences, but to do so virtually.

CHAPTER NINE

Virtual Eaves

I'm an eavesdropper. I listen in on conversations everywhere
I go ... I'm fascinated to hear little snippets of other people's
lives ... I love Facebook because it's even better than eavesdropping on people's conversations. You get to be part of
people's lives and know what's happening with them from
the mundane, to the bizarre, to the dramatic. And you can
insert yourself into the conversation, unlike when you're
eavesdropping!   Tara Mahady, age 20

Y EARS ago Richard Dawkins pointed out that if Nature
builds something, it will get used, even if it is no longer
beneficial or is counter-productive.[1] Like a battery that, as
advertised, "keeps on going and going," biological drives persistently look for ways to express themselves. When it was no longer
necessary to police their neighborhoods, people kept policing them
anyway. When it was no longer necessary to vet strangers, people
kept looking for cracks in human personas. People kept their eyes
and ears open, they told themselves, because it was only prudent to
do so. Lives worked better when they knew what others, including
social and business competitors, were planning and doing; and they
were respected, even admired, for knowing things that others did

not. But this functional perspective overlooks something. What if tuning in to each other's lives produced no tangible results at all? Would we quit eavesdropping if it were *only* enjoyable?

We have witnessed drives to display and monitor, and to conceal and eavesdrop, across a broad range of plants, birds, fish, and mammals, including the other primates. We have also discussed the adaptive value of eavesdropping in the evolution of our own species. The human drive to control what is known about others and ourselves has remained in force, and at high levels of operation, since its emergence. In the past ten to fifteen thousand years, however, there were enormous changes in domestic and personal life, and these changes altered the ways—and the reasons—that people would peer into the private lives of others.

The changes occurred in two major waves. The first involved increases in privacy, which began with the structural kind that afforded solitude, but subsequently expanded to include social and psychological means of isolation. In earlier chapters we saw that settlements, domestic walls, and cultural sequelae modified our ancestors' ability to control and access personal information. My purpose here is to discuss the second wave—a cascade of developments that prepared human minds for the new systems of personal display.

Internet diaries

English professor Laurie McNeill has written that the personal diary, once a life-history log that was strictly private, has become a genre of choice for the "life writers" on the Internet.[2] These "writers" are ordinary people who, before the emergence of the new modalities, had few if any ways to bring their stories to an audience of millions.[3] One diarist wrote that what she loved about online journals and diaries was "the paradoxical combination of *complete anonymity* and a *startling level of intimacy*."[4]

Life-readers on the Internet seem to love opportunities to sample the confessions of strangers, but McNeill was not all that charmed by the experience. "I've learned too much I didn't need to know about too many people's everyday lives—lives without anything particularly extraordinary to recommend them, except the diarists' own sense of importance and relevance," she wrote. "Some journals make me feel guilty, as if I have been looking at texts I should not be reading, that are too personal and not intended for me to see. I 'lurk' on diary sites." As a researcher, McNeill knew that she was not the intended audience for this material, nor did she have anything in common with the writers. "Consequently," she confessed, "I felt as if I was an eavesdropper...not a welcomed participant."[5]

One of the electronic diary systems, Facebook, began in 2004 as a social network site. It now has at least 400 million members, and has daily site visits that number in the *billions*. Each member posts personal material on a "wall" and sets up links with "friends." Having spent some time reading the interactions among these friends, one Facebook user wrote, "it's even better than eavesdropping on people's conversations."

Two years after the launch of Facebook another life-writing system began. It was twitter, a social networking and "micro-blogging" system that enables users to send messages and read the "tweets" of others. Tweets are short (140-character) comments about some aspect of the twitterers' lives—famously, what they had for breakfast that morning. Senders can elect to restrict transmission to those in their circle of friends or allow access to anyone. What makes twitter interesting to eavesdroppers is that each member has a number of approved followers, and these individuals can *lurk*, that is, can monitor each other's "tweets," as if listening to a large group conversation with perfect intelligibility and no interruptions. Like an eavesdropper, they can choose merely to "listen" and remain silent.

The humans that lived fifteen thousand years ago were no less human than we. But their brains, like ours, were outfitted with mechanisms that were preconfigured to take the perspectives of others. If they had stumbled across computers or cell phones they could not have guessed their intended uses. Nothing in their life experiences would have prepared them for twitter. But something happened—quite a few things, in fact—that helped to ready us, their descendants, for what was to come.

Cultural adaptations

The new biographical systems that seemed to burst on the scene overnight are actually rooted in a number of ancient developments. The first involved a reduction in direct perceptual experience. Walls and population increases made it necessary to take in information about others when they were physically absent, relying on the representations—the gossip—of intermediaries. The advent of widespread literacy and new forms of creativity made it possible to appraise the moods, sentiments, and subtle behaviors of others in complete solitude. In time there were letters, diaries, biographies, and novels, all of which offered intimate experience to others, known or unknown to the author, who would sample that experience at later times and different places, and interpret it from a perspective provided by a wholly different culture. These new modalities altered the physical and psychological relationship of humans-in-interaction and, in doing so, boosted the role of imagery and imagination.

Passing almost unnoticed was a change in the *functions* of perceptual exploration. Where observation had been, and continued to be, carried out directly, individuals remained concerned with information that might help them to ward off or solve environmental problems. With a tilt toward mediated experience, however, the subject matter often was individuals known only to one of the parties; and in literature there was a shift of focus to beings that were *not even real*. If there was no need to keep track of these *fictitious beings*, the motive for an increasing share of this sort of *virtual eavesdropping* would have to be found elsewhere.

When eavesdropping was stripped of its ultimate and objective functions, it could now be seen, with unprecedented clarity, that eavesdroppers were exercising an evolved disposition, and doing so on a proximate motive, an incentive that involved little more than a pleasurable sensation. This, by definition, was psychological. In their attention to beings that were constructed and not real, eavesdroppers were drawn to activities, frequently, that were *merely intimate*. It was finally possible to view eavesdropping as an act that was functional in some new and more internal way, a way that could be seen as purely hedonic.

These trends continued and intensified with the advent of photography and the printed media, including gossip columns and glossy photo magazines; and of telephones, films, radio, and television, including soap operas, talk shows, and reality TV.

If unintelligible to our ancestors, alphabets and computers are now considered good ways to display and sample intimate behavior—*virtually*. Not that this poses a challenge to human beings. Purely by living in groups, individuals must regularly infer the mental states of others, and act *as though* their inferences are correct. Studies of brain and other physiological functions indicate that real and virtual experience recruit or precipitate similar neural and hormonal activity. But how is it that human minds were conditioned to seek and interpret virtual experience *through the media*? How did the trend that led us to Internet diaries begin?

Autobiography then

"The present age," wrote Samuel Johnson in 1753, "may be styled with great propriety *The Age of Authors*; for, perhaps, there was never a time, in which men of all degrees of ability, of every kind of education, of every profession and employment, were posting with ardour so general to the press."[6] Many of these "postings" were personal diaries. In the eighteenth century, record numbers of French and English citizens began to keep personal diaries. Many of these, like the diaries maintained by Samuel Pepys in the 1660s, were intended to be private but were later published by others. Some, like James Lackington's *Memoirs of the First Forty-Five Years*, which appeared in 1791, were published by the authors themselves.

The appearance of personal diaries is thought to reflect a growing need for individuals to make sense of their lives, and in a time of increasing individuation, a belief that one's own experiences were significant in some way. Such diaries, it was hoped, would have meaning for others, but some were mainly entertaining. In 1830 a series of autobiographies appeared in a special edition entitled *Autobiography; a Collection of the Most Instructive and Amusing Lives Ever Published*.

Many personal diaries came with locks and keys, and the material entered therein was surely too intimate for the eyes of others. In her book on the use of diaries to create self in seventeenth-century England, Brigitte Glaser concludes that life history writing paved the way for the novel, inasmuch as writers in both forms tread the boundaries between fact and fiction.[7] I believe that the structure and focus of novels, and the characteristics of their readers, can tell us a great deal about eavesdropping, particularly the category of eavesdropping that focuses on intimate experience.

Pamela *and the romance novel*

Intimate scenes, especially ones that included sex and adultery, have featured prominently in novels since the inception of the genre. In 1740 Samuel Richardson published a novel featuring Pamela Andrews, a fifteen-year-old waiting-maid to a woman referred to only as "Lady B." The story is epistolary, much of it told through letters that Pamela writes to her father or mother, some of it through a journal or diary that she kept. When Lady B dies, Pamela, though virtuous and virginal, is beset first by Mr. B's son, then other men. Each time, through her own wits, she narrowly escapes moral disaster. Eventually Mr. B begins to pursue Pamela as well. Though concerned about the social distance between them, he eventually casts misgivings aside and marries his servant.

When *Pamela* hit the bookshops, it caused a sensation. In the first year there were five printings and total sales of approximately 20,000 copies. But *Pamela* also inspired a riot of unauthorized appropriations, begat a series of like-structured novels, and launched a whole new industry.[8] Romance novels were in, and they stayed in. In the early nineteenth century the vast majority of the books in commercial lending libraries were romance novels.

In epistolary novels, readers have the experience, as John Vernon pointed out, of reading someone else's mail. "If novels tell secrets," he wrote, "what else is a reader but a kind of eavesdropper?"[9] "Richardson's work demands that the reader continually be the voyeur," wrote Lennard Davis. Reading *Pamela*, he said, is not different from "staring through the keyhole...Bared bosoms, stolen kisses, and supine, helpless figures are the essence of Richardson's eroticism, and the reader of the work is placed within the text as voyeur."[10]

Like eavesdropping, novels once had an illicit quality. They featured rogues and courtesans that readers were unlikely to encounter in genteel life. In the eighteenth century, the prime ingredient of romance novels was bodice-ripping sex. A century later simple sex was no longer sufficient. People wanted adultery.

And they got it. If novels needed to address issues that intrigued prospective consumers, adultery was surely the way to go. The public sensorium was already attuned to it. In fact, many of the nineteenth-century novels that were canonized as *great*, wrote Tony Tanner in *Adultery in the Novel*, were built on adultery.

Exhibit 32 *Forbidden Books*, Alexander Rossi, 1897

Without it, he wrote, "the history of the novel would, indeed, have been very different—and much poorer."[11]

The desire to sample these illicit worlds was highlighted in several paintings depicting the pleasures of novel-reading. Titles such as *Forbidden Books* and *Forbidden Fruit* reinforce the impression that, for the educated classes at least, the novel was "clandestine reading." In one painting, an older woman eavesdrops on the romance readers, evidently to make sure their passions were not being dangerously inflamed.

If novel-reading shares properties with eavesdropping, there are other similarities between these means of accessing the intimate experiences of strangers. The novels themselves made frequent use of eavesdropping. Almost every novel by Balzac, Dickens, and Hardy contains at least one bout of eavesdropping, as did novels by Austen and Proust. Since readers would naturally take the eavesdroppers' perspective, and look at everything through their eyes, this made it easier for authors to portray the other characters as they would normally be in private—unguarded, unvarnished, and vulnerable.

Gender

As in intimate eavesdropping, the authors and readers of novels were, and still are, unevenly divided between the sexes. Relative to other books, the writers were disproportionately female, even if female novelists sometimes used male pen names in the belief that this would give them a commercial advantage. Male authors of romance novels tended to keep their authorship quiet. As for the readership, women predominated here, too, even though early eighteenth-century surveys revealed a lower literacy rate in women. Women were drawn to intimate portrayals of characters and detailed accounts of intimate relationships.[12] As we saw previously, these things have long concerned women, whose capacity to survive was historically tied to the quality and durability of marital relationships. Men enjoyed reading about these things too, but many were embarrassed to be "caught" reading romance novels. Today, according to literature professor Kay Mussell, romance novels "are with few exceptions written by women, read by women, and published for women."[13]

Most romance novels are written to a formula, one that, according to feminist scholar Tania Modleski, is invariant. In every book a young and innocent woman, of modest means, becomes involved with a man who is invariably handsome, strong, experienced, powerful, and wealthy, and usually about ten to fifteen years older. Although this "hero" is initially superior and arrogant, he falls in love with the woman and submits to her control. The heroine acquires power through her lover, and the story ends happily.[14]

Romance novels must be doing something right. One imprint, Harlequin, publishes over five hundred new titles every month, in twenty-five languages. The reason for their popularity is that romance novels offer images that appeal to evolved mechanisms. When women are asked what should *never* be included in a romance novel, their most frequent responses are promiscuity, a sad ending, rape, physical torture, and a weak hero—things that they would be expected to fear or avoid in real life. When asked *what they like to see in a hero*, their leading responses are intelligence, tenderness, a sense of humor, strength, and protectiveness. Since these are the qualities they seek in real-life partners, romance novels have been called "compensatory fiction."[15]

Novel reactions

In real life, people are able to control access to illicit scenes—that is the purpose of walls and keyhole covers. In novels, the authors exercise this control. But the scenes described in novels, if they had a liminal quality about them, were considered too accessible to proper young women. Critics worried about the ability of readers to distinguish fictive worlds from real ones. When they had finished reading a romance novel, wrote Jayne Ann Krentz, it was feared that, "the young women may not be able to step back out of the fantasy."[16]

Men had their own concerns. A pervasive element in romance novels is *female empowerment*. The woman always wins. By virtue of the heroine's courage, intelligence, and gentleness, wrote Krentz, she is able to bring "the most dangerous creature on earth, the human male, *to his knees*." She tames the hero, and forces him to acknowledge her power.[17] Romance novels can thus be seen as *subversive*, for they portray, and could be interpreted as recommending, a complete reversal of the power structure of patriarchal societies.

If men feared gossip and scolding, they were no less unnerved by romance novels. In his *Physiology of Marriage*, published in 1829, Balzac wrote that men should give their wives more things to do if they showed an affinity for novels. "To leave a woman free to read such books as the bent of her mind would lead her to choose," he wrote, "is to drop a spark in a gunroom. Nay, it is worse than that, it is *to teach your wife how to do without you*, to live in an imaginary world, a paradise. For what do women read? Works relating to the passions, Jean-Jacques' *Confessions*, novels, and all things that are likely powerfully to *agitate their feelings.*" Balzac went on to explain:

> In reading plays and novels, the woman, being a creature far more susceptible to loftier feelings than we are, must experience *the most intoxicating ecstasies*. She creates around her an ideal existence that makes everything else look pale; it is not long before she tries to realize this voluptuous life, and convey its magic into her actual life. Almost involuntarily she passes from the spirit to the letter, and from the letter to the senses.[18]

Balzac may have been writing in a semi-humorous vein, but there was serious concern among others, including parents, who were attempting to rear their daughters to be virtuous.

The soaps

Several writers have pointed to strong similarities between romance novels and soap operas.[19] Mary Ellen Brown described the common features: the centrality and power of female characters; the portrayal of male characters as sensitive; an emphasis on intimate conversation which carries the essence of the story; a focus on intimate relationships; and use of the home as the setting.[20]

It is clear from Brown's description that soaps appeal unusually to women. Indeed, they are the only type of national television drama that specifically targets females.[21] In the early 1980s the audience for network television soap operas in America included *two-thirds of all women living in homes with a TV.*[22] Only one in ten viewers was male.

It is easy to think of reasons why soaps' emphasis on romance would appeal to women viewers. The stories, like women's diaries, focus on love, romance, childbearing, health, manners, and morality.[23] Danielle Blumenthal suggested that women watch the soaps as a means of addressing their own romantic needs. Soap operas "pay a great deal of attention to the need to explore, express, and resolve all varieties of human emotion, romantic or otherwise," she wrote. "This is the true source of their appeal to women."[24]

Women do not just catch the odd soap opera when they can; they have favorite soaps, and view them *loyally*. Some have watched the same soap for their entire lives. The television soap opera *Love of Life* was aired from 1952 to 1980. John Keeler, writing in the *New York Times*, expressed wonder about the sort of "unsated curiosity" that could keep a single story going five days a week for 28 years.[25] Little did he know that *Guiding Light*, a sister program that took to the radio waves in 1937, would still be running on TV over seventy years later. But the soaps are not just popular in America. They also command considerable followings places as diverse as Australia, Cyprus, Britain, Pakistan, Canada, Mexico, Ireland, and Greece. Latin American soap operas, called *telenovas*, are the most popular genre of television program in the world, having a worldwide audience of at least *two billion*.

Biographies

In novels and soaps, the focus is on people that never existed and never will. But we are also drawn to the inner sanctums of real lives. In the late seventeenth century, John Aubrey published *Brief Lives*, a series of short biographies of over four hundred of his famous or unusual English countrymen.[26] Aubrey was clearly an eccentric, and there were few authors who could match his zeal for portraiture. But the desire for personal information about famous people was intense. In the early nineteenth century, American publishers printed hundreds of biographies. In an article in the *Yale Literary Magazine* in June, 1845, a writer said, "Biography has obtained within the last half century a degree of attention and importance it never before enjoyed. Lives of men eminent in art, distinguished for achievements, or notorious for misfortunes or wickedness, have, during this period, been more than quadrupled . . . Biography is the rage of the day."

Readers were hoping for some of the same things that eavesdroppers want. When they first appeared, biographies were the only way, except for eavesdropping and gossip, that ordinary people could learn about the private lives of public figures and strangers. Inside those lives, it was suspected, were the behaviors that facilitated success. If they knew what these behaviors were, readers could emulate them, and more easily ascend the economic ladder. Biographies, according to Scott Casper, were thus treated as "middle-class handbooks."[27]

If private lives conceal the secrets to success, readers would surely want access to this material. In 1816 a critic complained that readers were forced to "look, in vain, for those little foibles and weaknesses, which are inseparably attached to the nature of man." "We must follow him to his closet," the critic advised, "we must see him, in the bosom of his family; we must know, whether he acts the hero to his valet de chambre; it is in these situations only, that we can find the motives, that influence his actions."[28]

Writers' tendency to draw a veil over such private dramas went uncorrected, and the criticism of sanitized biographies continued. In 1827 the *American Quarterly Review* summed up the shortcomings of much American biography. "Your modern biographer," the *Review* said, "rarely leads you into the private lodgings of the hero—never places you before the poor reasonable animal, as naked as nature made him; but represents him uniformly as a demi-god." In the middle of the nineteenth century, Casper wrote, a growing number of critics was condemning "the didactic tendencies to whitewash flaws and make subjects into cookie-cutter models of specific virtues."[29]

Autobiographies now

Although diaries initially featured the public lives of men, they took a turn toward private life in the nineteenth century. In *A Day at a Time*, Margo Culley writes that the trend toward greater privacy was accompanied by an increase in self-examination, and it is around this time that women became more active in diary and journal writing than men. Their chosen topics were clearly intimate, from pregnancy and mothering to care giving and homemaking, and these were written in a more subjective, sentimental, and self-analytical style than comparable works by men.[30]

A spur was provided by Marie Bashkirtseff, a young Russian painter whose passionately self-oriented diaries were written in the 1880s. When these were translated into English, American women seemed to feel that they, too, could begin to stray from their largely familial orientation. At the turn of the century, a nineteen-year-old woman from Butte, Montana—still some decades ahead of her time—opened her diary with:

> I of womankind and of nineteen years, will now begin to set down
> as full and frank a Portrayal as I am able of myself, Mary MacLane,
> for whom the world contains not a parallel.
> I am convinced of this, for I am odd.
> I am distinctly original innately and in development.
> I have in me a quite unusual intensity of life.
> I can feel.
> I have a marvelous capacity for misery and for happiness.
> I am broad-minded.
> I am a genius.

Though Mary eventually moved on to other sentence structures, her diary shows a continuing fondness for the first person singular pronoun.[31]

Nicholas Humphrey has written that a key characteristic of human consciousness—the essential impenetrability of human thought—causes individuals to feel separate from each other. As a *species*, we humans are considered intensely social, so intent are we to find out what is in the minds of others. But as *individuals*, he wrote, our unavoidably separate consciousnesses make us "exceptionally lonely." In *The Pursuit of Happiness* David Myers wrote, "When a person realizes he has been deeply heard, his eyes moisten. I think in some real sense he is weeping for joy. It is as though he were saying, 'Thank God, somebody heard me. Someone knows what it's like to be me.' "[32]

Autobiography gave people a chance to do something about this—to say: look at me, understand me—and the new life-writers have availed themselves of this opportunity. The proliferation of life-writing spaces on the Internet, wrote Laurie McNeill, marks an equally unprecedented interest in the lives of ordinary individuals who, before the Internet, had few opportunities to publish their life stories on such a wide scale."[33]

Historically, ordinary people had public lives but very little privacy, and few wrote biographies. Now, ordinary people spend much of their time in private but are relatively less exposed to friends and neighbors. Perhaps this is why they feel a need to post tiny fragments about their lives online.

When behavior persistently occurs in the absence of discernible benefits, we see, with unusual clarity, the possibility that it may be due to a once-adaptive disposition that is still "in there." When people spend large amounts of time perusing the personal material on electronic diaries, some of which was composed by strangers or intended for other eyes, they do so not to minimize danger or acquire needed resources. They surf these diaries—and read romance novels—for a different reason, one that is self-evidently psychological. When all of the practical possibilities have been filtered out, the one thing that remains, the irreducible core, is the drive to access and savor the intimate experiences of others—preferably by theft.

CHAPTER TEN

Intimacy by Theft

He seeks to catch the other at an unguarded and intimate
moment, a moment when the other will be naked and
available to his concealed gaze . . . He wishes to experience
from the outside another's life as it is lived from the inside.

Edgar Dryden

W E have seen many reasons for eavesdropping, from
idle curiosity to concerns about personal or public
safety and maintenance of moral values. Here we
return to examine what, in modernity, may be the most important
motive. It is also the most mysterious, both because mystery is
created, enjoyed, and resolved by those who share intimate experience with others; and because the use of one mind to access
another is a process that, itself, works in mysterious ways.

In the previous chapter we were reminded by many things—
the street scene in *Paris, A Rainy Day*, the sheer number and
popularity of Parisian *physiologies*, and new forms of architectural
individuation—that, in most societies, every person has his own
life, with his own ideas, plans, and goals. Collectively we are, as
English psychologist Nicholas Humphrey has written, "a society of
selves."[1]

The minds of others *are* different from our own. We accept this because we, *as humans*, have consciousness—an awareness of our own mental activity—*paired with* what is commonly called a "theory of other minds," a conceptual awareness that others have mental activity too. Once this other-minds concept is activated, early in childhood, it continuously reminds us—and will keep doing so as long as we live—that others know, think, and feel things that may or may not correspond to our own knowledge, thoughts, and feelings.

Philosophers refer to these things as "qualia," a term my dictionary defines as "the internal and subjective component of sense perceptions, arising from stimulation of the senses by phenomena." Qualia are set up when we sense and interpret specific aspects of the environment. Examples include the taste of wine and the color of the sky at day's end. We and others sip the same wine and gaze together at the setting sun, but our responses are subjective, which makes our qualia different.[2]

Taken together, consciousness and the other-minds concept alert us to the possibility of *discrepancies* between other minds and our own, without actually telling us what they are. Sensing-without-understanding fuels the quest to explore, from the outside, the contents of minds that are not completely intelligible to their "owners." It is because we regularly exercise these gap-narrowing skills, according to Nicholas Humphrey, that we humans get along with each other as well as we do.

Empathy

These processes that pull together semi-isolated selves share properties with empathy. Normally we think of empathy as the disposition to help people who are suffering, and to feel what they are feeling. But it was pointed out many years ago that empathy has a *cognitive* component too. Except for emotions that are directly provoked by a perception, such as the sight or sound of a person suffering, there is usually a role for *understanding* that others are experiencing *something*, and knowing what that is.[3] Viewed in this light, it is possible to see empathic responding, to some degree, as a *product* of the fact that humans are more or less continuously scanning and reading each other.

That we do so is attested by the number of processes that are automatically set in motion by these scans. For example, it has long been known that people in groups tend spontaneously to adopt a rhythm, and to move in synchrony with each other, and that people in dyadic arrangements additionally tend to pick up, without intending to, a range of peculiarities of voice, speech, and body language. The relevant processes, convergence and contagion, ensure a measure of social coordination, their reliability virtually guaranteed by the fact that they operate unconsciously. But people around the world also take special delight in *perfecting* their capacity to coordinate temporally and substantively. These celebrations of coordination include chorus kick lines, barbershop quartets, and marching bands.[4] When sought and practiced as a goal, synchronicity may be responsible for even greater degrees of other-comprehension and unity. Indeed, it appears that the human brain has some highly specialized cells (mirror neurons) that are responsible for just such effects.[5]

If an adaptive species such as ours is outfitted with social sensors, we must also have the possibility of doing something with the input that they provide, and the challenge of understanding other minds is one that we *welcome*. Returning home from a dinner party, one finds oneself analyzing the behavior of the other guests, much as one relives a film, dissecting the plot and reviewing the performances. The degree of functionality is different in films and real life, but we approach the analyses with similar levels of enthusiasm.

Our goal, of course, is to relate all of this to our own lives. Here, the deck might seem to be stacked against us. "There are no wormholes between conscious minds," Humphrey has written.

"Really there are not." But, he added, this lack of connections "does not stop people avidly searching for them."[6] To the contrary, the absence of "wormholes" is the source of our Asmodean dispositions. We lack the magical powers of limping demons, but we can *do things* to establish connectivity. This is what creates the chase scenes in human life, the opportunities to use our interpretive systems for the things they were designed to do. Given half a chance, we know we will make a great deal of headway with these challenges. When the gaps are narrowed, we know that the narrowing is due to something that we did, to the skillful ways that we learned to apply our psychological capacities.

Of course we do not throw everything we've got at these human mysteries. Every investigation is guided by a theory. The kind I have in mind is what some lawyers call a "theory of the case." We direct our attention to particular things based on our sense of what is going on, or what *could be* going on. Eavesdropping on the thoughts and feelings of others is not just a matter of interpreting what we see and hear, but selectively looking and listening for, and to, particular elements that are embedded in the behaviors of others. In doing so, we are never unaware of what would make a compelling narrative for us, and for our friends.

We are drawn by mystery, and try to resolve it, but we do so half hoping that when the investigation is over, some mystery will remain; and to make sure that some does, we stand ready to envisage additional possibilities. The possible existence of an undiscovered "something" is intriguing. Did you: see the expression on her face when you asked ... notice that he looked away when you said ... sense their surprise when you tried to explain ...?

This is not to deny our relief, and occasional joy, at the discovery of common ground. But I think we usually do not want to understand *everything* about *everyone*—unless, perhaps, we are totally dependent on them. Do we want everyone in our social circle to be *exactly* like us; to associate only with individuals who can finish our sentences, and we theirs? Or do we prefer the company, at least part of the time, of people whose minds have been in places that ours have never gone?

The experience of understanding others *partially,* but *not completely,* is a boundary experience, like several others that we will see. This is largely responsible for the allure of eavesdropping.

Perceptual trespassing

Like many other animal species, we humans are territorial. If people walk onto our property, our "zone of immunity," to reuse French historian Georges Duby's phrase, we are entitled to react defensively. Studies of proxemics indicate that people can be extraordinarily unnerved if a stranger, or mere acquaintance, stands a few inches closer than he should. What if someone enters our *mental territory,* a region that was designed by nature, and molded by culture, to be exclusively our own? What if they situate themselves too close to the face of our private self?

Many people fear that their privacy might be breached, and this feeling undergirds, and perhaps reflects, the laws that were passed to forbid such violations. What is less obvious is *why* people are frightened. Locating the source may help us to isolate the experience of the intruder.

A brief look at some legal history will be helpful. In a landmark article that appeared in the *Harvard Law Review* in 1890, Richard Warren and his law partner, Louis Brandeis, argued that every citizen has a "right to privacy." "The common law," they wrote, "secures to each individual the right of determining, ordinarily, to what extent his thoughts, sentiments, and emotions shall be communicated to others."[7] Their concern in the late nineteenth century was with the press, as it would now be with a broader range of media.

There were at least two reasons for the article. For some years a general trend had been building, away from strictly physical definitions of a person and toward more psychological interpretations. Though Warren and Brandeis made repeated references to traditional laws against *trespassing*, that is, laws that criminalized "physical interference with life and property," they understood that cultural changes justified new concerns about violations of "man's spiritual nature, of his feelings and his intellect."[8] It was becoming clear, they thought, that only a fraction of life's pleasures lay in physical things. More could be found in thoughts, emotions, and sensations, and these were demanding legal recognition.[9] Just two years before they argued their case for a right to privacy a respected jurist, Thomas Cooley, alluded to a growing recognition of the "right of each individual *to be let alone.*"[10]

Richard Warren also had personal reasons to feel strongly about the right of private individuals to be let alone. He was not being afforded this privilege himself. In January of 1883 Warren married Mabel Bayard, daughter of a U.S. senator, and began an elegant style of life in the Back Bay section of Boston. News of his social activities regularly appeared in the *Saturday Evening Gazette.* A Boston "blueblood," Warren may have been irritated by this tendency of the press to expose the activities of the socially prominent. In June of 1890 the *Gazette* published a short item indicating that the Warren home had been transformed into a "veritable flower bower" for a breakfast celebrating the wedding of Warren's cousin. Six months later his article with Louis Brandeis was published.

Stalking intimacy

One can violate the personal space of another, purely as a proxemic matter—by staring, standing too close, or displaying other physically dominant behaviors—without actually trespassing upon a private place. In recent years, individuals who might have been arrested for eavesdropping in previous centuries have been charged with *stalking.*

Stalking is a "modern" crime in the sense that there were no laws against it until the 1990s. In most cases of stalking, the perpetrator physically follows the victim. That's because the latter, usually a female, is on the move. The stalker's desire is to watch—to follow his victim *perceptually*. He usually follows his prey, stands outside her home and stares, or otherwise physically intrudes on her zone of privacy, even if in public. For this reason, surveillance is specifically identified in most of the state laws against stalking.

Research conducted by a California professor of criminal justice, Doris Hall, found that eighty-four percent of the stalks include surveillance of the home.[11] That's four percent more than were guilty of following, the hallmark of stalking. "Peeping Toms," according to two English barristers, Paul Infield and Graham Platford, "have all the attributes of the stalker who loiters."[12] A recent bulletin in America warned potential stalking victims to "trim the bushes beside your home."

Just as over eighty percent of the ancient under-the-eaves type of eavesdropping was committed by men, modern stalking is also dominated by men. The percentage of stalking due to males varies, depending on the study, from eighty-four to eighty-seven percent. A similar majority of stalking *victims*—from seventy-eight to eighty-three percent—are female.[13]

Over seventy percent of male stalkers are considered "intimacy seekers."[14] Intimacy seekers, like a related class—incompetent suitors—are among the most numerous and persistent of all male stalkers. "Both groups," according to Paul Mullen and his associates, "are attempting to establish a relationship with the object of their unwanted attentions."[15] The prime motivation of intimacy seekers is "to enable their love to find expression in an intimate relationship." Most of these individuals are shy, live a solitary and lonely life, and have consistently failed in intimate relationships.[16]

Liminality

The crime in intimate following, and in perceptual trespassing, derives its meaning from the concept of personal territory or thresholds. It was predictable that the monitoring of private behavior would come to be seen as a transgression of the victim's personal boundaries. The French philosopher Maurice Merleau-Ponty suggested that perceiving a place was equivalent, on some level, to actually being in that place. To illustrate this, he suggested that his readers close their eyes and then open them again. "Do you have the impression that you are staring out upon the world," he asked, "as though you were looking through the windows of your unlit house, having opened the shutters? Far from it," he wrote, "you are out there yourself, shamelessly mingling with all you see."[17]

In a book on eavesdropping in the novel, Ann Gaylin wrote that the essence of eavesdropping, the property responsible for its special allure, is that it "represents *liminality*." Eavesdroppers straddle two worlds. Indeed, we would not be as acutely aware of the boundaries between public and private if there were no people who sought to violate them.[18]

Gaylin's reference to liminality was perceptive. Privacy is not about *being* alone, or in any other physical or social context. It is about the desire to maintain unbreachable barricades around our *life*. Foremost, here, is a psychological life, one that is truly and completely our own. Legal definitions of privacy began to reflect a general desire to block unwarranted forays into psychological territory. Law professor Anita Allen argued that "personal privacy is a condition of inaccessibility of the *person*," including any mental states that others might be able to sense. To say that a person is private, she wrote, is to say that his "*conduct, thought, belief, or emotion*" are beyond the sensory range of others.[19]

Allen was not alone in stressing the territoriality of thought and feeling. "The *boundary* between what we *reveal* and what we do not," wrote philosopher Thomas Nagel, "and some control over that *boundary*, are among the most important attributes of our humanity." Nagel wrote that inner life would be impossible if our thoughts, feelings, and private behaviors were exposed to public view. "The division of the self protects the limited public space from unmanageable *encroachment* and the unruly inner life from excessive inhibition."[20]

If laws protected privacy, then penalties for breaking these laws would need to be meted out. Decisions would have to be made about the severity of violations, the extent of damages. In the 1960s and 1970s, several theorists identified an important condition of life that would be compromised if privacy were infringed—a condition that is now familiar to us here. It was intimacy.

Intimacy

The question was, how to define it, not just semantically, but in a way that could be used in a courtroom. A respected jurist, Charles Fried, was among the first to give it a try. In his definition, intimacy was "the sharing of information about one's actions, beliefs, or emotions which one does not share with all, and which one has the right not to share with anyone."[21] Philosopher Jeffrey Reiman objected to elements of Fried's definition, claiming that intimate relationships involve a "reciprocal desire to share present and future intense and important experiences together, not merely to swap information."[22] Julie Innes seemed to agree, for she argued that intimacy had less to do with any acts and activities than the participants' motivation to engage in them. Where intimacy is involved, the motivation, she suggested, will be "love, liking, or care."[23]

All of these definitions stress intimate *relationships*, but there is no reason why intimacy should be defined in exclusively social terms. Humans also have a desire to relate to themselves, and a need to do so. This has less to do with observable acts and activities than opportunities to be alone with one's feelings and thoughts. Thomas Nagel's definition of intimacy is salient here. Intimacy, he wrote, "is the situation where the *interior of the self* is most exposed."[24]

What makes the interior of a person so special, so in need of protection against the senses of others? When jailed for crimes uncovered by the Whitewater investigation in the late 1990s, Associate Attorney General Webster Hubbell, like other prisoners, involuntarily relinquished control of certain privacies. Journalists obtained transcripts of his personal telephone conversations with Mrs. Hubbell. In one transcript, she discusses her plans for dinner, remarking that the children wanted meatloaf. Hubbell reminds his wife that meatloaf is not among his favorite foods. "Have it before I get home," he tells his wife. "I just don't like meatloaf—O.K.?" His wife, in mock sympathy, responds "Poor Webby."

He doesn't like meatloaf. She calls him "Webby." These are the kinds of things that really hurt when they become public, and the hurt is hard to describe. When The *Washington Post* published details of his personal diary, former U.S. Senator Robert Packwood complained that the most painful revelations were not the "lewd and foolish" acts that had been alleged and about which the public wanted to know. They were his favorite recipe for baked apples, preferred local supermarket, and fondness for the music of Edvard Grieg. Packwood said these irrelevant disclosures left him "feeling violated."

These kinds of revelations are reminiscent of reactions to domestic burglaries. Typically, the victims of these break-ins comment that even if *nothing was taken* they experience the distress that comes from knowing that things normally seen only by them were briefly in the perceptual possession, and may persist in the memory, of persons unknown. In research carried out in France, victims said they were particularly bothered by burglars looking into containers that were usually kept closed—boxes, safes, drawers, and cupboards. A thirty-five-year-old man told interviewers that burglars had "seen things which belong to us, which are, if you like, our little secrets." A woman of the same age said that her apartment "had been visited in all its nooks and crannies and really in the most private of places." What bothered her the most, she said, was that the burglars had seen her cosmetics.[25]

There are gendered influences here, as there are throughout the study of human intimacy. In evaluations of the meaning assigned to domestic objects, it has been consistently found that women, more than men, place a high value on photographs, mementoes, souvenirs, and other items that symbolize emotional relationships.[26]

We saw in Chapter 3 that some groups of hunter-gatherers store ordinary things, for example, cooking utensils and extra clothing, *in* their huts, but do intimate things, such as sleeping, *in front* of them. Now, in ironic reversal, we keep our intimate things inside our homes and display our ordinary behaviors outside of them. As a consequence, we are horrified at the thought that thieves might see *our things*, for this would tell them more about who we are, as we think of ourselves, than an *actual view of us* would.

It has long been known that humans have anthropomorphic dispositions—we tend to endow animals and objects with human qualities—but we also look for evidence of intimate qualities where they may not exist. A century ago, Leslie Stephen wrote about the "organic" approach to literature. When people read organically, Stephen said, they struggle to acquaint themselves with the author, even where the work is not autobiographical or the topic approached from a personal perspective. "The ultimate source of pleasure derivable from all art," on Stephen's view, "is that it brings you into communication with the artist. What you really love in the picture or the poem is the painter or poet."[27]

The extent of this would be easy to underestimate. When viewers look *at* a landscape painting, they search *for* personal messages that may be embedded in the hues and brush strokes. "His verve and feeling for the dramatic are of a piece with his temperament," wrote J. P. Hodin in reference to Charles François Daubigny. "All are there to be read in his nervous and clamant brushwork." Van Gogh's work, Hodin continued, "is a personal expression of utmost intensity. Its rhythm is that of heartbeats which become ever wilder as his mortal sickness grows upon him."[28]

Most of us are naturally quite good at these inferences. It is the rare person, one who lacks an *intimate mind*, that is not. This exceptional individual, proving the rule, may at some point in his life be diagnosed with a condition that is an obstacle to intimacy. One such condition is Asperger's syndrome, a mild form of autism that occurs disproportionately in males.

Liminal intimacy

The desire to observe the unaware, who cannot protect or modify their images, is a product of human evolution, but what is the nature of the psychological experience? What is it that the observer senses or feels? What can be said about the "liminal" experience for the observer? Is it the experience of operating *near* a boundary, or *crossing* it, or *being on the other side of it*? The art historian David Freedberg wrote that sexuality does not work if it is blatant. In such cases, "there is none of the frisson, the tension, or the still stronger arousal that arises from a sense of the image being on the *borderline* of what is art... and what is not art." If it is art, he wrote, "it transgresses—just—the limits of the admissible and the tolerable. This *borderline* position is what gives so many of these images their sexual potential."[29]

We normal human eavesdroppers are particularly drawn to the partially open door, the dimly lit room, the whispered confession. Even as they seek to thwart, they invite, and if a border is crossed, reward. In her book *On Photography*, Susan Sontag wrote, "There is something on people's faces when they don't know they are being observed that never appears when they do."[30] To Sartre, the problem with looking *visibly* is that it attracts a look in return. When that happens, he said, one loses the appearance of the eyes. "It is never when eyes are looking at you that you can find them beautiful or ugly, that you can remark on their color," he wrote. "The Other's look hides his eyes."[31]

These are simple things, and our perceptual wants are simple, according to postmodern theorist Jean Baudrillard. The "other" need not *do anything*, he wrote. "We ask him only to *be* other, to have that minimal glimmer of otherness."[32] One sees this in

"The adventure of a photographer," a short story by Italo Calvino. The story centers on the obsession of a photographer, Antonino Paraggi, to "capture" on film a young woman named Bice. What Paraggi sought, Calvino wrote, was a *"presence that presupposed his own absence and that of others."*

Paraggi's objective was to catch Bice when she didn't know he was watching her: *"to surprise her as she was in the absence of his gaze, of any gaze."*[33] What Calvino's photographer knew was this: if Bice saw him, the threshold experience would disappear and the image would vanish. At the same moment, the observer's privileges would change as well. If the observer is seen, a new set of rules goes into effect. One of these rules is "no staring."

Street photographers

The work, and the confessions, of real photographers—especially those who have sought images of people as they really are—provide additional insights. Frequently, the objective of street photographers is to photograph people who are alone, when they are wearing no particular face. The original practitioners were naturalists, amateur ethologists, who set out to observe human animals in their natural habitat. The problem, of course, was the difficulty of remaining obscure. When photographers first took to the streets of New York, they were unable to hide their bulky cameras. What they sought was a subject that would be blind to their existence. "I felt," wrote Paul Strand, "that one could get a *quality of being* through the fact that the person did not know he was being photographed."[34] Strand got the naturalness he sought by photographing a person who was *actually* blind. In 1916, he took a picture called *Blind Woman*.

There is room for discomfort here, but this cannot be because the woman was unable to see the camera; the camera goes unnoticed by the subjects of many popular street photographs taken later. It seems more likely that it is because we sighted individuals are aware of our images and are conscious that others regularly partake of

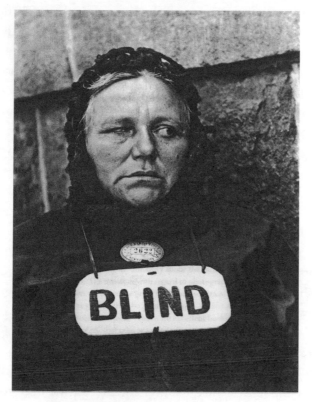

Exhibit 33 *Blind woman*, Paul Strand, 1916

them, but blind individuals may not understand that they have such a visual presence—and, therefore, that it can be "taken" from them. They may not fully appreciate that unknown others—filing through art galleries or leafing through photography books—can study these unguarded representations of their selves.

Even sighted individuals may not know that the visual image given off by their face or body is *them*. We take for granted that the person we see in the mirror is "us," but this sense of self does not exist in all primate species, nor are human infants born with it. There is an age when normally developing infants pass the "mirror recognition test." In this test, a bit of rouge is surreptitiously applied to the tip of the infant's nose. The infant is then exposed to his image in a mirror. If he attempts to rub off the rouge, which usually does not happen until about twenty-four months, it is assumed that the infant knows that the person in the mirror is *him*.[35]

The first street photographers to reach public attention were Humphrey Spender and Henri Cartier-Bresson. Spender documented the lives of ordinary English people in the 1930s and 1940s. His pictures were enormously successful, partly because, as he wrote a half-century later, he "believed obsessionally that truth would be revealed only when people were not aware of being photographed. I had to be invisible."[36] Spender's counterpart in France, Cartier-Bresson, wrote that he "prowled the streets all day... determined to '*trap*' life—to preserve life in the act of living."[37]

Perhaps the photographer most intent on capturing private moments was an American, Walker Evans. Between 1938 and 1941, when Spender and Cartier-Bresson were photographing people wherever they found them, Walker took more than six hundred pictures of people on the subways of New York. He used a camera that was concealed in his coat.[38]

Evans' photos show subway riders with their masks off. Whatever influences their countenance is known only to them, and possibly not even to them—perhaps a personal problem, or the anticipation of something they will experience when they get home. Inspecting the photographs, one is freed from the observational rules that normally apply. It is not just that the subjects are unaware of us. They also cannot see that we are inspecting or examining them.

The subway photos are liminal in more ways than one. "The subway," wrote photography historian Luc Sante, "is a neutral zone in which people are free to consider themselves invisible; time spent commuting is a hiatus from social interaction."[39] The poet Billy Collins also commented on this. In the introduction to a later book of subway photographs he wrote, "the subway is a place, but the human subjects are in transit. They are neither here nor there. These travelers often wear their 'subway face,' that look of

Exhibit 34 *Subway Passengers*, Walker Evans

self-absorption, the middle-distance stare that suggests that life has been temporarily suspended only to resume back on street level."[40]

Most of the subway riders are not doing anything. There is little in their activities that would be legally actionable, but their images tell inferencing others something about their relationships, their selves, and their lives. This is why some countries have laws that protect the unauthorized use of a person's image. In 1999 photographer Luc Delahaye was forced to publish his book, *L'Autre* ("The Other"), outside France (in England). The reason is that it contained close-up photographs of ninety ordinary French people— each taken surreptitiously by Delahaye on the Paris Metro. In France, Delahaye could have been sued for "stealing" their images.

It is no longer what people *do* in the privacy of their own *homes*— like the hoarding of meat by the Kung and the Samoans, or the adultery of English villagers living in lightly built seventeenth-century houses—but what they *experience* in the privacy of their own *minds*. To the observer, this experience is both liminal and psychological. No longer seeking information about what people *do* in private, observers ask what they are *like* in private, enjoying spectatorial experience in its own right.

In unseeing faces, the absolute separateness of individual souls becomes fully evident. The photographer Peter Peter said he thought there was something *beautiful* about the subjects in his own subway photos, a beauty that derived from their spontaneity and openness, and their honesty.[41] He felt this particularly when something about the strap-hangers gave clues to their thoughts and feelings, something he could have used to relate to them had his purpose been social.

I too believe there is something beautiful and pristine about humans in their natural monadic state. There may even be a nobility of sorts, much as there is nobility in animals in the wild, unaware that they are being watched. The subways are the natural habitat for some members of the species *Homo sapiens*. It is their wilderness. When people appear in public there are display rules to follow, and they follow them. But occasionally they forget, and when they do, we discover what is happening on the other side of the display faces. We encounter experiences that resemble our own.

Photographer Diane Arbus once remarked, "it's impossible to get out of your skin and into somebody else's." That other person's tragedy, she wrote, "is not the same as your own."[42] This may be true, but we are intent on finding the areas of commonality. For any differences we discover are likely to tell us as much about ourselves as they do about the others.

We have consciousness for a particular reason, according to Nicholas Humphrey. It evolved, he suggested, because it "makes life more worth living."[43] Those who look for intimate experience in other minds are seeking to extend the sphere of their own consciousness. Walker Evans would have approved. "Stare, pry, listen, eavesdrop," he wrote. "Die knowing something. You are not here long."[44]

Notes

Prologue

1 Wiener 1954, p. 16.

Chapter One: Passionate Spectators

1 Crawford & Gowing 2000.
2 Thurston 1987, p. 131.
3 Rupp & Wallen 2008.
4 Brown 1994, p. 131.
5 Gouge 1622, p. 156.
6 Le Sage 1707, p. 38.
7 Hawthorne 1831/1974, p. 192.
8 Dickens 1848/1987, p. 648.
9 Baudelaire 1863/1995, p. 10.
10 Bill Buford, "Thy Neighbor's Life," *The New Yorker*, January 5, 1998.
11 Haviland & Haviland 1983, p. 347.
12 Shils 1966, p. 286.
13 Miller 1983.
14 Sobel et al. 1998.
15 Frank et al. 2006.
16 Cirillo 2003.
17 Gregor 1970, p. 235.
18 Kundera 1995, p. 259.
19 Hochschild 1983.
20 Régnier-Bohler 1988, p. 331; also see Udry 2002.
21 Bearman 2005, p. 109.
22 André Breton, *Entretiens*, in Cartier-Bresson 1976.
23 Hotchkiss 1967, p. 715.
24 Benn 1971, p. 4.
25 Simmel 1906, p. 455, italics mine.
26 McConville & Shepherd 1992, p. 92.
27 "A Lady Resident" 1889, pp. 43, 44.
28 Kuper 1953, p. 14.

29 Randy Kennedy, "'Rear Window,' Brooklyn Style," *The New York Times*, October 24, 2004.
30 Silber 1971, p. 228.
31 Goffman 1958.
32 Kaya & Erkíp 1999.
33 Tickner 2003, p. 384.
34 Hiatt 1947.
35 Trapnell 1987, p. 22.
36 Murray 2003.
37 Franklin 1842.
38 Truffaut 1986, p. 321.
39 Gaylin 2002, p. 8.
40 Tamar Levin, "Intimate strangers across the street, just don't get too close," *The New York Times* (The City), May 26, 2002.

Chapter Two: Under the Leaves

1   Frank 1966, p. 1.
2   Von Uexküll 1934/1957, p. 5.
3   Partan & Marler 2002.
4   Cited in von Uexküll 1992, p. 295.
5   Morand-Ferron et al. 2007.
6   Vitousek et al. 2007.
7   Lea et al. 2008.
8   Hall & DeVore 1965.
9   Pipitone & Gallup 2008.
10 Badyaev & Hill 2003; Jawor & Breitwisch 2003; Leitão et al. 2006.
11 Weatherhead & Robertson 1979.
12 McGregor 2005.
13 Baldwin et al. 2002.
14 Gershenzon 2007, p. 5257; see also Ballaré 1999; Dicke & Bruin 2001; Heil & Bueno 2007; Kobayashi & Yamamura 2003, 2007.
15 Endler 1992, 1993.
16 Christy 1995; Endler & Basolo 1998; Guilford & Dawkins 1991.
17 Silk 2007.
18 Leboucher & Pallot 2004; Vallet & Kreutzer 1995.
19 Doutrelant & McGregor 2000; Kunc et al. 2006; Leboucher & Pallot, 2004.
20 Berglund et al. 1996; Cox & Le Boeuf 1977; Maestripieri & Roney 2005; O'Connell & Cowlishaw 1994; Semple 2001; Semple et al. 2002.
21 Apicella et al. 2007; Collins 2000; Dabbs & Mallinger 1999.
22 Evans et al. 2006; Braun & Bryan 2006.
23 Symons et al. 1997.

24 Malek 1992, pp. 74, 75.

25 Briggs et al. 1996; Dugatkin 1998; Galef & White 1998; Grant & Green 1996; White & Galef 2000; Witte & Noltemeier 2002; Witte & Ryan 1998, 2002.

26 Dugatkin & Godin 1993; Vukomanovic & Rodd 2007.

27 Matessi et al. 2005.

28 Oliveira et al. 2001.

29 Bernhardt et al. 1998.

30 Deecke et al. 2005.

31 Dabelsteen et al. 1998.

32 Herb et al. 2003.

33 Choudhury 1995; Mennill et al. 2003.

34 Hauser 1990.

35 Goodall 1986; McGinnis 1979; Tutin 1979.

36 Dally et al. 2005.

37 Emery & Clayton 2001.

38 Hare et al. 2001.

39 Hare et al. 2006.

40 Melis et al. 2006.

41 Brauer et al. 2008.

42 Hare & Tomasello 2004.

43 Galton 1871, p. 356.

44 Elgar 1989; see also Quenette 1990; in actuality, several things co-vary with group size, and any of these could independently reduce predator vigilance besides the hypothesized tendency to share watchfulness.

45 Clark & Mangel 1986.

46 Bräuer et al. 2007; van Schaik et al. 1983.

47 Wrangham & Peterson 1997.

48 Hare 2001, p. 271.

49 Caine & Marra 1998.

50 Bygott 1979; Blurton-Jones & Trollope 1968; Gautier & Gautier-Hion 1977; Smuts 1987a.

51 Smuts 1987b.

52 Cooper & Bernstein 2000.

53 Blount 1985.

54 Greeno & Semple 2009.

55 Tennis & Dabbs 1975.

56 Hall 1984, 1996 [others].

57 Aiello 1977; Baxter 1970; Sommer 1959.

58 Silk 2007.

59 Baldellou & Henzi 1992; Boesch & Boesch 1984; Fragaszy 1990; Gould et al. 1997; Rose 1994; Rose & Fedigan 1995; Treves 1998, 1999, Treves et al. 2001; also see reviews in Quenette 1990; Steenbeek et al. 1999.

60 Quenette 1990; Rose & Fedigan 1995; Treves 1999.

61 Baldellou & Henzi 1992. I base this on data presented in Table 1 of Treves 1999 and Table 2 of Treves 1998.

62 Treves et al. 2001.

63 Biben et al. 1989; Leighton-Shapiro 1986; Treves et al. 2001.

64 Leighton-Shapiro 1986.

65 Mailer, N. Birds and lions: writing from the inside out. *The New Yorker*, December 23 & 30, 2002, p. 82.

66 Innocenti & Kaas 1995; Kaas 1995.

67 Silk 2007, p. 1348.

68 Dunbar 1993; Dunbar 2007; Dunbar & Shultz 2007.

69 Lindenfors et al. 2004, p. S102.

70 Dunbar & Shultz 2007.

71 Dunbar & Shultz 2007.

72 Dunbar & Shultz 2007, p. 1346.

73 Humphrey 1976, p. 311.

74 Byrne & Whiten 1992.

75 Byrne & Corp 2004; Crockford et al. 2007.

76 Dunbar 2007, p. 280.

77 Ruby & Decety 2001, 2003, 2004; Decety & Grèzes 2006.

Chapter Three: Open-plan Living

1 Groves & Sabater Pi 1985; Hediger 1977.

2 Hediger 1977, p. 174.

3 Reynolds 1972; nearly two million years ago a camp was built in eastern Africa that was later discovered by archeologist Mary Leakey. She found that this camp, known as the Stone Circle, conformed to a plan that was practically identical in size and shape to camps built by freely living groups just a few generations ago. The Circle, Leakey wrote, "resembles temporary structures often made by present-day nomadic peoples" (Leakey 1971, p. 24).

4 Hedge 1982; Oldham 1988; Sundstrom et al. 1982.

5 The correct spelling is actually !Kung, where the first symbol represents a lingual (alveopalatal) click. This tribe is also known as the Ju/'hoansi (or Ju/wasi).

6 Yellen 1977, p. 134.

7 Briggs 1971, p. 77.

8 Yellen 1977.

9 Lee 1979b, p. 461.

10 Gould 1977.

11 Groves & Sabater Pi 1985.

12 Dentan 1968, p. 29.
13 Dentan 1968, pp. 28–29.
14 Dentan 1968, p. 29.
15 Bird-David 1994.
16 Bird-David 1994, pp. 590–591.
17 Shore 1982, p. 179.
18 Shore 1982, p. 180.
19 Roberts & Gregor 1971.
20 Sundstrom et al. 1982.
21 Archea 1977, p. 121.
22 Dentan 1968, p. 29.
23 Foster 1960.
24 Forge 1972, p. 374.
25 Humphrey 2007, p. 752.
26 Fejos 1943.
27 Fried 1968, p. 475.
28 Narroll 1959.
29 Foster 1960, p. 177.
30 Forge 1972, p. 375.

Chapter Four: Reluctant Domestication

1 Leyhausen 1971.
2 Gregor 1977, p. 244; Klopfer & Rubenstein 1977, p. 62; Thomas Nagel, "The shredding of public privacy," *Times Literary Supplement*, August 14, 1998; Schwartz 1968, p. 741.
3 Excavation of a camp found on the French Riviera indicates that the ability to build existed three to four hundred thousand years ago (de Lumley 1969; Kostof 1995).
4 Cohen 1977, pp. 122–123.
5 Hitchcock 1987.
6 Cohen 1977, p. 133.
7 Wilson 1988.
8 Barker 2006; Cohen 1977. Wilson 1988 interprets early fishing settlements to mean that it was population pressures more than agriculture that produced the drift into sedentism.
9 Barker 2006.
10 Kent 1989; Lee 1979b.
11 Rapoport 1969, p. 20, italics mine.
12 Cooper 1946, pp. 110–111.
13 Rapoport 1969, p. 21, italics mine.

14 Carpenter 1966, p. 221.

15 Wilson 1988, p. 173.

16 Roberts & Gregor 1971.

17 Draper 1973.

18 Feeley-Harnik 1980, p. 562.

19 Feeley-Harnik 1980, p. 564.

20 Feeley-Harnik 1980, p. 568.

21 Feeley-Harnik 1980, p. 581.

22 Feeley-Harnik 1980, p. 580.

23 Haviland & Haviland 1983.

24 Haviland & Haviland 1983, p. 347.

25 Haviland & Haviland 1983, p. 347, italics theirs.

26 Haviland & Haviland 1983, p. 354.

27 Haviland & Haviland 1983, p. 349.

28 Barker 2006.

29 Byrd 2005.

30 Foster 1960.

31 Wilson 1988, p. 104.

32 Gregor 1970.

33 Gregor 1970, p. 244.

34 Gregor 1970, p. 244, italics mine.

35 Smith 1997.

36 Weitman 1973, p. 230, italics mine.

37 Flannery 1972.

Chapter Five: Privacy, Intimacy, and The Selves

1 Wilson 1988, p. 173.

2 Campbell 1964, pp. 292–293.

3 Allen 1988, p. 15, italics mine.

4 Arendt 1959, p. 58.

5 Delany 1969, p. 21.

6 Muchembled 1985, p. 41, italics his.

7 Duby 1987, p. viii.

8 Hamill 1969, p. 151.

9 Le Roy Ladurie 1978, p. 256.

10 Bok 1982, p. 13.

11 Glassie 1972, p. 43, italics mine.

12 Muchembled 1985, pp. 34, 35.

13 Ward 1999.

14 Stevenson 1879/1992, p. 173.

15 Muchembled 1985.

16 Sarti 2002, pp. 121–122.

17 Smith 2000, p. 20.

18 Gadlin 1976, p. 305.

19 Smith 2000, p. 204.

20 Allen 1988.

21 These concerns are reflected today in the authorship of books on privacy. Do a literature search and you will find, as I have, that many of the books written by men warn of creeping surveillance by the government, or of threats to privacy in the context of business, banking, or computing. Women's books, on the other hand, stress the importance of privacy in the context of relations and family life.

22 Ellis 1899/1942.

23 Parker 1974, p. 280.

24 Sarti 2002.

25 Ariès 1989.

26 Corbin 1990.

27 Corbin 1990; Ariès 1989.

28 Mansfield & Winthrop 2000.

29 Gadlin 1976, p. 306.

30 Bagehot 1853/1911, p. 134.

31 Duby 1987, p. viii.

32 Baumeister 1986, p. v.

33 Le Sage 1707, p. 39.

34 Ames 1973.

Chapter Six: Personal Power and Social Control

1 Hunter 1994.

2 Hunter 1994, p. 117.

3 Hunter 1994.

4 Hunter 1994, p. 83.

5 Bateson et al. 2006.

6 Maloney 1976, p. vii.

7 Ginsburg & Shechtman 1993, p. 1851.

8 McAdams 1996, pp. 2266–2267.

9 Wilson 2003.

10 Posner 1993.

11 Fletcher 1993, p. 1626.

12 Thompson 1975.

13 Walker 1960, p. 21.

14 Thompson 1983.

15 Farge 1989, p. 578.

16 Perrot 1990, p. 228.

17 In Perrot 1990, p. 228.

18 Ernaux 1992, pp. 15–16.

19 Crawford and Gowing 2000, quotes from pp. 156–157.

20 Le Roy Ladurie 1978, p. 258.

21 Gouge 1622/1976, p. 259.

22 For additional details, see Castan, N. 1989, among many sources.

23 Castan, N. 1989, p. 417.

24 Castan, N. 1989, p. 417.

25 Locke & Bogin 2006.

26 Bott 1971, p. 67.

27 Emler 1992, pp. 23, 24.

28 Walsh 1977.

29 The term may have come from the Old Norse *upsardropi*, derived from *ups* "eaves" + *dropi* "a drop."

30 Blackstone 1796, p. 169.

31 McIntosh 1996, p. 93.

32 McIntosh 1998.

33 McIntosh 1991, p. 68.

34 *The Legal News*, 30 July 1887, p. 241.

35 McIntosh 1991, p. 68.

36 Russell 1958.

37 Stone 1977, p. 98.

38 McIntosh 1998, p. 175.

39 Mendelson & Crawford 1998, p. 212.

40 McIntosh 1996.

41 McIntosh 1998.

42 William Sheppard (or Shepherd), *A Grand Abridgment of the Common and Statute Law of England* (London, 1675), quoted in Boose 1991, p. 189.

43 Blackstone 1796, ch. 13.

44 Gowing 1996, p. 2.

45 Goldberg 1995.

46 Springer 1998.

47 *Poor Robin's True Character of a Schold, or, the Shrews Looking Glass*. London: Printed for L. C. 1678.

48 Roberts 1616.

49 Shoemaker 2004, p. 62.

50 Harper 1638.

51 Plot 1686, p. 389.

52 Blacklock 1897.

53 Brushfield 1855, p. 37.

54 Lackington 1795, p. 278.

55 Boose 1991, p. 206.

56 Fabre 1989, p. 535.

57 Davis 1975.

58 Fabre 1989, p. 535; Alford 1959.

59 Thompson 1991; Ingram 1984.

60 Fletcher 1995, pp. 271–2.

61 Ingram 1994.

62 Fletcher 1995, p. 272.

Chapter Seven: Passionate Exhibitors

1 Balzac 1847/1968.

2 Geist 1983, p. 67.

3 Benjamin 1973.

4 Prendergast 1992.

5 Featherstone 1998.

6 Benjamin 1983, p. 36.

7 Tester 1994.

8 Baudelaire 1863/1995, p. 10.

9 Baudelaire 1869/1970, p. 20, quoted by Tester 1994, p. 3.

10 Shaya 2004, p. 49.

11 See Forgione 2005, p. 680.

12 Hamilton 1929; Kinsey et al. 1953.

13 Tjaden and Thoennes 1997; Locke 2005.

14 Gleber 1999, p. 171.

15 Figure 12 in Sieburth 1984.

16 Addison 1711, p. 51.

17 Prendergast 1992, p. 134.

18 Smith 1841.

19 Sieburth 1984, p. 175 and p. 166.

20 Prendergast 1992.

21 Murkowski 1933/1970, p. 406.

22 Humphrey 2007, p. 749.

23 Individuation is also evident in *Pont Neuf*, painted by Renoir in 1872 (Forgione 2005).

24 Benjamin 1973, p. 35.

25 Sieburth 1984.

26 Prendergast 1992, p. 134.

27 Ferguson 1994, pp. 27–28.

28 Benjamin 1973, p. 175.

29 Poe 1840, pp. 63, 64. In fact, Poe's account was the inspiration for Baudelaire's; Mazlish 1994.

30 Bédarida & Sutcliffe 1980; Buck-Morss 1986; Featherstone 1998; Forgione 2005.

31 Miller 1981.

32 Forgione 2005.

33 Zola 1881/2001, p. xxii.

34 Steele 1985.

35 Miller 1981, p. 192.

36 R. Dupouy, De la kleptomanie. *Journal de Psychologie Normale et Pathologique* (1905), 413, cited in Miller 1981, p. 204.

37 Friedberg 1994, p. 36.

38 Williams 1902, p. 69.

39 Bédarida & Sutcliffe 1980; Buck-Morss 1986; Featherstone 1998.

40 Prendergast 1992.

41 Prendergast 1992.

42 Corfield 1990.

43 Cranz 1980, p. S80 and S81.

44 Love 1973.

45 Lyle 1970, p. 51.

46 Lennard & Lennard 1984.

47 Oosterman 1992, p. 162.

Chapter Eight: What Will the Servants Say?

1 *Trials for adultery; or, the history of divorces. Being select trials at Doctors commons, for adultery, fornication, cruelty, impotence, & c. From the year 1760, to the present time. Including the whole of the evidence on each cause.* New York: Garland, 1985. Quotations from vol. I, pp. 20–24.

2 Kent 1989.

3 Hobsbawm 1968, cited in Robbins 1986, p. 15.

4 Veblen 1899/1957, p. 39.

5 Turner 1962.

6 Kussmaul 1981.

7 Hunter 1994; Sarti 2002; Dawes 1973; Dutch art reveals this integration of employers and staff. It is difficult to distinguish servants and family members, wrote Simon Schama, since the former were "axiomatically included" in domestic scenes (Schama 1991). In the seventeenth century, according to Wayne Franits, Dutch maids frequently ate at the same table as the family, even when they had dinner guests (Franits 1993).

8 Fairchilds 1984.

9 Blackstone 1796, cited in Steedman 2003, p. 320.

10 In Steedman 2003, p. 321.

11 Sarti 2002, p. 144.

12 Turner 1962, p. 15.

13 Hecht 1980, p. 221.

14 McBride 1974, p. 53.

15 Sarti 2002.

16 Adams & Adams 1825, p. 20.

17 May 1998.

18 Braddon 1863/1998, p. 245.

19 *Town & Country Magazine*, 10.234 (1778), 222; in Stone 1990, p. 222.

20 *Selections from the Letters of Geraldine Endsor Jewsbury to Jane Welsh Cashyle*, ed. Mrs Alexander Ireland. London: Longmans, Green, and Co., 1892. Letter dated 3 August 1852. Quoted in Flanders 2003, 152–153.

21 Flanders 2003, pp. 152–153.

22 Mainardi 2003, p. 61.

23 Hunter 1994.

24 Stone 1990, p. 222.

25 Stone 1990, p. 221.

26 *Trials for adultery*, vol. 3, p. 15.

27 *Trials for adultery*, vol. 3, p. 24.

28 *Trials for adultery*, vol. 6, p. 70.

29 Trodd 1989, p. 162.

30 Schama 1991.

31 Robinson 1987.

32 Trodd 1989, p. 246.

33 Stone & Stone 1984.

34 Boswell 1758, p. 226.

Chapter Nine: Virtual Eaves

1 Dawkins 1982.

2 McNeill 2003, p. 25.

3 McNeill 2003.

4 McNeill 2003, p. 27; italics mine.

5 McNeill 2003, p. 32.

6 Johnson 1753, p. 515.

7 Glaser 2001.

8 Keymer & Sabor 2001.

9 Vernon 1982, p. 87.

10 Davis 1983, pp. 187–188.

11 Tanner 1979, p. 377, italics mine; also Phillips 1992.

12 Brown 1994.

13 Mussell 1984, p. 3.

14 Modleski 1982.

15 Radway 1984, p. 113.

16 Krentz 1992.

17 Krentz 1992, p. 5.

18 Balzac, *Physiology of Marriage* (1829), quoted in Mainardi: 2003, p. 157.

19 Cantor & Pingree 1983; Modleski 1982.

20 Brown 1994.

21 Blumenthal 1997; Cantor & Pingree 1983.

22 Allen 1988.

23 Cantor & Pingree 1983.

24 Blumenthal 1997, p. 58.

25 John Keeler, "Soaps: counterpart to the 18th century's quasi-moral novel."
    New York Times, March 16, 1980.

26 Dick 1972.

27 Casper 1999, p. 17.

28 Delaplaine 1816, p. 286.

29 Casper 1999, p. 5.

30 Culley 1985, p. 188.

31 Culley 1985.

32 Myers 1992, p. 152.

33 McNeill 2003, p. 26.

Chapter Ten: Intimacy by Theft

1 Humphrey 2007, p. 753.

2 Humphrey 2000.

3 Deutsch & Madle 1975.

4 McNeill 1995.

5 Humphrey 2007.

6 Humphrey 2007, p. 753.

7 Warren & Brandeis 1890, p. 193.

8 Warren & Brandeis 1890, p. 193.

9 Warren & Brandeis 1890, p. 195.

10 Cooley 1888, p. 195, my italics.

11 Hall 1998.

12 Infield & Platford 2000, p. xxxiii.

13 Hall 1998; Tjaden & Thoennes 1997.

14 Mullen et al. 2000.

15 Mullen et al. 2000.

16 Meloy 1998; Mullen et al. 2000.

17 Merleau-Ponty 1962.

18 Gaylin 2002, p. 2.

19 Allen 1988, p. 15, italics mine.

20 Thomas Nagel, "The shredding of public privacy," *Times Literary Supplement*, August 14, 1998.

21 Fried 1968, p. 484.

22 Reiman 1976, p. 44.

23 Inness 1992, pp. 83–84.

24 See Nagel 1998a and 1998b.

25 Korosec-Serfaty & Bolitt 1986.

26 Csikszentmihalyi & Rochberg-Halton 1981; Dittmar 1991; Dittmar et al. 1995; Wallendorf & Arnould 1988.

27 Stephen 1909, p. 155.

28 Hodin 1966, p. 155, 159.

29 Freedberg 1989, p. 355–356, my italics.

30 Sontag 1977, p. 37.

31 Sartre 1956.

32 Baudrillard 1999.

33 Calvino n.d., p. 10.

34 Dyer 2005, p. 44.

35 Suddendorf et al. 2007.

36 Spender 1987, p. 15.

37 Cartier-Bresson 1999, P. 22, my italics.

38 Rosenheim 2004; Sante 2004.

39 Sante 2004, p. 11.

40 Collins 2004.

41 Peter 2004.

42 Arbus 1972.

43 Humphrey 2008, p. 269.

44 Evans 1982, p. 161

References

"A Lady Resident" ("Sketch of life in buildings") (1889). In *Life and labour of the people in London*. Ed. Charles Booth. London: Macmillan and Company.

Adams, S. & Adams, S. (1825/1989). *The complete servant*. Lewes, East Sussex: Southover Press.

Addison: Selections from Addison's Papers Contributed to the Spectator, 1711. Ed. Thomas Arnold. London: Macmillan and Company.

Aiello, J. R. (1977). Visual interaction at extended distances. *Personality and Social Psychology Bulletin, 3*, 83–86.

Alford, V. (1959). Rough music or charivari. *Folklore, 70*, 505–518.

Allen, A. L. (1988). *Uneasy access: privacy for women in a free society*. Totowa, NJ: Rowman & Little.

Ames, S. M. (ed.) (1973). *County Court Records of Accomack-Northampton, Virginia, 1640–1645*. Charlottesville, VA: University Press of Virginia.

Apicella, C. L., Feinberg, D. R., & Marlowe, F. W. (2007). Voice pitch predicts reproductive success in male hunter-gatherers. *Biology Letters, 3*, 682–684.

Arbus, D. (1972). *Diane Arbus*. New York: Aperture.

Archea, J. (1977). The place of architectural factors in behavioral theories of privacy. *Journal of Social Issues, 33*, 116–137.

Arendt, H. (1959). *The human condition*. New York: Doubleday Anchor.

Ariès, P. (1989). Introduction. In Chartier, R. (ed.), *A history of private life. III. Passions of the Renaissance*. Cambridge, MA: Harvard University Press.

Badyaev, A. V., & Hill, G. E. (2003). Avian sexual dichromatism in relation to phylogeny and ecology. *Annual Review of Ecology, Evolution, and Systematics, 34*, 27–49.

Bagehot, W. (1853/1911). Shakespeare—the man. *Literary Studies*, Vol. 1. New York: Dutton.

Baldellou, M., & Henzi, P. (1992). Vigilance, predator detection and the presence of supernumerary males in vervet monkey troops. *Animal Behaviour, 43*, 451–461.

Baldwin, I. T., Kessler, A., & Halitschke, R. (2002). Volatile signaling in plant-plant-herbivore interactions: what is real? *Current Opinion in Plant Biology, 5*, 351–354.

References

Ballaré, C. L. (1999). Keeping up with the neighbours: hytochrome sensing and other signalling mechanisms. *Trends in Plant Science, 4,* 97–102.

Balzac, H. de (1847/1968). *Cousin Pons.* Trans. H. J. Hunt. London: The Folio Society.

Barker, G. (2006). *The agricultural revolution in prehistory: why did foragers become farmers?* Oxford: Oxford University Press.

Barth, F. (1975). *Ritual and knowledge among the Baktaman of New Guinea.* New Haven, CT: Yale University Press.

Bateson, M., Nettle, D., & Roberts, G. (2006). Cues of being watched enhance cooperation in a real-world setting. *Biology Letters, 2,* 412–14.

Baudelaire, C. (1863/1995). The painter of modern life. In Mayne, J. (ed.), *The painter of modern life and other essays.* Trans. Jonathan Mayne. Oxford: Phaidon Press.

Baudelaire, C. (1869/1970). *Paris Spleen.* Trans. L. Varèse. New York: New Directions.

Baudrillard, J. (1999). Poetic transference of situation. Translated by Chris Turner. In Delahaye, L., *L' Autre.* London: Phaidon Press.

Baumeister, R. F. (1986). Preface. In Baumeister, R. F. (ed.), *Public self and private self.* New York: Springer-Verlag.

Baxter, J. C. (1970). Interpersonal spacing in natural settings. *Sociometry, 33,* 444–456.

Bearman, P. (2005). *Doormen.* Chicago, IL: University of Chicago Press.

Bédarida, F., & Sutcliffe, A. (1980). The street in the structure and life of the city: reflections on nineteenth-century London and Paris. *Journal of Urban History, 6,* 379–396.

Benjamin, W. (1973). *Charles Baudelaire: a lyric poet in the era of high capitalism.* Trans. by Harry Zohn. London: New Left Books.

Benjamin, W. (1983). *Charles Baudelaire: A lyric poet in the era of high capitalism.* Trans. by H. Zohn. London: New Left Books.

Benn, S. I. (1971). Privacy, freedom, and respect for persons. In Pennock, J. R., & Chapman, J. W. (eds.), *Privacy.* New York: Atherton Press.

Berglund, A., Bisazza, A., & Pilastro, A. (1996). Armaments and ornaments: an evolutionary explanation of traits of dual utility. *Biological Journal of the Linnean Society, 58,* 385–399.

Bernhardt, P. C., Dabbs, J. M., Jr., Fielden, J. A., & Lutter, C. D. (1998). Testosterone changes during vicarious experiences of winning and losing among fans at sporting events. *Physiology and Behavior, 65,* 59–62.

Biben, M., Symmes, D., & Bernhards, D. (1989). Vigilance during play in squirrel monkeys. *American Journal of Primatology, 17,* 41–49.

Billington, J. H. (1980). *Fire in the minds of men: origins of the revolutionary faith.* New Brunswick, NJ: Transaction Publishers.

Bird-David, N. (1994). Sociality and immediacy: or, past and present conversations on bands. *Man (N.S.), 29,* 583–603.

Blacklock, F. G. (1897/1999). *The suppressed Benedictine Minster and other ancient and modern institutions of the Borough of Leominster.* Leominster, UK: The Mortimer Press.

Blackstone, W. (1796). *Commentaries on the laws of England. Vol. 4.* Dublin: John Enshaw and others.

Blount, B. G. (1985). "Girney" vocalizations among Japanese Macaque females: context and function. *Primates, 26,* 424–435.

Blumenthal, D. (1997). *Women and soap opera: a cultural feminist perspective.* Westport, CT: Praeger.

Blurton-Jones, N. H., & Trollope, J. (1968). Social behaviour of stump-tailed macaques in captivity. *Primates, 9,* 365–394.

Boesch, C., & Boesch, H. (1984). Possible causes of sex differences in the use of natural hammers by wild chimpanzees. *Journal of Human Evolution, 13,* 415–440.

Bok, S. (1982). *Secrets: on the ethics of concealment and revelation.* New York: Pantheon Books.

Boose, L. E. (1991). Scolding brides and bridling scolds: taming the woman's unruly member. *Shakespeare Quarterly, 42,* 179–213.

Boswell, J. (1758–1777/1924). *Letters of James Boswell,* collected and ed. Chauncey B. Tinker. Oxford: Clarendon Press.

Bott, E. (1971). *Family and social network: roles, norms, and external relationships in ordinary urban families.* London: Tavistock Publications.

Braddon, M. (1863/1998). *Aurora Floyd.* Vol. I. Elibron Classics.

Bräuer, J., Call, J., & Tomasello, M. (2007). Chimpanzees really know what others can see in a competitive situation. *Animal Cognition, 10,* 439–448.

Bräuer, J., Call, J., & Tomasello, M. (2008). Chimpanzees do not take into account what others can hear in a competitive situation. *Animal Cognition, 11,* 175–178.

Braun, M. F. & Bryan, A. (2006). Female waist-to-hip and male waist-to-shoulder ratios as determinants of romantic partner desirability. *Journal of Social and Personal Relationships, 23,* 805–819.

Briggs, J. (1971). *Never in anger: portrait of an Eskimo family.* Cambridge, MA: Harvard University Press.

Briggs, S. E., Godin, J.-G., & Dugatkin, L. A. (1996). Mate-choice copying under predation risk in the Trinidadian guppy. *Behavioural Ecology, 7,* 151–157.

Brown, M. E. (1994). *Soap opera and women's talk: the pleasure of resistance.* Thousand Oaks, CA: Sage Publications.

Brushfield, T. N. (1855–1862). On obsolete punishments, with particular reference to those of Cheshire. Part I. The brank, or scold's bridle. *Journal of the Architectural, Archaeological, and Historic Society, County, City, and Neighbourhood of Chester, 2,* 31–48.

Buck-Morss, S. (1986). The *flâneur*, the sandwichman, and the whore: the politics of loitering. *New German Critique, 39,* 99–140.

Bygott, J. D. (1979). Agonistic behavior, dominance, and social structure in wild chimpanzees of the Gombe National Park. In Hamburg, D. A., & McCown, E. R. (eds.), *The great apes.* Menlo Park, CA: Benjamin/ Cummings.

Byrd, B. F. (2005). Reassessing the emergence of village life in the Near East. *Journal of Archaeological Research, 13,* 231–290.

Byrne, R. W., & Corp, N. (2004). Neocortex size predicts deception rate in primates. *Proceedings of the Royal Society London B, 271,* 1693–1699.

Byrne, R. W., & Whiten, A. (1992). Cognitive evolution in primates: evidence from tactical deception. *Man (N.S.), 27,* 609–627.

Caine, N. G., & Marra, S. L. (1998). Vigilance and social organization in two species of primates. *Animal Behaviour, 36,* 897–904.

Calvino, I. (n.d.). The adventure of a photographer. Trans. from Italian William Weaver. (http://home.pacbell.net/ishmael9/calvino.htm)

Campbell, J. K. (1964). *Honour, family and patronage: a study of institutions and moral values in a Greek mountain community.* Oxford: Clarendon Press.

Cantor, M. G., & Pingree, S. (1983). *The soap opera.* Beverly Hills, CA: Sage.

Carpenter, E. (1966). Image making in Arctic art. In Kepes, G. (ed.), *Sign, image, symbol.* New York: George Braziller.

Cartier-Bresson, H. (1976). *Henri Cartier-Bresson.* London: Aperture.

Cartier-Bresson, H. (1999). *The mind's eye: writings on photography and photographers.* London: Aperture.

Casper, S. E. (1999). *Constructing American lives: biography and culture in nineteenth-century America.* Chapel Hill, NC: University of North Carolina Press.

Castan, N. (1989). The public and the private. In Chartier, R. (ed.), *A history of private life. III. Passions of the Renaissance.* Cambridge, MA: Harvard University Press.

Choudhury, S. (1995). Divorce in birds: a review of the hypotheses. *Animal Behaviour, 50,* 413–429.

Christy, J. H. (1995). Mimicry, mate choice, and the sensory trap hypothesis. *American Naturalist, 146,* 171–181.

Cirillo, J. (2003). Social and psychobiological aspects of whispered speech. Dissertation, Department of Biology, Chemistry, and Pharmacology, Free University, Berlin.

Clark, C. W., & Mangel, M. (1986). The evolutionary advantages of group foraging. *Theoretical Population Biology, 30,* 45–75.

References

Cohen, M. N. (1977). *The food crisis in prehistory: overpopulation and the origins of agriculture.* New Haven, CT: Yale University Press.

Collins, B. (2004). Foreword. In Peter, P., *The subway pictures.* New York: Random House.

Collins, S. A. (2000). Men's voices and women's voices. *Animal Behaviour, 60,* 773–80.

Cooley, T. M. (1888). *A treatise on the law of torts, or, the wrongs which arise independent of contract.* Chicago: Callaghan & Co.

Cooper, J. M. (1946). The Ona. In Steward, J. H. (ed.), *Handbook of South American Indians: the marginal tribes.* Vol. I. Washington: U. S. Government Printing Office.

Cooper, M. A., & Bernstein, I. S. (2000). Social grooming in assamese macaques *(Macaca assamensis). American Journal of Primatology, 50,* 77–85.

Corbin, A. (1990). Backstage. In Ariès, P., & Duby, G. (eds.), *A history of private life. IV. From the fires of revolution to the great war.* Cambridge, MA: Harvard University Press.

Corfield, P. J. (1990). Walking the city streets: the urban odyssey in eighteenth-century England. *Journal of Urban History, 16,* 132–174.

Cox, C. R., & Le Boeuf, B. J. (1977). Female incitation of male competition: a mechanism in sexual selection. *American Naturalist, 111,* 317–335.

Cranz, G. (1980). Women in urban parks. *Signs: Journal of Women in Culture and Society, 5,* S79–S95.

Crawford, P., & Gowing, L. (2000). *Women's worlds in seventeenth-century England.* London: Routledge.

Crockford, C., Wittig, R. M., Seyfarth, R. M., & Cheney, D. L. (2007). Baboons eavesdrop to deduce mating opportunities. *Animal Behaviour, 73,* 885–890.

Csikszentmihalyi, M., & Rochberg-Halton, E. (1981). *The meaning of things: domestic symbols and the self.* Cambridge: Cambridge University Press.

Culley, M. (1985). *A day at a time: the diary literature of American women from 1764 to the present.* New York: The Feminist Press at the City University of New York.

Dabbs, J. M., & Mallinger, A. (1999). High testosterone levels predict low voice pitch among men. *Personality and Individual Differences, 27,* 801–804.

Dabelsteen, T., McGregor, P. K., Lampe, H. M., Lagmre, N. E., & Holland, J. (1998). Quiet song in song birds: an overlooked phenomenon. *Bioacoustics, 9,* 89–105.

Dally, J. M., Emery, N. J., & Clayton, N. S. (2005). Cache protection strategies by western scrub-jays, *Aphelocoma californica:* implications for social cognition. *Animal Behaviour, 70,* 1251–1263.

Davis, L. J. (1983). *Factual fictions: the origins of the English novel*. New York: Columbia University Press.

Davis, N. Z. (1975). *Society and culture in early modern France*. London: Duckworth.

Dawes, F. V. (1973). *Not in front of the servants: a true portrait of upstairs, downstairs life*. London: Century.

Dawkins, R. (1982). *The extended phenotype*. Oxford: Freeman.

Decety, J., & Grèzes, J. (2006). The power of simulation: imagining one's own and other's behavior. *Brain Research, 1079*, 4–14.

Deecke, V. B., Ford, J. K. B., & Slater, P. J. B. (2005). The vocal behaviour of mammal-eating killer whales: communicating with costly calls. *Animal Behaviour, 69*, 395–405.

Delany, P. (1969). *British autobiography in the seventeenth century*. London: Routledge & Kegan Paul.

Delaplaine's *Repository of the lives and portraits of distinguished American* (1816). *Portico, 2*, 282–293.

de Lumley, H. (1969). A paleolithic camp at Nice. *Scientific American, 220*, 42–50.

Delvau, A. (1862). *Histoire anecdotique des cafés et cabarets de Paris*. Paris: Dentu. In Marcus, S. (1999), *Apartment stories: city and home in nineteenth-century Paris and London*. Berkeley, CA: University of California Press.

Dentan, R. K. (1968). *The Semai: a nonviolent people of Malaya*. New York: Holt, Rinehart and Winston.

Deutsch, F., & Madle, R. (1975). Empathy: historic and current conceptualizations, measurement, and a cognitive theoretical perspective. *Human Development, 18*, 267–278.

Dick, O. L. (ed.) (1972). *Aubrey's brief lives*. Harmondsworth, UK: Penguin Books.

Dicke, M., & Bruin, J. (2001). Chemical information transfer between plants: back to the future. *Biochemical Systematics and Ecology, 29*, 981–994.

Dickens, C. (1848/1987). *Dealings with the firm of Dombey and Son: wholesale, retail, and for exportation*. Fairclough, P. (ed.). Oxford: Oxford University Press.

Dittmar, H. (1991). Meanings of material possessions as reflections of identity: gender and social-material position in society. *Journal of Social and Behavior Personality, 6*, 491–511.

Dittmar, H., Beattie, J., & Friese, S. (1995). Gender identity and material symbols: objects and decision considerations in impulse purchases. *Journal of Economic Psychology, 16*, 491–511.

Doutrelant, C., & McGregor, P. K. (2000). Eavesdropping and mate choice in female fighting fish. *Behaviour, 137*, 1655–1669.

Draper, P. (1973). Crowding among hunter gatherers: the !Kung Bushmen. *Science, 182*, 301–303.

Duby, G. (1987). Foreword. In Ariès, P., & Duby, G. (eds.), *A history of private life. I. From pagan Rome to Byzantium*. Cambridge, MA: Harvard University Press.

Dugatkin, L. A. (1998). Genes, copying, and female mate choice: shifting thresholds. *Behavioral Ecology, 9,* 323–327.

Dugatkin, L. A., & Godin, J.-G. (1993). Female mate copying in the guppy (Poecilia reticulata): age-dependent effects. *Behavioral Ecology, 4,* 289–292.

Dunbar, R. I. M. (1993). Coevolution of neocortical size, group size and language in humans. *Behavioral and Brain Sciences, 16,* 681–694.

Dunbar, R. I. M. (2007). Evolution of the social brain. In Gangestad, S. W., & Simpson, J. A. (eds.), *The evolution of mind: fundamental questions and controversies*. New York: Guilford Press.

Dunbar, R. I. M., & Shultz, S. (2007). Evolution in the social brain. *Science, 317,* 1344–1347.

Dyer, G. (2005). *The ongoing moment*. New York: Pantheon Books.

Elgar, M. A. (1989). Predator vigilance and group size in mammals and birds: a critical review of the empirical evidence. *Biological Reviews, 64,* 13–33.

Ellis, H. (1899/1942). *Studies in the psychology of sex*. New York: Random House.

Emery, N. J., & Clayton, N. S. (2001). Effects of experience and social context on prospective caching strategies by scrub jays. *Nature, 414,* 443–446.

Emler, N. (1992). The truth about gossip. *Social Psychology Newsletter, 27,* 23–37.

Endler, J. A. (1992). Signals, signal conditions, and the direction of evolution. *American Naturalist, 139,* S125–S153.

Endler, J. A. (1993). Some general comments on the evolution and design of animal communication systems. *Philosophical Transactions of the Royal Society of London B, 340,* 215–225.

Endler, J. A., & Basolo, A. L. (1998). Sensory ecology, receiver biases and sexual selection. *Trends in Ecology and Evolution, 13,* 415–420.

Ernaux, A. (1992). *A man's place*. Trans. Leslie, T., of *La Place*. New York: Four Walls Eight Windows.

Evans, S., Neave, N., & Wakelin, D. (2006). Relationships between vocal characteristics and body size and shape in human males: an evolutionary explanation for a deep male voice. *Biological Psychology, 72,* 160–163.

Evans, W. (1982). *Walker Evans at work*. New York: Harper & Row.

Fabre, D. (1989). Families: privacy versus custom. In Chartier, R. (ed.) *A history of private life. III. Passions of the Renaissance*. Cambridge, MA: Harvard University Press.

Fairchilds, C. (1984). *Domestic enemies: servants and their masters in Old Regime France*. Baltimore, MD: Johns Hopkins University Press.

Farge, A. (1989). The honor and secrecy of families. In Chartier, R. (ed.), *A history of private life. IV.* Cambridge, MA: Harvard University Press.

Featherstone, M. (1998). The *flâneur*, the city and virtual public life. *Urban Studies, 35,* 909–925.

Feeley-Harnik, G. (1980). The Sakalava house (Madagascar). *Anthropos, 75,* 559–585.

Fejos, P. (1943). *Ethnography of the Yagua.* Viking Fund Publications in Anthropology, Number 1. New York.

Ferguson, P. P. (1994). The *flâneur* on and off the streets of Paris. In Tester, K. (ed.), *The flâneur.* London: Routledge.

Fischer, D. H. (1989). *Albion's seed: four British folkways in America.* Oxford: Oxford University Press.

Flanders, J. (2003). *Inside the Victorian home: a portrait of domestic life in Victorian England.* New York: W. W. Norton.

Flannery, K. V. (1972). The origins of the village as a settlement type in Mesoamerica and the Near East: a comparative study. In Ucko, P. J., Tringham, R., & Dimbleby, G. W. (eds.), *Man, settlement and urbanism.* London: Duckworth.

Fletcher, A. (1995). *Gender, sex and subordination in England 1500–1800.* New Haven, CT: Yale University Press.

Fletcher, G. P. (1993). Blackmail: the paradigmatic crime. *University of Pennsylvania Law Review, 141,* 1617–1638.

Forge, A. (1972). Normative factors in the settlement size of neolithic cultivators (New Guinea). In Ucko, P. J., Tringham, R., & Dimbleby, W. (eds.), *Man, settlement and urbanism.* Cambridge: Schenkman Publishing Company.

Forgione, N. (2005). Everyday life in motion: the art of walking in late-nineteenth-century Paris. *Art Bulletin, 87,* 664–687.

Foster, G. (1960). Interpersonal relations in peasant society. *Human Organization, 19,* 174–178.

Fragaszy, D. M. (1990). Age and sex differences in the organization of behavior in wedge-capped capuchins, *Cebus olivaceus. Behavioral Ecology, 1,* 81–94.

Franits, W. E. (1993). *Paragons of virtue: women and domesticity in seventeenth-century Dutch art.* Cambridge: Cambridge University Press.

Frank, L. K. (1966). The world as a communication network. In Kepes, G. (ed.), *Sign, image, symbol.* New York: George Braziller.

Frank, R. A., Gesteland, R. C., Bailie, J., Rybalsky, K., Selden, A., & Dulay, M. F. (2006). Characterization of the sniff magnitude test. *Archives of Otolaryngology and Head and Neck Surgery, 132,* 532–536.

Franklin, B. (1842). *The life of Benjamin Franklin.* Philadelphia: Thomas, Cowperthwait and Company.

Freedberg, D. (1989). *The power of images: studies in the history and theory of response.* Chicago, IL: University of Chicago Press.

Fried, C. (1968). Privacy. *Yale Law Journal, 77,* 475–493.

Friedberg, A. (1994). *Window shopping: cinema and the postmodern.* Berkeley, CA: University of California Press.

Gadlin, H. (1976). Private lives and public order: a critical view of the history of intimate relations in the U.S. *Massachusetts Review, 17,* 304–330.

Galef, B. G., & White, D. J. (1998). Mate-choice copying in Japanese quail, Coturnix coturnix japonica. *Animal Behaviour, 55,* 545–552.

Galton, F. (1871). Gregariousness in cattle and in men. *MacMillan's Magazine, 23, 353–357.*

Gardner, A. R. L. (1931). *The art of crime.* London: Philip Allan.

Gautier, J.-P., & Gautier-Hion, A. (1977). Vocal communication in Old World primates. In Sebeok, T. A.. (ed.), *How animals communicate.* Bloomington, IN: Indiana University Press.

Gaylin, A. (2002). *Eavesdropping in the novel from Austen to Proust.* Cambridge: Cambridge University Press.

Geist, J. F. (1983). *Arcades: the history of a building type.* Cambridge, MA: MIT Press.

Gershenzon, J. (2007). Plant volatiles carry both public and private messages. *Proceedings of the National Academy of Science, 104,* 5257–5258.

Ginsburg, D. H., & Shechtman, P. (1993). Blackmail: an economic analysis of the law. *University of Pennsylvania Law Review, 141,* 1849–1876.

Glaser, B. (2001). *The creation of the self in autobiographical forms of writing in seventeenth-century England.* Heidelberg: Universitätsverlag.

Glassie, H. (1972). Eighteenth-century cultural process in Delaware Valley folk building. *Winterthur Portfolio, 7,* 29–57.

Gleber, A. (1999). *The art of talking a walk: flânerie, literature, and film in Weimar culture.* Princeton, NJ: Princeton University Press.

Godkin, E. L. (1890). The rights of the citizen. IV. To his own reputation. *Scribner's Magazine, 8,* July, 58–67.

Goffman, E. (1958). *The presentation of self in everyday life.* Edinburgh: University of Edinburgh.

Goldberg, P. J. P. (1995). *Women in England c. 1275–1525: documentary sources.* Manchester: Manchester University Press.

Goodall, J. (1986). *The chimpanzees of Gombe: patterns of behavior.* Cambridge, MA: Harvard University Press.

Gouge, W. (1622/1976). *Of domesticall duties: eight treatises.* Amsterdam: Theatrum Orbis Terrarum and Norwood, NJ: Walter J. Johnson.

Gould, R. (1977). Puntutjarpa Rockshelter and the Australian desert culture. Vol. 54, Part I. Anthropological Papers of the American Museum of Natural History. New York.

Gould, L., Fedigan, L. M., & Rose, L. M. (1997). Why be vigilant? The case of the alpha animal. *International Journal of Primatology, 18,* 401–414.

Gowing, L. (1996). *Domestic dangers: women, words, and sex in early modern London.* Oxford: Clarendon Press.

Grant, J. W. A., & Green, L. D. (1996). Mate copying versus preference for actively courting males by female Japanese medaka (Oryzias latipes). *Behavioral Ecology, 7,* 165–167.

Greeno, N., & Semple, S. (2009). Sex differences in vocal communication among adult rhesus macaques. *Evolution in Human Behaviour, 30,* 141–145.

Gregor, T. (1970). Exposure and seclusion: a study of institutionalized isolation among the Mehinacu Indians of Brazil. *Ethnology, 9,* 234–250.

Gregor, T. (1977). *Mehinaku: the drama of daily life in a Brazilian Indian village.* Chicago, IL: University of Chicago Press.

Groves, C. P., & Sabater Pi, J. (1985). From ape's nest to human fix-point. *Man, 20,* 22–47.

Guilford, T., & Dawkins, M. S. (1991). Receiver psychology and the evolution of animal signals. *Animal Behaviour, 42,* 1–14.

Hall, D. M. (1998). The victims of stalking. In Meloy, J. R. (ed.), *The psychology of stalking: clinical and forensic perspectives.* San Diego, CA: Academic Press.

Hall, J. A. (1984). *Nonverbal sex differences: communication accuracy and expressive style.* Baltimore, MD: Johns Hopkins University Press.

Hall, J. A. (1996). Touch, status, and gender at professional meetings. *Journal of Nonverbal Behavior, 20,* 23–44.

Hall, K. R. L., & De Vore, I. (1965). Baboon social behavior. In De Vore, I. (ed.), *Primate behavior: field studies of monkeys and apes.* New York: Holt, Rinehart and Winston.

Hamill, P. (1994). *A drinking life.* Boston: Little Brown.

Hamilton, G. V. (1929). *A research in marriage.* New York: Lear Publishers.

Hare, B. (2001). Can competitive paradigms increase the validity of experiments on primate cognition? *Animal Cognition, 4,* 269–280.

Hare, B., Call, J., & Tomasello, M. (2001). Do chimpanzees know what conspecifics know? *Animal Behaviour, 61,* 139–151.

Hare, B., Call, J., & Tomasello, M. (2006). Chimpanzees deceive a human competitor by hiding. *Cognition, 101,* 495–514.

Hare, B., & Tomasello, M. (2004). Chimpanzees are more skilful in competitive than in cooperative cognitive tasks. *Animal Behaviour, 68,* 571–581.

Harper, R. (1638). *The anatomy of a woman's tongue. London.* In Harleian Miscellany II (1744), 167–178.

Hauser, M. D. (1990). Do female chimpanzee copulation calls incite male–male competition? *Animal Behaviour, 39,* 596–597.

Haviland, L. K., & Haviland, J. B. (1983). Privacy in a Mexican Indian village. In Benn, S. I., & Gaus, G. F. (eds.), *Public and private in social life.* London: Croom Helm.

Hawthorne, N. (1831/1974). Sights from a steeple. In *Twice-told tales.* Columbus, OH: Ohio State University Press.

Hecht, J. Jean (1980). *The domestic servant in eighteenth-century England.* London: Routledge & Kegan Paul.

Hedge, A. (1982). The open-plan office: a systematic investigation of employee reactions to their work environment. *Environment and Behavior, 14,* 519–542.

Hediger, H. (1977). Nest and home. *Folia Primatologica, 28,* 170–187.

Heil, M., & Bueno, J. C. S. (2007). Within-plant signaling by volatiles leads to induction and priming of an indirect plant defense in nature. *Proceedings of the National Academy of Science, 104,* 5467–5472.

Herb, B. M., Biron, S. A., & Kidd, M. R. (2003). Courtship by subordinate male Siamese fighting fish, Betta splendens: their response to eavesdropping and naïve females. *Behaviour, 140,* 71–78.

Hiatt, V. E. (1947). Eavesdropping in Roman comedy. Ph.D. dissertation, Department of Latin Language and Literature, University of Chicago.

Hitchcock, R. (1987). Sedentism and site structure: organizational changes in Kalahari Basarwa residential locations. In Kent, S. (ed.), *Method and theory for activity area research: an ethnoarchaeological approach.* New York: Columbia University Press.

Hobsbawm, E. J. (1968). *Industry and empire.* Harmondsworth, UK: Penguin.

Hochschild, A. R. (1983). *The managed heart: commercialization of human feeling.* Berkeley, CA: University of California Press.

Hodin, J. P. (1966). The painter's handwriting. In Kepes, G. (ed.), *Sign, image, symbol.* New York: George Braziller.

Hotchkiss, John C. (1967). Children and conduct in a Ladino community of Chiapas, Mexico. *American Anthropologist, 69,* 711–718.

Humphrey, N. (1976). The social function of intellect. In Bateson, P. P. G., & Hinde, R. A. (eds.), *Growing points in ethology.* Cambridge: Cambridge University Press.

Humphrey, N. (2000). The privatization of sensation. In Huber, L., & Heyes, C. (eds.), *The evolution of cognition.* Cambridge, MA: MIT Press.

Humphrey, N. (2007). The society of selves. *Philosophical Transactions of the Royal Society B, 362,* 745–754.

Humphrey, N. (2008). Getting the measure of consciousness. *Progress of Theoretical Physics Supplement, 173,* 264–269.

Hunter, V. J. (1994). *Policing Athens: social control in the attic lawsuits, 420–320 B. C.* Princeton, NJ: Princeton University Press.

Infield, P., & Platford, G. (2000). *The law of harassment and stalking.* London: Butterworths.

Ingram, M. (1984). Ridings, rough music and the "reform of popular culture" in early modern England. *Past and Present, 105,* 79–113.

Ingram, M. (1994). "Scolding women cucked or washed": a crisis in gender relations in early modern England? In Kermode, J., & Walker,

G. (eds.), *Women, crime and the courts in early modern England*. London: UCL Press.

Inness, J. C. (1992). *Privacy, intimacy, and isolation*. Oxford: Oxford University Press.

Innocenti, G. M., & Kaas, J. H. (1995). The cortex. *Trends in Neuroscience, 18*, 371–372.

Jawor, J. M., & Breitwisch, R. (2003). Melanin ornaments, honesty, and sexual selection. *The Auk, 120*, 249–265.

Johnson, S. (1753). The adventurer. Number 119. In Arthur Murray (ed.), *The Works of Samuel Johnson*. London: S. and R. Bentley.

Kaas, J. (1995). The evolution of isocortex. *Brain, Behavior, and Evolution, 46*, 187–196.

Kaya, N., & Erkíp, F. (1999). Invasion of personal space under the condition of short-term crowding: a case study on an automatic teller machine. *Journal of Environmental Psychology, 19*, 183–189.

Kent, D. A. (1989). Ubiquitous but invisible: female domestic servants in mid-eighteenth century London. *History Workshop, 28*, 111–128.

Keymer, T., & Sabor, P. (2001). *The Pamela controversy: criticisms and adaptations of Samuel Richardsons' Pamela 1740–1750*. Vol. I. Richardson's apparatus and Fielding's *Shamela* verse responses. London: Pickering & Chatto.

Kinsey, A. C., Pomeroy, W. B., Martin, C. E., & Gebhard, P. H. (1953). *Sexual behavior in the human female*. Philadelphia: W. B. Saunders.

Klopfer, P. H., & Rubenstein, D. I. (1977). The concept *privacy* and its biological basis. *Journal of Social Issues, 33*, 52–65.

Kobayashi, Y., & Yamamura, N. (2003). Evolution of signal emission by non-infested plants growing near infested plants to avoid future risk. *Journal of Theoretical Biology, 223*, 489–503.

Kobayashi, Y., & Yamamura, N. (2007). Evolution of signal emission by non-infested plants to help nearby infested relatives. *Evolution and Ecology, 21*, 281–294.

Korosec-Serfaty, P., & Bolitt, D. (1986). Dwelling and the experience of burglary. *Journal of Environmental Psychology, 6*, 329–344.

Kostof, S. (1995). *A history of architecture: settings and rituals*. New York: Oxford University Press.

Krentz, J. A. (1992). Introduction. In Krentz, J. A. (ed.), *Dangerous men and adventurous women: writers on the appeal of the romance*. Philadelphia: University of Pennsylvania Press.

Kunc, H. P., Amrhein, V., & Naguib, M. (2006). Vocal interactions in nightingales, Luscinia megarhynchos: more aggressive males have higher pairing success. *Animal Behaviour, 72*, 25–30.

Kundera, M. (1995). *Testaments betrayed*. London: Faber and Faber.

Kuper, L. (1953). Blueprint for living together. In Kuper, L. (ed.), *Living in towns*. London: The Cresset Press.

Kussmaul, A. (1981). *Servants in husbandry in early modern England*. Cambridge: Cambridge University Press.

Lackington, J. (1795). *Memoirs of the forty-five first years of the life of James Lackington*. Finsbury Square, London: Moorfields.

Latham, R., & Matthews, W. (1970–1983). *The diary of Samuel Pepys*. Berkeley, CA: University of California Press.

Lea, A. J., Barrera, J. P., Tom, L. M., & Blumstein, D. T. (2008). Heterospecific eavesdropping in a nonsocial species. *Behavioral Ecology*, 1041–1046.

Leakey, M. D. (1971). *Olduvai Gorge: excavations in beds I and II 1980–1983*. Cambridge: Cambridge University Press.

Leboucher, G., & Pallot, K. (2004). Is he all he says he is? Intersexual eavesdropping in the domestic canary, *Serinus carina*. *Animal Behaviour*, *68*, 957–63.

Lee, R. B. (1979a). *The Dobe !Kung*. New York: Holt, Rinehart and Winston.

Lee, R. B. (1979b). *The !Kung San: men, women, and work in a foraging society*. Cambridge: Cambridge University Press.

Leighton-Shapiro, M. E. (1986). Vigilance and the costs of motherhood to rhesus monkeys (abstract). *American Journal of Primatology*, *10*, 414–415.

Leitão, A., ten Cate, C., & Riebel, K. (2006). Within-song complexity in a songbird is meaningful to both male and female receivers. *Animal Behaviour*, *71*, 1289–1296.

Lennard, S. H. C., & Lennard, H. L. (1984). *Public life in urban places: social and architectural characteristics conducive to public life in European cities*. Southampton, NY: Gondolier Press.

Le Roy Ladurie, E. (1978). *Montaillou: Cathars and Catholics in a French village*. London: Scolar Press.

Le Sage, A. R. (1707). *The devil upon two sticks* (trans. from *Le Diable Boiteux*). London: John Bell.

Leyhausen, P. (1971). Dominance and territoriality as complemented in mammalian social structure. In Esser, A. H. (ed.), *Behavior and environment: the use of space by animals and men*. New York: Plenum Press.

Lindenfors, P., Fröberg, L., & Nunn, C. L. (2004). Females drive primate social evolution. *Proceedings of the Royal Society of London B (Suppl.)*, *271*, S101–S103.

Locke, J. L. (2005). Looking for, looking at: social control, honest signals, and intimate experience in human evolution and history. In McGregor, P. K. (ed.), *Animal communication networks*. Cambridge: Cambridge University Press.

Locke, J. L., & Bogin, B. (2006). Language and life history: a new perspective on the evolution and development of linguistic communication. *Behavioral and Brain Science*, *29*, 259–325.

Love, R. L. (1973). The fountains of urban life. *Urban Life and Culture*, *2*, 161–209.

Lumley, H. de (1969). A Paleolithic camp site at Nice. *Scientific American, 220,* 42–50.

Lyle, J. T. (1970). People-watching in parks: a report from France and California. *Landscape Architecture, 61,* 31, 51–53.

Maestripieri, D., & Roney, J. R. (2005). Primate copulation calls and postcopulatory female choice. *Behavioral Ecology, 16,* 106–113.

Mainardi, P. (2003). *Husbands, wives, and lovers: marriage and its discontents in nineteenth-century France.* New Haven, CT: Yale University Press.

Malek, D. O. (1992). Mad, bad, and dangerous to know: the hero as challenge. In Krentz, J. A. (ed.), *Dangerous men and adventurous women: romance writer on the appeal of the romance.* Philadelphia: University of Pennsylvania Press.

Maloney, C. (1976). Introduction. In Maloney, C. (ed.) (1976). *The evil eye.* New York: Columbia University Press.

Mansfield, H. C., & Winthrop, D. (2000). *Alexis de-Tocqueville: democracy in America.* Chicago, IL: University of Chicago Press.

Matelski, M. J. (1988). *The soap opera evolution.* Jefferson, NC: McFarland.

Matessi, G., McGregor, P. K., Peake, T. M., & Dabelsteen, T. (2005). Do male birds intercept and use rival courtship calls to adjust paternity protection behaviours? *Behaviour, 142,* 507–524.

May, T. (1998). *The Victorian domestic servant.* Market Harborough, UK: Shire Press.

Mazlish, B. (1994). The *flâneur*: from spectator to representation. In Tester, K. (ed.), *The flâneur.* London: Routledge.

McAdams, R. H. (1996). Group norms, gossip, and blackmail. *University of Pennsylvania Law Review, 144,* 2237–2292.

McBride, T. M. (1974). Social mobility for the lower classes: domestic servants in France. *Journal of Social History* (Autumn), 63–78.

McConville, M., & Shepherd, D. (1992). *Watching police, watching communities.* London: Routledge.

McGinnis, P. R. (1979). Sexual behavior in free-living chimpanzees: consort relationships. In Hamburg, D. A., & McCown, E. R. (eds.), *The great apes. Perspectives on human evolution, Vol. 5.* A publication of the Society for the Study of Human Evolution, Inc., Berkeley and Menlo Park, CA: Benjamin/Cummings.

McGregor, P. (2005). Introduction. In McGregor, P. (ed.), *Animal communication networks.* Cambridge: Cambridge University Press.

McIntosh, M. K. (1991). *A community transformed: the manor and liberty of Havering, 1500–1620.* Cambridge: Cambridge University Press.

McIntosh, M. K. (1996). Finding language for misconduct: jurors in fifteenth-century local courts. In Hanawalt, B. A., & Wallace, D. (eds.), *Bodies and disciplines: intersections of literature and history in fifteenth-century England.* Minneapolis, MN: University of Minnesota Press.

References

McIntosh, M. K. (1998). *Controlling misbehavior in England, 1370–1600*. Cambridge: Cambridge University Press.

McNeill, L. (2003). Teaching an old genre new tricks: the diary on the internet. *Biography, 26*, 24–47.

McNeill, W. H. (1995). *Keeping together in time: dance and drill in human history.* Cambridge, MA: Harvard University Press.

Melis, A. P., Call, J., & Tomasello, M. (2006). Chimpanzees (Pan troglodytes) conceal visual and auditory information from others. *Journal of Comparative Psychology, 120*, 154–162.

Meloy, J. R. (1998). The psychology of stalking. In Meloy, J. R. (ed.), *The psychology of stalking: clinical and forensic perspectives*. San Diego, CA: Academic Press.

Mendelson, S., & Crawford, P. (1998). *Women in early modern England, 1550–1720*. Oxford: Oxford University Press.

Mennill, D. J., Boag, P. T., & Ratcliffe, L. M. (2003). The reproductive choices of eavesdropping female black-capped chickadees, *Poecile atricapillus*. *Naturwissenschaften, 90*, 577–582.

Merleau-Ponty, M. (1962). Eye and mind. *Phenomenology of perception*. Translated by C. Smith. London: Routlege & Kegan Paul.

Miller, G. A. (1983). "Informavores." In Machlup, F., & Mansfield, U. (eds.), *The study of information: interdisciplinary messages*. New York: John Wiley & Sons.

Miller, M. B. (1981). *The Bon Marché: bourgeoise culture and the department store, 1869–1920*. Princeton, NJ: Princeton University Press.

Modleski, T. (1982). *Loving with a vengeance: mass-produced fantasies for women*. Hamden, CT: The Shoestring Press.

Morand-Ferron, J., Sol, D., & Lefebvre, L. (2007). Food stealing in birds: brain or brawn? *Animal Behaviour, 74*, 1725–1734.

Muchembled, R. (1985). *Popular culture and elite culture in France 1400–1750*. Translated by Lydia Cochrane. Baton Rouge, LA: Louisiana State University Press.

Mullen, P. E., Pathé, M., & Purcell, R. (2000). *Stalkers and their victims*. Cambridge: Cambridge University Press.

Murkowski, E. (1933/1970). *Lived time: phenomenological and psychological studies*. Translated by Nancy Metzel. Evanston, IL: Northestern University Press.

Murray, S. B. (2003). The spy, a shill, a go-between, or a sociologist: unveiling the "observer" in participant observer. *Qualitative Research, 3*, 377–95.

Mussell, K. (1984). *Fantasy and reconciliation: contemporary formulas of women's romance fiction*. Westport, CT: Greenwood Press.

Myers, D. G. (1992). *The pursuit of happiness: discovering the pathway to fulfillment, well-being, and enduring personal joy.* New York: Avon.

Nagel, T. (1998a). Concealment and exposure. *Philosophy & Public Affairs, 27*, 3–30.

Nagel, T. (1998b). The shredding of public privacy. *Times Literary Supplement*, August 14.

Narroll, R. (1959). A tentative index of culture stress. *International Journal of Social Psychiatry, 5*, 107–116.

O'Connell, S. M., & Cowlishaw, G. (1994). Infanticide avoidance, sperm competition and mate choice: the function of copulation calls in female baboons. *Animal Behaviour, 48*, 687–694.

Oldham, G. R. (1988). Effects of changes in workspace partitions and spatial density on employee reactions: a quasi experiment. *Journal of Applied Psychology, 73*, 253–258.

Oliveira, R. F., Lopes, M., Carneiro, L. A. & Canário, A. V. M. (2001). Watching fights raises fish hormone levels. *Nature, 409*, 475.

Oosterman, J. (1992). Welcome to the pleasure dome: play and entertainment in urban public space: the example of the sidewalk café. *Built Environment, 18*, 155–164.

Parker, R. B. (1974). A definition of privacy. *Rutgers Law Review, 27*, 275–296.

Partan, S., & Marler, P. (2002). The *Umwelt* and its relevance to animal communication: introduction to special issue. *Journal of Comparative Psychology, 116*, 116–119.

Perrot, M. (1990). Roles and characters. In Ariès, P., & Duby, G. (eds.), *A history of private life. IV. From the fires of revolution to the great war*. Cambridge, MA: Harvard University Press.

Peter, P. (2004). *The subway pictures*. New York: Random House.

Phillips, S. E. (1992). The romance and the empowerment of women. In Krentz, J. A. (ed.), *Dangerous men and adventurous women: writers on the appeal of the romance*. Philadelphia: University of Pennsylvania Press.

Pipitone, R. N., & Gallup, G. G. (2008). Women's voice attractiveness varies across the menstrual cycle. *Evolution and Human Behavior, 29*, 268–274.

Plot, R. (1686). *The natural history of stafford-shire*. Oxford: Printed at the Theater.

Poe, E. A. (1840). *The works of Edgar Allan Poe*. Volume 2. Chicago: Stone & Kimball.

Posner, R. A. (1993). Blackmail, privacy, and freedom of contract. *University of Pennsylvania Law Review, 141*, 1817–1847.

Prendergast, C. (1992). *Paris and the nineteenth century*. Oxford: Blackwell.

Quenette, P.-Y. (1990). Functions of vigilance behaviour in mammals: a review. *Acta Œcologica, 11*, 801–818.

Rachels, J. (1975). Why privacy is important. *Philosophy & Public Affairs, 4*, 323–333.

References

Radway, J. (1984). *Reading the romance: women, patriarchy, and popular literature.* Chapel Hill, NC: University of North Carolina Press.

Rapoport, A. (1969). *House form and culture.* Englewood Cliffs, NJ: Prentice-Hall.

Régnier-Bohler, D. (1988). Imagining the self: exploring literature. In Duby, G. (ed.), *A history of private life. II. Revelations of the medieval world.* Cambridge, MA: Harvard University Press.

Reiman, J. H. (1976). Privacy, intimacy, and personhood. *Philosophy & Public Affairs, 6,* 26–44.

Reynolds, V. (1972). Ethology of urban life. In Ucko, P. J., Tringham, R., & Dimbleby, G. W. (eds), *Man, settlement and urbanism.* London: Duckworth.

Richardson, S. (1741/2001). *Pamela; or, virtue rewarded.* Ed. with explanatory notes by Thomas Keymer and Alice Wakely. Oxford: Oxford University Press.

Robbins, B. (1986). *The servant's hand: English fiction from below.* New York: Columbia University Press.

Roberts, A. (1616). *A treatise of witchcraft: wherein sundry propositions are laid down, plainly discovering the wickednesses of that damnable art, with diverse other special points annexed, not impertinent to the same, such as ought diligently of every Christian to be considered.* London.

Roberts, J. M., & Gregor, T. (1971). Privacy: a cultural view. In Pennock, J. R., & Chapman, J. W. (eds.), *Privacy.* NOMOS 13. New York: Atherton Press.

Robinson, W. W. (1987). The *Eavesdroppers* and related paintings by Nicolaes Maes. In *Jahrbuch Preußischer Kulturbesitz Sonderband 4.* Berlin: Mann Verlag.

Rose, H., & Rose, S. (2000). (eds.). *Alas, poor Darwin: arguments against evolutionary psychology.* London: Jonathan Cape.

Rose, L. M. (1994). Benefits and costs of resident males to females in white-faces capuchins (*Cebus capucinus*). *American Journal of Primatology, 32,* 235–248.

Rose, L. M., & Fedigan, L. M. (1995). Vigilance in white-faced capuchins, *Cebus capucinus,* in Costa Rica. *Animal Behaviour, 49,* 63–70.

Rosenheim, J. L. (2004). Afterword. In Evans, W., *Many are called.* New Haven, CT: Yale University Press.

Ruby, P., & Decety, J. (2001). Effect of subjective perspective taking during simulation of action: a PET investigation of agency. *Nature Neuroscience, 4,* 546–550.

Ruby, P., & Decety, J. (2003). What you believe versus what you think they believe: a neuroimaging study of conceptual perspective taking. *European Journal of Neuroscience, 17,* 2475–2480.

Ruby, P., & Decety, J. (2004). How would you feel versus how do you think she would feel? A neuroimaging study of perspective taking with social emotions. *Journal of Cognitive Neuroscience, 16,* 988–999.

Rupp, H. A., & Wallen, K. (2008). Sex differences in response to visual sexual stimuli: a review. *Archives of Sexual Behavior, 37,* 206–18.

Russell, J. C. (1958). Late ancient and medieval population. *Transactions of the American Philosophical Society, 48,* Part 3.

Sante, L. (2004). Foreword. In Evans, W., *Many are called.* New Haven, CT: Yale University Press.

Sarti, R. (2002). *Europe at home: family and material culture 1500–1800.* Translated by Allan Cameron. New Haven, CT: Yale University Press.

Sartre, J.-P. (1956). *Being and nothingness: an essay in phenomenological ontology.* Special abridged edn. Translated by Hazel E. Barnes. Seacaucus, NJ: The Citadel Press.

Schama, S. (1991). *The embarrassment of riches: an interpretation of Dutch culture in the Golden Age.* London: Fontana Press.

Schwartz, B. (1968). The social psychology of privacy. *American Journal of Sociology, 73,* 741–752.

Semple, S. (2001). Individuality and male discrimination of female copulation calls in the yellow baboon. *Animal Behaviour, 61,* 1023–1028.

Semple, S., McComb, K., Alberts, S., & Altmann, J. (2002). Information content of female copulation calls in yellow baboons. *American Journal of Primatology, 56,* 43–56.

Shaya, G. 2004). The *flâneur,* the *badaud,* and the making of a mass public in France, circa 1860–1910. *American Historical Review, February,* 41–77.

Shils, E. (1966). Privacy: its constitution and vicissitudes. *Law and Contemporary Problems, 31,* 281–306.

Shoemaker, R. B. (2004). *The London mob: violence and disorder in eighteenth-century England.* London: Hambledon and London.

Shore, B. (1982). *Sala 'Ilua: a Samoan mystery.* New York: Columbia University Press.

Sieburth, R. (1984). Same difference: the French *physiologies,* 1840–1842. In Cantor, N. F. (ed.), *Notebooks in cultural analysis.* Durham, NC: Duke University Press.

Silber, J. R. (1971). Masks and fig leaves. In Pennock, J. R., & Chapman, J. W. (eds.), *Privacy.* New York: Lieber-Atherton.

Silk, J. B. (2007). Social components of fitness in primate groups. *Science, 317,* 1347–1351.

Simmel, G. (1906). The sociology of secrecy and of secret societies. *American Journal of Sociology, 11,* 441–498.

Smith, A. (1841). *Social zoologies: the natural history of the idler upon town.* London: D. Bogue.

Smith, J. M. (1997). *Private matters: in defense of the personal life.* Reading, MA: Addison-Wesley.

References

Smith, R. E. (2000). *Ben Franklin's web site: privacy and curiosity from Plymouth Rock to the Internet*. Providence, RI: Privacy Journal.

Smuts, B. B. (1987a). Gender, aggression, and influence. In Smuts, B. B., Cheney, D. L., Seyfarth, R. M., Wrangham, R. W., & Struhsaker, T. T. (eds.). *Primate societies*. Chicago, IL: University of Chicago Press.

Smuts, B. B. (1987b). Sexual competition and mate choice. In Smuts, B. B., Cheney, D. L., Seyfarth, R. M., Wrangham, R. W., & Struhsaker, T. T. (eds.). *Primate societies*. Chicago, IL: University of Chicago Press.

Sobel, N., Prabhakaran, V., Desmond, J. E., Glover, G. H., Goode, R. L., Sullivan, E. V., & Gabrieli, J. D. E. (1998). Sniffing and smelling: separate subsystems in the human olfactory cortex. *Nature, 392*, 282–286.

Sommer, R. (1959). Studies in personal space. *Sociometry, 22*, 247–260.

Sontag, S. (1977). *On photography*. New York: Farrar, Straus and Giroux.

Spender, H. (1987). *'Lensman.' Photographs 1932–1952*. Introd. Humphrey Spender. London: Chatto & Windus.

Springer, J. (1998). *Ringmaster!* New York: St. Martin's Press.

Steedman, C. (2003). Servants and their relationship to the unconscious. *Journal of British Studies, 42*, 316–50.

Steele, V. (1985). *Fashion and eroticism: ideals of feminine beauty from the Victorian era to the jazz age*. New York: Oxford University Press.

Steenbeek, R., Piek, R. C., Buul, M. van, & Hooff, J. A. R. A. M. van (1999). Vigilance in wild Thomas langurs (*Presbytis thomasi*): the importance of infanticide risk. *Behavioral Ecology and Sociobiology, 45*, 137–150.

Stephen, L. (1909). *Hours in a library*. Vol. 1. London: Smith, Elder & Company.

Stevenson, R. L. (1879/1992). *Travels with a donkey in the Cevennes*. Oxford: Oxford University Press.

Stone, L. (1977). *The family, sex and marriage in England 1500–1800*. London: Weidenfeld and Nicolson.

Stone, L. (1990). *Road to divorce: England 1530–1987*. Oxford: Oxford University Press.

Stone, L., & Stone, J. C. F. (1984). *An open elite? England 1540–1880*. Oxford: Clarendon Press.

Suddendorf, T., Simcock, G., & Nielsen, M. (2007). Visual self-recognition in mirrors and live videos: evidence for a developmental asynchrony. *Cognitive Development, 22*, 185–196.

Sundstrom, E., Herbert, R. K., & Brown, D. W. (1982). Privacy and communication in an open-plan office: a case study. *Environment and Behavior, 14*, 379–392.

Symons, D., Salmon, C., & Ellis, B. (1997). Unobtrusive measures of human sexuality. In Betzig, L. (ed.), *Human nature: a critical reader*. Oxford: Oxford University Press.

Tanner, T. (1979). *Adultery in the novel: contract and transactions*. Baltimore, MD: Johns Hopkins University Press.

Tennis, G. H., & Dabbs, J. M. (1975). Sex, setting and personal space: first grade through college. *Sociometry, 38*, 385–394.

Tester, K. (1994). Introduction. *The flâneur.* London: Routledge.

Thompson, E. P. (1975). The crime of anonymity. In Hay, D., Linebaugh, P., Rule, J. G., Thompson, E. P., & Winslow, C. (eds.), *Albion's fatal tree: crime and society in eighteenth-century England.* New York: Pantheon Books.

Thompson, E. P. (1991). *Customs in common.* London: Merlin Press.

Thompson, R. (1983). "Holy Watchfulness" and communal conformism: the functions of defamation in early New England communities. *New England Quarterly, 56*, 504–522.

Thurston, C. (1987). *The romance revolution: erotic novels for women and the quest for a new sexual identity.* Urbana, IL: University of Illinois Press.

Tickner, L. (2003). A strange alchemy: Cornelia Parker. *Art History, 26*, 364–391.

Tjaden, P., & Thoennes, N. (1997). *Stalking in America: findings from the National Violence against Women Survey.* Denver, CO: Center for Policy Research.

Trapnell, W. H. (1987). *Eavesdropping in Marivaux.* Genève: Librairie Droz.

Treves, A. (1998). The influence of group size and neighbors on vigilance in two species of arboreal monkeys. *Behaviour, 135*, 453–481.

Treves, A. (1999). Within-group vigilance in red colobus and redtail monkeys. *American Journal of Primatology, 48*, 113–126.

Treves, A., Drescher, A., & Ingrisano, N. (2001). Vigilance and aggregation in black howler monkeys (Alouatta pigra). *Behavioral Ecology and Sociobiology, 50*, 90–95.

Trials for adultery; or, the history of divorces. Being select trials at Doctors Commons, for adultery, fornication, cruelty, impotence, &c. From the year 1760, to the present time. Including the whole of the evidence on each cause. New York: Garland, 1985.

Trodd, A. (1989). *Domestic crime in the Victorian novel.* London: Macmillan.

Truffaut, F. (1986). *Le cinéma selon Hitchcock.* London: Paladin.

Turner, E. S. (1962). *What the butler saw: two hundred and fifty years of the servant problem.* London: Penguin.

Tutin, C. E. G. (1979). Mating patterns and reproductive strategies in a community of wild chimpanzees (*Pan troglodytes schweinfurthii*). *Behavioral Ecology and Sociobiology, 6*, 29–38.

Udry, S. (2002). Robert de Blois and Geoffroy de la Tour Landry on feminine beauty: two late medieval French conduct books for women. *Essays in Medieval Studies, 19*, 90–102.

Uexküll, J. von (1934/1957). A stroll through the worlds of animals and men. In Schiller, Claire H. (ed. and trans.), *Instinctive behavior: the development of a modern concept.* Introd. Karl S. Lashley. New York: International Universities Press, 5–80.

References

Uexküll, von T. (1992). Introduction: the sign theory of Jakob von Uexkull. *Semiotica, 89,* 279–315.

Vallet, E., & Kreutzer, M. (1995). Female canaries are sexually responsive to special song phrases. *Animal Behaviour, 49,* 1603–10.

van Schaik, C. P., van Noordwijk, M. A., Warsono, B., & Sutriono, E. (1983). Party size and early detection of predators in Sumatran forest primates. *Primates, 24,* 211–221.

Veblen, T. (1899/1957). *The theory of the leisure class.* London: Allen and Unwin.

Vernon, J. (1982). Reading, writing, and eavesdropping: some thoughts on the nature of realistic fiction. *Kenyon Review, 4,* 44–54.

Vitousek, M., Adelman, J. S., Gregory, N. C., & St. Clair, J. J. H. (2007). Heterospecific alarm call recognition in a non-vocal reptile. *Biology Letters, 3,* 632–634.

Vukomanovic, J., & Rodd, R. H. (2007). Size-dependent female mate copying in the guppy (*Poecilia reticulate*): large females are role models but small ones are not. *Ethology, 113,* 579–586.

Walker, W. (1960). *The creeds and platforms of Congregationalism.* Boston: The Pilgrim Press.

Wallendorf, M., & Arnould, E. J. (1988). "My favorite things": a cross-cultural inquiry into object attachment, possessiveness and social linkage. *Journal of Consumer Research, 14,* 531–547.

Walsh, M. E. (1977). *The fence: a new look at the world of property theft.* Westport, CT: Greenwood Press.

Ward, P. (1999). *A history of domestic space: privacy and the Canadian home.* Vancouver, Canada: UBC Press.

Warren, S. D., & Brandeis, L. D. (1890). The right to privacy. *Harvard Law Review, 4,* 193–220.

Weatherhead, P. J., & Robertson, R. J. (1979). Offspring quality and the polygyny threshold: "The sexy son hypothesis." *American Naturalist, 113,* 201–208.

Weitman, S. R. (1973). Intimacies: notes toward a theory of social inclusion and exclusion. In Birenbaum, A., & Sagarin, E. (eds.), *People in places: the sociology of the familiar.* New York: Praeger.

White, D. J., & Galef, B. G. (2000). 'Culture' in quail: social influences on mate choices of female *Coturnix japonica. Animal Behaviour, 59,* 975–979.

Wiener, N. (1954). *The human use of human beings: cybernetics and society.* New York: Da Capo Press.

Williams, J. L. (1902). *New York sketches.* New York: Charles Scribner's Sons.

Wilson, F. (2003). *The courtesan's revenge: Harriette Wilson, the woman who blackmailed the king.* London: Faber and Faber.

Wilson, P. J. (1988). *The domestication of the human species.* New Haven, CT: Yale University Press.

Witte, K., & Noltemeier, B. (2002). The role of information in mate-choice copying in female sailfin mollies (*Poecilia latipinna*). *Behavioral Ecology and Sociobiology, 52,* 194–202.

Witte, K., & Ryan, M. J. (1998). Male body length influences mate-choice copying in the sailfin molly *Poecilia latipinna. Behavioral Ecology and Sociobiology, 9,* 534–539.

Witte, K., & Ryan, M. J. (2002). Mate choice copying in the sailfin molly, *Poecilia latipinna,* in the wild. *Animal Behaviour, 63,* 943–949.

Wrangham, R., & Peterson, D. (1997). *Demonic males: apes and the origins of human violence.* London: Bloomsbury.

Yellen, J. E. (1977). *Archaeological approaches to the present: models for reconstructing the past.* New York: Academic Press.

Zola, D. (1881/2001). *Au bonheur des dames.* Trans. R. Buss. Harmondsworth: Penguin.

Index

Index

Index

participant-observers in
    experiments 34
paternity, doubt in 13
Pears Annual 19
Pepys, Samuel 194
Perrot, Michelle 116
personal privacy 103–5
personal space 32
    optimum 76–7
    violations 209–10
perspective
    imagining others' 60–1
    individual 40–1
Peter, Peter 220
photography, covert 216–20, *219*
Physiologie du flâneur (Huart) *154*
physiologies of Parisians 157–9
Physiology of Marriage (Balzac) 198–9
Pigal, Edme-Jean *146*
Pitjantjatjara people 66–7
plants, communication in 44
Plato 109–10
Poe, Edgar Allen 159
Policing Athens (Hunter) 111
population growth
    and fear of strangers 95, 132
    in Paris 155–6
Posner, Richard 114
possessions, private 105
predators
    avoiding by listening for clues 42–3
    of plants 44
Prendergast, Christopher 155, 158
primates 16, 20
    courtship rituals 50
    group behavior 53–4, 59
    interpreting behavior 58–9
    sex differences 54–7
    stealth 51
privacy
    averted gaze 73–4

and choice in sharing 101–2
defending 208–9
individual 103–5
in mating chimpanzees 50
and privation 94
psychological 73, 211–12, 220
and public personas 25, 105–7
and secrecy 90–1, 96–7
from servants 186–8, *187*
and solitude 88–9, 93–4
from strangers 95
and trust 102–3
violations 213
Private Letter Drawer, The
    (Simonetti) *181*
private spaces 64–6
promenades 161–3
"proximate mechanism" 125
proximity, and need for escape 73
psychological barriers 31–2
psychological privacy 73, 211–12,
    220
public persona 105–7
    vs. private persona 25
punishments
    for observed wrongdoing 143–7
    for scolding 140–2, *141*
Pursuit of Happiness, The (Myers)
    202–3
"qualia" 205

Rapoport, Amos 81, 86
Rear Window 30–1
"recreational eavesdropping" 37
Reiman, Jeffrey 212
relationships
    animals eavesdropping on 45–6
    inferring from observation 24
remarriage, punishments for 144–5
Republic, The (Plato) 109–10
Richardson, Samuel 194–5